International
Criminal Law

Editorial Advisors

Vicki Been
Elihu Root Professor of Law
New York University School of Law

Erwin Chemerinsky
Dean and Distinguished Professor of Law
University of California, Irvine, School of Law

Richard A. Epstein
James Parker Hall Distinguished Service Professor of Law
University of Chicago Law School
Peter and Kirsten Bedford Senior Fellow
The Hoover Institution
Stanford University

Ronald J. Gilson
Charles J. Meyers Professor of Law and Business
Stanford University
Marc and Eva Stern Professor of Law and Business
Columbia Law School

James E. Krier
Earl Warren DeLano Professor of Law
The University of Michigan Law School

Richard K. Neumann, Jr.
Professor of Law
Hofstra University School of Law

Robert H. Sitkoff
John L. Gray Professor of Law
Harvard Law School

David Alan Sklansky
Professor of Law
University of California at Berkeley School of Law

Kent D. Syverud
Dean and Ethan A. H. Shepley University Professor
Washington University School of Law

Elizabeth Warren
Leo Gottlieb Professor of Law
Harvard Law School

ASPEN PUBLISHERS

essentials

International Criminal Law

Ronald C. Slye
Associate Professor of Law
Seattle University School of Law
Honorary Professor of Law
University of the Witwatersrand

Beth Van Schaack
Associate Professor
Santa Clara University School of Law

Wolters Kluwer
Law & Business

AUSTIN   BOSTON   CHICAGO   NEW YORK   THE NETHERLANDS

To contact Customer Care, e-mail customer.care@aspenpublishers.com, call 1-800-234-1660, fax 1-800-901-9075, or mail correspondence to:

Aspen Publishers
Attn: Order Department
PO Box 990
Frederick, MD 21705

Printed in the United States of America.

1 2 3 4 5 6 7 8 9 0

ISBN 978-0-7355-6553-1

Library of Congress Cataloging-in-Publication Data

Slye, Ronald.
  International criminal law : the essentials / Ronald C. Slye, Beth Van Schaack.
    p. cm.
  Includes bibliographical references and index.
  ISBN 978-0-7355-6553-1 (pbk. : alk. paper) 1. International offenses. 2. Crimes against humanity. 3. War crimes. I. Van Schaack, Beth. II. Title.

KZ6326.S589 2008
345—dc22
                                                    2008040741

About Wolters Kluwer Law & Business

Wolters Kluwer Law & Business is a leading provider of research information and workflow solutions in key specialty areas. The strengths of the individual brands of Aspen Publishers, CCH, Kluwer Law International and Loislaw are aligned within Wolters Kluwer Law & Business to provide comprehensive, in-depth solutions and expert-authored content for the legal, professional and education markets.

CCH was founded in 1913 and has served more than four generations of business professionals and their clients. The CCH products in the Wolters Kluwer Law & Business group are highly regarded electronic and print resources for legal, securities, antitrust and trade regulation, government contracting, banking, pension, payroll, employment and labor, and healthcare reimbursement and compliance professionals.

Aspen Publishers is a leading information provider for attorneys, business professionals and law students. Written by preeminent authorities, Aspen products offer analytical and practical information in a range of specialty practice areas from securities law and intellectual property to mergers and acquisitions and pension/benefits. Aspen's trusted legal education resources provide professors and students with high-quality, up-to-date and effective resources for successful instruction and study in all areas of the law.

Kluwer Law International supplies the global business community with comprehensive English-language international legal information. Legal practitioners, corporate counsel and business executives around the world rely on the Kluwer Law International journals, loose-leafs, books and electronic products for authoritative information in many areas of international legal practice.

Loislaw is a premier provider of digitized legal content to small law firm practitioners of various specializations. Loislaw provides attorneys with the ability to quickly and efficiently find the necessary legal information they need, when and where they need it, by facilitating access to primary law as well as state-specific law, records, forms and treatises.

Wolters Kluwer Law & Business, a unit of Wolters Kluwer, is headquartered in New York and Riverwoods, Illinois. Wolters Kluwer is a leading multinational publisher and information services company.

To Harold Hongju Koh
Our mentor, friend, and inspiration
R.C.S. & B.V.S.

Table of Contents

CHAPTER 5

The Principle of Legality in International Criminal Law 121

PART II

INTERSECTIONS 145

CHAPTER 6

The Legal Regulation of Armed Conflict 149

CHAPTER 7

The Crimes of Terrorism

CHAPTER 8

Genocide and Crimes
Against Humanity

CHAPTER 9

Immunities, Amnesties, and Excuses 241

CHAPTER 10

Forms of Individual Responsibility 269

Acknowledgments

The authors express their sincere thanks to the many people who contributed to this volume, and especially the anonymous reviewers recruited by Aspen Publishers who provided very detailed and helpful feedback. We would also like to thank several students from Santa Clara University School of Law — Adam Birnbaum, Leslie Frost, Jeffrey Larson, Kevin Osborne, Monica Toole, and Nicholas Webber — and Marsha Mavunkel from Seattle University School of Law for their expert research assistance. We would also like to thank Bob Menanteaux of the Seattle University School of Law library for excellent research, and Deans Kellye Testy and Donald Polden for providing us with the time and resources to make this project possible. We also appreciate the reviews provided by Eric Van Schaack and Bill Slye. Finally, thanks go out to the staff at Aspen Publishers for their support, assistance, and patience throughout this project.

Preface

International criminal law (ICL) can be, and is, taught in a number of different ways depending on the text utilized and the interests and expertise of the particular professor. ICL can be taught as a subset of public international law, with an emphasis on relevant treaties and customary international law and the institutions and organizations that adjudicate ICL. ICL can also be taught as a specialized criminal law course, with an emphasis on the elements of crimes, the burdens on the prosecution and defense, and the parties' strategic moves in the adversarial or inquisitorial context. Given that many professors come to the field with a domestic law background, the course can also be taught as the transnational extension of domestic criminal law. This approach would focus on interstate cooperation in law enforcement matters. It is hoped that this book will complement all of these approaches.

With these different approaches in mind, we discuss the major institutions and international crimes, emphasizing some of their unique features. In these materials, we do not dwell on the minutiae of ICL on the assumption that the cases highlighted in the primary text will. Instead, the book outlines the origins and elements of the major international crimes and identifies doctrinal areas that remain the subject of litigation, advocacy, and negotiation. We also present some of the jurisdictional issues surrounding the major fora in which ICL norms are adjudicated: international tribunals, hybrid tribunals, and domestic courts. In addition to these more standard topics, we have endeavored to fill in some gaps in what is usually taught in a two- or three-unit course on ICL. For example, we have included chapters on the history of the field and the sources of ICL that are more detailed than what is provided by many primary texts. In addition, we have included a chapter on a defense that is almost ubiquitous in ICL — that of *nullum crimen sine lege* — that provides insights into ICL reasoning and rhetoric. In so doing, we hope to convey some of the deep structure of the field, with all its uncertainties, inconsistencies, *lacunae*, and idealism. Throughout the book, we move between macro and micro perspectives to convey the full panoply of issues presented by this relatively new area of law. As a result, this book is meant to operate only partially as a comprehensive "nutshell" text for the field of ICL. Taken as a whole, we hope this book will provide a useful framework for understanding the fascinating field of ICL.

Although we touch on some central questions of procedure concerned with enforcement and adjudicative jurisdiction, we primarily approach the field as one of substantive international law adjudicated before international, or quasi-international, institutions. We are thus concerned with the origins, elements, and evolution of international crimes. In this regard, we focus on what we consider to be the core ICL crimes: genocide, crimes against humanity, and war crimes. These are also termed *atrocity crimes* in the literature to distinguish them from other crimes that may also be the subject of international law, such as drug trafficking or money laundering. These atrocity crimes are within the subject matter jurisdiction of the ad hoc tribunals and the International Criminal Court (ICC). These are also the crimes over which many states can by treaty or statute exercise universal jurisdiction. As such, although most of the case law mentioned in the text forms part of the jurisprudence of the international (and hybrid) criminal tribunals, we occasionally address proceedings in national courts because ICL is subject to a high degree of concurrent jurisdiction, with domestic and international authorities having a role to play in ensuring comprehensive and complementary enforcement.

From this core, we also venture into the periphery by providing materials on the crimes of aggression and the so-called treaty crimes (such as torture and terrorism). The prohibition against torture is universally accepted. Nonetheless, as a result of the so-called "war on terrorism," the definition of torture is today contested. The crimes of terrorism and aggression give rise to unique conceptual difficulties. The crime of international terrorism, to the extent that there is such a concept in general international law, is often implicated in circumstances in which the prohibitions against war crimes, crimes against humanity, and even genocide may be equally applicable. Nonetheless, a strong sentiment has emerged that terrorism *stricto sensu* is something altogether different and deserves separate treatment in the canon of ICL. The crime of aggression is also a disputed concept, in part because it has the potential to complicate determinations of threats to the peace that are textually committed in the United Nations Charter to the "political" branches — the Security Council and, to a lesser extent, the General Assembly. A determination in a penal proceeding that the crime of aggression has occurred has the potential to contradict political determinations involving the same situation or state and thus to invite institutional conflicts.

Our focus is primarily on *international* criminal law. We do, however, make reference to some crimes that more accurately may be considered *transnational* crimes. Transnational criminal law encompasses crimes with a transnational dimension that are prohibited and prosecuted primarily at the domestic level (although they may also be the subject of multilateral treaties). The emphasis on transnational implies that the borders of at least two states are crossed in some fashion during the inception or commission of the offense, or where the offense creates direct or indirect effects on more than one country. For some crimes, this transnational dimension is inherent to the offense itself (as in export crimes or various forms of trafficking or smuggling). Other crimes may be committed domestically or transnationally, depending on the circumstances (such as mail fraud or money laundering).

In light of our focus on substantive law, this book gives only cursory treatment to procedural issues relevant to the domestic prosecution of crimes with international dimensions, such as questions of extradition, transnational mutual assistance, choice of law, and the recognition of foreign penal judgments. On the whole, we think these topics are best taught as specialized courses in transnational criminal law and procedure. Although the international community is increasingly generating international law to address these dimensions of transnational crime, solutions are largely the product of the unique constitutional, statutory, and jurisprudential frameworks of individual nations and adjudicative institutions. We also spend little time on the growing international body of criminal procedural and evidentiary law being developed by the ad hoc criminal tribunals. Although the international law governing criminal procedure and evidence presents a fascinating and *sui generis* blend of elements from the common law and civil law traditions, this material is also best covered in a specialized procedural or comparative law course. The field of international criminal procedural law is destined to continue to evolve in the next few years as the ad hoc tribunals wind down their work and the ICC becomes the primary game in town.

Although ICL is ultimately a course of substantive law, it is impossible to consider the relevant law without reference to background issues of state sovereignty, foreign policy, national security, and the exercise of power in international relations. The international community and individual states do not resort to ICL in a vacuum. Rather, choosing to implement a regime of international criminal justice is a political choice. The decision to pursue criminal trials is influenced by a number of variables often at odds with the legalistic principles underlying criminal justice in its platonic state. Thus it is important to consider what role ICL is playing in the particular historical moment in which it has been invoked and what other options may have been available to elites with decision-making power. These other options — such as amnesties, reparations, efforts at reconciliation and rehabilitation, symbolic memorials, and so on — are the subject of our final chapter on alternatives to ICL. ICL is often an exercise in idealism reflecting the belief in a world governed by law and altruism rather than power or apathy. At the same time, it is a course on the limits of such idealism in the face of *realpolitik*.

Although ICL is at its height of codification, the field is still very much in a state of evolution, and the ad hoc tribunals and the ICC continue to issue important judgments that resolve outstanding doctrinal issues. This text, by providing the basic framework for understanding the field of ICL, will lay the foundation for understanding and assimilating new developments when they inevitably occur. Although the contexts and institutions of ICL may vary, the substantive law is converging to a certain extent, making this one of the most dynamic topics of public international law and a fascinating addition to a course of legal study.

Ronald Slye
Seattle, Washington
Beth Van Schaack
Santa Clara, California

November 2008

essentials

International Criminal Law

part I
The Discipline of International Criminal Law

This part addresses fundamental questions concerning international criminal law as a distinct discipline of public international law. It begins here by tackling the question of what areas of law the field of international criminal law encompasses. This preliminary definitional discussion is followed in Chapter 1 by a concise history of this body of law, with reference to key treaties, instruments, institutions, and historical moments. Chapter 2 introduces the primary institutions that adjudicate international criminal law and the way in which these institutions mediate, accommodate, and threaten the principle of state sovereignty — a foundational principle of international relations. Chapter 3 addresses the way in which international criminal law is made, with reference to the traditional sources of public international law. Chapter 4 discusses the justifications for raising certain crimes to the international level; in other words, why a particular set of killings should trigger international, as well as domestic, jurisdiction. Finally, Chapter 5 considers the way in which tribunals have addressed situations in which the extant international criminal law is incomplete, vague, or indeterminate while remaining faithful to the principle of legality. These chapters should enable you to better evaluate the relative authoritativeness of the various sources of law being cited by parties and tribunals as they resolve contested doctrinal issues before them in the cases you read.

WHAT IS INTERNATIONAL CRIMINAL LAW?

Academics and practitioners often do not agree on the full contours of the field of international criminal law (ICL) as a distinct discipline. In fact, we suspect that the readers of this volume may be taught very different subjects in their respective courses on ICL. Part of this definitional disagreement stems from the fact that ICL is a relatively new discipline. Although ICL has a few long taproots (as discussed in the chapter on the history of ICL), most of its history starts with the post–World War II period when two major bodies of law converged. Modern ICL sits at the intersection of public international law — which historically regulated the behavior of states on the world scene — and domestic criminal law — which metes out individualized criminal penalties for breaches of the peace. Although the individual arrived late on the scene as a full subject of public international law, she now sits front and center in ICL as victim and perpetrator.

This definitional disagreement also reflects the fact that contemporary devotees (both practitioners and scholars) have entered the field from different places, including the disciplines of domestic criminal law, international human rights law (IHR), and international humanitarian law (IHL). One's understanding of a field is heavily influenced by one's point of entry. Criminalists therefore tend to build the field outward from a domestic foundation to cover the transnational dimensions of domestic criminal law and the various ways that states endeavor to extend their penal law abroad. Some of this body of law is more accurately described as transnational criminal law, rather than ICL *stricto sensu*, although the two bodies of law often draw from and influence each other. Transnational criminal law focuses in part on issues of substantive law — such as the ways in which states incorporate international crimes into their domestic penal codes or otherwise criminalize conduct with extraterritorial dimensions — but also on procedural issues, such as the provision of mutual legal assistance among states, processes of extradition and prisoner transfer, and the recognition of foreign judgments. Individuals who approach the field from the human rights tradition tend to focus on the prosecution of so-called atrocity crimes — genocide, war crimes against civilians, and crimes against humanity. When human rights advocates take up ICL, they adopt a different orientation from their brethren working in the domestic realm, who are often most concerned with the rights of the accused and executive overreaching rather than with the prerogatives of the prosecutor and under-enforcement. Finally, individuals who approach ICL from the perspective of military justice are primarily interested in crimes committed in the context of armed conflicts involving prohibited tactics of war and protected persons. This dimension of the field at times requires a high degree of technical knowledge about military tactics and technology.

In this text, and in our work, we approach the field first and foremost as a subset of public international law involving the use of criminal sanctions to enforce law that is primarily international in its origins. We thus define ICL as the body of law that assigns individual criminal responsibility for breaches of public international law. Given this emphasis on the field's international law pedigree, we take international law sources — treaties, international custom, general principles of law, jurisprudence generated by international institutions, jurisprudence generated by domestic institutions applying substantive international law, and the writings of publicists — as our point of departure. To facilitate this approach, this text provides an overview chapter on the sources of ICL for those students who have not yet taken a basic course in public international law or who would value a refresher of basic principles from an ICL perspective. At the same time, we recognize that ICL is not purely a field of international law. States have incorporated many substantive norms of ICL — with varying degrees of fealty to their international origins — into their domestic penal codes. On the basis of these statutes, domestic courts are increasingly prosecuting international crimes under various forms of extraterritorial jurisdiction. The contemporary field is thus characterized by a fascinating cross-fertilization between domestic and international legislative, judicial, and executive actions.

Modern ICL has gathered together once unconnected strands of public international law under one rubric. Some elements of ICL have their origins in the IHR edifice. Many multilateral IHR treaties, conventions, and covenants (such as the International Covenant for Civil and Political Rights) and the human rights machinery they created (such as the Human Rights Committee) concern themselves with the allocation of state responsibility. Other treaties (such as the Convention Against Torture and Other Cruel, Inhuman or Degrading Treatment or Punishment) also envision criminal penalties for individuals who violate treaty provisions. Thus, acts of genocide, torture, slavery, and other crimes against humanity may give rise to both state civil responsibility as IHR violations and individual criminal responsibility as ICL violations. Other elements of ICL have their origins in IHL, also called the law of war or the law of armed conflict. Although much of IHL concerns state responsibility, certain violations of this body of law also carry criminal penalties when committed in the context of armed conflict. Such "war crimes" include abuses of civilians or prisoners of war (POWs), using weapons calculated to cause unnecessary suffering, or employing methods of war that cause harm disproportional to the military advantage to be gained.

ICL materialized into a discrete field of law in the modern period as a reaction to a global war of catastrophic proportions. Since then, it has been a feature of civil war armistices and postwar occupations. During the democratic transitions in Latin America and elsewhere, ICL has become part of the repertoire of any transitional government moving from a period of repression and state terror to one in which the rule of law can take root. ICL is also employed outside of conflict zones in states with only transient custody over offenders, but scant other connection to the crimes in question. Even more controversially, states sometimes attempt to assert jurisdiction over individuals who are not in their custody and who have never stepped foot on their territories. ICL thus supports expansive assertions of international and extraterritorial jurisdiction, although the outer limits are still in flux. The cases and materials you will no doubt read in your ICL course will be drawn from these disparate contexts. The next chapter on the history of ICL outlines how the field reached this point.

~ 1 ~

A Concise History of International Criminal Law

INTRODUCTION: THE GENESIS STORY

The international criminal proceedings following World War II (1939–1945) are credited with launching the modern regime of international criminal law (ICL). Antecedents, however, trace back for centuries and across the globe. In particular, ICL draws on four main strands of international law history: nineteenth-century prohibitions against piracy, the subsequent regulations of slavery and the slave trade, the once theological and later secular theory of just war, and international humanitarian law (IHL) or the law of armed conflict. On this foundation, the international community gradually built the norms, rules, instruments, and institutions that now make up the modern ICL machinery. This chapter interweaves the history of substantive norms with that of evolving principles of domestic and international jurisdiction, as these narratives are virtually inseparable in ICL.

Several features of this evolution are worth pointing out at the outset. First, with the exception of the post–World War II period, when the international community created tribunals and the law they were to apply virtually simultaneously, many ICL norms developed well before there were judicial institutions available to enforce them. In the terminology of Dan-Cohn, ICL had conduct rules without corresponding enforcement rules (rules directing officials to enforce the conduct rules).[1] As is the case with much public international law, it took some time before the international community was willing to put principle into practice. Second, until very recently, the design of much of the system was ad hoc and reactive to world events rather than the result of any sort of coherent forward-looking process. A notable exception is the permanent International Criminal Court (ICC), which has only prospective jurisdiction. Third, the history of ICL is marked by greater and greater incursions into arenas that were historically the exclusive province of sovereign states. Thus, ICL norms increasingly govern the treatment a state can legally accord its citizens and others under its jurisdiction, and such acts are increasingly the subject of international scrutiny, condemnation, and criminal prosecution.

SUBSTANTIVE LAW ANTECEDENTS TO MODERN ICL

Just War: *Jus Ad Bellum*

Although early Christian theology manifested an "extreme pacifism" that prohibited participation in war, by the time of St. Augustine (C.E. 354-430) a theory of *just war* had developed, which stated that resort to war was permitted only if the ends were just. Other religious and national traditions also preserved the right to engage in war against "infidels" or to avenge a wrong. Efforts to identify the necessary conditions for war constitute the *jus* (or *ius*) *ad bellum* — the set of rules regulating the decision to use military or armed force in international relations.

In his *Summa Theologica*, for example, St. Thomas Aquinas (C.E. 1225-1274) set forth the following requirements for a war to be considered just: (1) it must be authorized by a legitimate sovereign; (2) it must be necessary for the achievement of a just cause; and (3) it must be for a "right intention," that is, the restoration of a good and just order and not in furtherance of injustice.[2] Self-defense against an unjust act of aggression, punishment for an unjust act of aggression, or recovery of something wrongly taken all qualified as just causes for Aquinas.

By the sixteenth century, however, it became accepted that there may be a just war on both sides, and the laws of war gradually shifted attention away from identifying the acceptable reasons for going to war to regulating the effects of war — the *jus* (or *ius*) *in bello*. Eventually, the notion of just war dissipated almost entirely. By the time of World War I, war was viewed as the prerogative of the sovereign and a valid instrument of foreign policy. International law had thus dramatically shifted focus. It went from evaluating the morality and justice of going to war, but only weakly regulating the means and methods of warfare, to a resignation that the justness of war was too difficult to universalize combined with renewed efforts to humanize the means and methods of warfare. This shift in emphasis from *jus ad bellum* to *jus in bello* still largely describes the state of the law of armed conflict today, although the halting development of the crimes of terrorism and aggression harkens back to the *jus ad bellum* tradition.

Penal Antecedents: Piracy and Slavery

Piracy and the practices of slavery and the slave trade were some of the earliest international crimes outside of war that states coordinated among themselves to criminalize and prosecute. Up until this point, ICL primarily focused on acts committed by one state against the nationals of another state — the traditional paradigm for war crimes. With the recognition of piracy and slavery as international crimes, ICL turned its attention to private actors that operated within the interstitial space separating nation states. We thus see a shift from a focus solely on activity that is international, in the sense of activity between distinct nation states, to an acceptance of international jurisdiction over activity that affects the efficient operation of the international system (piracy) or that implicates universal moral values (slavery).

Piracy—widespread in the eighteenth and nineteenth centuries—was a crime that, in the absence of any international tribunal and because it was committed on the high seas, could long be prosecuted before the courts of any nation able to apprehend the perpetrators. The prohibition against piracy thus gave rise to the notion of universal jurisdiction, now a central feature of modern ICL.

Collective efforts to combat piracy in many respects began with the 1856 Paris Declaration Respecting Maritime Law, which abolished forms of piracy in armed conflict and was signed by nearly all the imperial powers. As the international community convened the League of Nations, there was talk of regulating piracy more generally through international agreements; however, this effort was abandoned as delegates thought it insufficiently pressing to merit international attention and got bogged down in distinctions between definitions of piracy under international and municipal law. It was not until the first Law of the Sea Convention was drafted in 1958 that an omnibus treaty-based definition emerged. Article 15 of the Geneva Convention of the High Seas defines piracy as:

> (1) Any illegal acts of violence, detention or any act of depredation, committed for private ends by the crew or the passengers of a private ship or a private aircraft, and directed:
>> (a) On the high seas, against another ship or aircraft, or against persons or property on board such ship or aircraft;

(b) Against a ship, aircraft, persons or property in a place outside the jurisdiction of any State;

(2) Any act of voluntary participation in the operation of a ship or of an aircraft with knowledge of facts making it a pirate ship or aircraft;

(3) Any act of inciting or of intentionally facilitating an act described in sub-paragraph 1 or sub-paragraph 2 of this article.[3]

This definition appears, with stylistic changes, in Article 101 of the 1982 United Nations Law of the Sea Convention.[4] The once customary practice of universal jurisdiction over piracy finds expression in the 1982 Convention at Article 105: "On the high seas, or in any other place outside the jurisdiction of any State, every State may seize a pirate ship . . . and arrest the persons and seize the property on board . . . [and] may decide upon the penalties to be imposed."

The abolition of slavery and the slave trade is another important chapter in the story of ICL and international human rights. Abolitionists working across the globe were responsible for gaining the passage of domestic laws outlawing slavery and the slave trade and convincing nation states to enter into multilateral treaties doing the same. Great Britain led the charge, entering into a network of bilateral and multilateral treaties that both permitted the searching of ships suspected of transporting individuals to be sold into slavery and established mixed tribunals in ports around the world to condemn slave ships. As early as the 1815 Congress of Vienna, signatories called for the voluntary abolition of the slave trade, which it described as "repugnant to the principles of humanity and universal morality."

The 1890 General Act for the Repression of the African Slave Trade ("the Brussels Act") finally called on all signatories to criminalize slave trading and to prosecute offenders — an early example of the concept of treaty-based universal

jurisdiction.* States also established an international moni-
toring commission, the Temporary Slavery Commission (1924-
1925), which expanded its own mandate to consider analogous
practices of forced labor, debt slavery, and sexual slavery. This
was followed a year later by the relatively anodyne Slavery
Convention of 1926, which called for the "progressive" suppression of slavery, but contained no concrete enforcement
regime. The subsequent Supplementary Convention on the
Abolition of Slavery, the Slave Trade, and Institutions and
Practices Similar to Slavery (1956) returned to the regime of
the Brussels Act and required domestic criminalization and prosecution. In particular, Article 6(1) provided that:

> The act of enslaving another person or of inducing another
> person to give himself or a person dependent upon him into
> slavery, or of attempting these acts, or being accessory
> thereto, or being a party to a conspiracy to accomplish any
> such acts, shall be a criminal offence under the laws of the
> States Parties to this Convention and persons convicted
> thereof shall be liable to punishment.

This legal response to slavery and related acts finds expression
in more modern international treaties prohibiting forced labor,
such as the 1932 Convention Concerning Forced or Com-
pulsory Labour, and the trafficking of persons, such as the
Protocol to Prevent, Suppress and Punish Trafficking in Persons Especially Women and Children (2000), which supplements the United Nations Convention against Transnational
Organized Crime (2000).

---

*The Act's effects were not all beneficial or beneficent; part of its enforce-
ment regime involved establishing colonial administrations in the African inter-
ior, putting "an anti-slavery guise on the colonial occupation and exploitation of
Africa." Suzanne Miers, *Slavery and the Slave Trade as International Issues 1890-
1939*, 19(2) Slavery and Abolition 19 (1998).

International Humanitarian Law

Modern international criminal law also borrows heavily from IHL. IHL describes those international rules governing armed conflict. As long as groups of people, and later states, have waged war, there have been rules in place governing acceptable behavior in armed conflict. Although the history of the law of war is often told from the perspective of international conferences held in The Hague and Geneva, as described in more detail later, all human cultures manifest efforts to regulate this seemingly inherent aspect of our shared humanity. Recorded history confirms that the ancient Israelites, Greeks, and Romans, for example, distinguished between combatants and civilians and made only the former the lawful object of attack. There are African and Islamic traditions dictating that captured combatants and civilians should be humanely treated. Likewise, in ancient combat, certain weapons or tactics were prohibited if they caused excessive damage. The codes of chivalry developed in Medieval Europe set forth rules of combat that applied within the knighthood. In 1139, for example, the Second Lateran Council condemned the use of the crossbow, foreshadowing subsequent efforts to ban the use of weapons viewed as unnecessarily cruel or inhumane. Many of these ancient principles and rules are now contained in a web of bilateral and multilateral treaties, making IHL the most codified area of ICL. A rich body of customary international law supplements this extensive treaty regime to this day.

From the perspective of the development of positive law, IHL rules historically evolved along parallel tracks. The set of treaties emerging from international conferences in The Hague and elsewhere concerned the means and methods of warfare and sought to limit the tactics of war and prohibit the use of certain weapons designed to cause excessive suffering

("Hague Law"). Treaties sponsored by the International Committee of the Red Cross (ICRC) in Geneva established protections for individuals uniquely impacted by war, especially those who do not — or who no longer — participate directly in hostilities, such as the shipwrecked, prisoners of war (POWs), and civilians and noncombatants ("Geneva Law"). In addition, whereas the law of war originally and almost exclusively addressed international armed conflicts, with notable exceptions such as the 1863 Lieber Code governing the U.S. Civil War, IHL rules increasingly apply to noninternational armed conflicts. Over time, these various strands of IHL have converged to create a more complete corpus of law. Article 8 of the Statute of the International Criminal Court reflects this gradual merging of Hague and Geneva Law and of the law applicable in international and noninternational armed conflicts.

The first multilateral IHL treaty in the strict sense was the 1856 Paris Declaration Respecting Maritime Law, referenced earlier in connection with the history of piracy, which addressed privateering and the neutrality of commercial ships in times of war, among other topics. It was followed by the First Geneva Convention of 1864. This treaty was the brainchild of Henry Dunant, an inadvertent witness to the Battle of Solferino between Austria and the kingdom of Sardinia prior to the Italian unification. After seeing thousands of soldiers lying wounded and dying on the battlefield, Dunant organized Italian citizens to provide care. He later wrote a highly influential book, *Un Souvenir de Solferino* ("A Memory of Solferino"), in which he advocated the creation of a neutral organization to care for the wounded in war. He also convinced the Swiss government to convene a diplomatic conference of states to draft rules to prevent the suffering he had witnessed. The conference led to the signing of the first Geneva Convention by several European and American states.

Aside from creating the ICRC,* the treaty established rules governing the duty to provide relief to the wounded without distinction of nationality, confirmed the neutrality of medical units, and designated the red cross symbol as a protected insignia.

By the turn of the century, the international community increasingly turned its attention to codifying the laws of war. Peace conferences were held in The Hague in 1899 and 1907 that led to the conclusion of multiple conventions addressing land and maritime war. (Ironically, preparations for a third conference were interrupted by World War I.) The 1899 Hague Conventions, signed but never ratified, addressed themselves to the Pacific Settlement of International Disputes (Hague I), the Laws and Customs of War on Land (Hague II), Maritime Warfare (Hague III), the Launching of Projectiles and Explosives from Balloons (Hague IV, 1), Asphyxiating Gases (Hague IV, 2), and Expanding Bullets (Hague IV, 3). Delegates reconvened in The Hague in 1906 to draft additional treaties, which have superseded their predecessors and expanded consideration to the Opening of Hostilities (Hague III), the Rights and Duties of Neutral Powers and Persons in Case of War on Land (Hague V), the Status of Enemy Merchant Ships at the Outbreak of Hostilities (Hague VI), the Laying of Submarine Automatic Contact Mines (Hague VIII), Bombardment by Naval Forces in Time of War (Hague IX), and the Discharge of Projectiles and Explosives from Balloons (Hague XIV).

The most important treaty to emerge from this latter Conference was undoubtedly the fourth, Respecting the Laws and

---

*The ICRC is a nongovernmental organization based in Geneva, Switzerland, that operates as a neutral, impartial, and independent organization to protect victims of armed conflict. In this capacity, the ICRC monitors compliance with the Geneva Conventions by warring parties, organizes care for those wounded on the battlefield, supervises the treatment of POWs, traces those missing in armed conflict, and mediates between warring parties.

Customs of War on Land,[5] which contained a detailed set of regulations in its annex. The fundamental principle of *jus in bello* is found in Article 22, which states that "[t]he right of belligerents to adopt means of injuring the enemy is not unlimited." The regulations go on to forbid poisoned weapons; the killing or wounding of those belligerents who are *hors de combat* (i.e., those who have laid down their weapons and no longer present a threat); means of warfare "calculated to cause unnecessary suffering"; the destruction or seizure of enemy property unless "imperatively demanded by the necessities of war"; and the attack of undefended towns, villages, dwellings, or buildings.

The Hague Conventions also introduced the so-called Martens Clause, named after the Russian delegate to the first Hague Conferences. The Clause appears in the preamble of the Hague Conventions of 1899 and 1907, in a modified form in the 1949 Geneva Conventions and Protocol II, and in the main text of Protocol I of 1977 of the Geneva Conventions. In its inaugural formulation, it provided that:

> Until a more complete code of the laws of war is issued, the High Contracting Parties think it right to declare that in cases not included in the Regulations adopted by them, populations and belligerents remain under the protection and empire of the principles of international law, as they result from the usages established between civilized nations, from the laws of humanity and the requirements of the public conscience.

Martens introduced the declaration after delegates at the Peace Conference failed to agree on the status of civilians who took up arms against an occupying force. Large military powers argued that they should be treated as *francs-tireurs* — a term first used to describe irregular military formations that had taken up arms against the Germans during the Franco-Prussian War (1870-1871) and from then on used to refer more generally to guerrilla fighters. Conversely, smaller states contended that these irregular fighters should be treated as privileged combatants. Although the clause was originally formulated to resolve this particular dispute, it has subsequently reappeared in various but similar forms in later treaties regulating armed conflicts.

The clause, although somewhat abstruse, contains several important ideas. First, it highlights the legal and moral bases of humanitarian obligations by making reference to natural law ideas, such as the sentiments of humanity. Second, by making reference to the practices of "civilized states," the clause directly incorporates customary law principles as a source of rules to fill in gaps in codified law. Third, although framed from the perspective of potential victims of violations ("populations and belligerents"), it also suggests a role for courts acting in an enforcement capacity to refer to principles of international law and morality in assigning responsibility for abuses.

Although the Fourth Hague Convention retains modern currency, today's rules of IHL are largely founded on the four Geneva Conventions of 1949, drafted on the heels of World War II and supplemented by their two 1977 Protocols.* The 1949 Conventions were developed to provide specific protections to four classes of individuals not actively involved in combat: the wounded and the sick in the field (Geneva Convention I), wounded and sick at sea (Geneva Convention II), prisoners of war (Geneva Convention III), and civilians and other noncombatants (Geneva Convention IV). The four Geneva Conventions primarily apply to international armed conflicts, although common Article 3 as a "convention in miniature" applies to conflicts "not of an international character." The four Conventions criminalize so-called "grave breaches," which in Geneva Convention III include willful killing, torture

---

*In 2005, a third Protocol recognized the red crystal as a fourth protected symbol alongside the red cross, the red crescent, and the lion and sun, and put to rest a long-standing dispute between the ICRC and the State of Israel, which had long advocated a nonsectarian symbol.

or inhuman treatment, including biological experiments, willfully causing great suffering or serious injury to body or health, depriving a POW of the rights of fair and regular trial, and the taking of hostages and extensive destruction and appropriation of property not justified by military necessity and carried out unlawfully and wantonly. It is notable that these provisions protect core due process rights alongside the physical and mental integrity of persons affected by armed conflict.

The international community adopted two Protocols to the Geneva Conventions in 1977 in response to the changing nature of armed conflict. Protocol I provides a detailed set of rules concerning the obligation to discriminate between military and civilian targets, defines international conflicts as including "armed conflicts in which people are fighting against colonial domination and alien occupation and against racist regimes in the exercise of their right of self-determination," expands the category of privileged combatants to include some members of guerrilla movements, and further defines and clarifies the rules with respect to mercenaries. Protocol II elaborates on the minimum rules in common Article 3 governing noninternational armed conflicts.

EFFORTS TO ENFORCE INTERNATIONAL CRIMINAL LAW

Pre–World War I: Antecedents

The original customary and conventional law of war implicated only state responsibility. In the event of a breach, responsible states were liable to pay reparations or provide other civil remedies to aggrieved nations. Only later did states begin to impose individual criminal liability on breaches of the law of war. Although many point to the trial of Peter von Hagenbach in 1474 in Austria for war crimes as the first prosecution of an individual for war crimes, the earliest recorded trial of an individual for war crimes appears to be the prosecution by an English court in 1305 of Scottish national hero and warrior Sir William Wallace. Sir Wallace was charged with, convicted of, and executed gruesomely for waging a war against the English "sparing neither age nor sex, monk nor nun."[6] The first treaty mention of individual criminal liability for breaches of IHL is found in the work of the Brussels Conference of 1874, which produced a final protocol that was signed by 15 European states but never ratified. Paragraph III stated:

> The laws and customs of war not only forbid unnecessary cruelty and acts of barbarism committed against the enemy; they demand also, on the part of the appropriate authorities, the immediate punishment of these persons who are guilty of these acts, if they are not caused by an absolute necessity.[7]

Jurisdictionally, most early prosecutions for violations of the laws and customs of war were based on the territorial or nationality principles of jurisdiction. A prominent example of an early war crimes prosecution is the 1865 military commission trial of Henry Wirz, a Confederate Captain accused of mistreating and murdering Union soldiers detained in Andersonville prison in violation of the laws and customs of war. Wirz argued that he was unable to ensure proper conditions in the prison and was otherwise just following orders. In pleading his case, he wrote:

> I do not think that I ought to be held responsible for the shortness of rations, for the overcrowded state of the prison (which was in itself a prolific cause of the fearful mortality), for the inadequate supplies of clothing, and of shelters &c. Still I now bear the odium, and men who were prisoners here seemed disposed to wreak their vengeance upon me for what they have suffered, who was only the medium, or I may better say, the tool in the hands of my superiors.[8]

The military commission rejected Wirz's defense and sentenced him to death by hanging. Notwithstanding that many wrote to President Andrew Johnson pleading Wirz's pardon or at least the commutation of the death sentence, Wirz was hanged on November 10, 1865. On the gallows, he reputedly stated: "I know what orders are. And I am being hanged for obeying them."

At the turn of the twentieth century, during an insurrection in the Philippines launched in opposition to U.S. annexation of the territory following the Spanish-American War (1898), the United States convened a number of military commissions to prosecute Filipino insurgents and courts martial to prosecute U.S. service members. These institutions adjudicated both war crimes and common crimes, the latter of which were prosecuted as a function of the U.S. obligations as occupier to maintain public order. Most of the 800 military commission cases involved abuses against Filipino victims (so-called *Americanistas*) who had been accused of collaborating with the American occupiers or opposing the guerillas. These institutions confronted a number of key issues that continue to vex the modern tribunals, such as the definition of crimes triable under the laws of war; forms of liability for lesser participants, accomplices, superiors, and co-conspirators; and legal defenses. The Filipino insurrection marks one of the few times that the U.S. Congress suspended the writ of *habeas corpus*.*

World War I: A False Start

The first modern world war launched the first genuine global effort to address international crimes through the exercise of international and domestic criminal jurisdiction. World War I (1914-1918)—which pitted the Central Powers (composed of

---

*Additional suspensions occurred in the South to combat the Ku Klux Klan and in Hawaii during World War II.

the German, Austro-Hungarian, Bulgarian, and Ottoman Empires) against the Allied and Associated Powers (Great Britain, France, Imperial Russia, later the United States, and others)—precipitated the commission of abuses against combatants, POWs, and civilians on an unprecedented scale. German atrocities included unrestricted submarine warfare, brutal occupations, the targeting of civilians and undefended towns, breaches of neutrality, and—from the perspective of the rest of Europe—the initiation of the war in the first place. The Ottoman Empire, with the Young Turks at the helm, was accused of staging one of the first genocides of the twentieth century in its effort to eradicate the Christian Armenian population of what is now Turkey. Under the pretext of averting an Armenian revolutionary uprising or a "treasonous" alliance with Russia during the war, the Ottoman Empire launched wholesale deportations and massacres that amounted to a virtual extermination of the Armenian population. In all, more than a million people were reportedly killed.

In the face of these offenses, the Allies convened a Commission on the Responsibility of the Authors of the War and on Enforcement of Penalties to inquire into culpable conduct by the Central Powers during the "Great War." The Commission was also to consider the propriety and feasibility of asserting penal jurisdiction over particular individuals—"however highly placed"—accused of committing such breaches. During the ensuing debates over the notion of ascribing individual criminal responsibility for crimes of war, a confluence of ideological and pragmatic objections emerged. On the merits, naysayers—led primarily by the Americans—took issue with the very premise that the principle of state sovereignty could be pierced so dramatically as to hold heads of state and other state actors liable for the collective actions of their sovereigns. Objectors also noted the lack of precedent for such a project and pointed to gaping lacunae in available substantive law. Others argued that trials could lengthen the war if the threat of prosecution was hanging over the parties. As the war ended, realists argued that trials would exacerbate instability in the fledgling Weimar Republic and in Turkey, where new governments were struggling to consolidate their authority in the wake of the war. Others warned that trials could create a dangerous precedent that might come back to bite the Allies in subsequent conflicts. Even where there was support for holding trials in theory, there was little agreement on secondary issues of venue, rules of procedure and evidence, standards of proof, and so on.

In 1919, the Commission presented its final report to the Paris Peace Conference that was at the time negotiating peace agreements with the Central Powers. This report documented "outrages of every description committed on land, at sea, and in the air, against the laws and customs of war and of the laws of humanity."* The report concluded that such crimes should be prosecuted before an international "high tribunal" composed of representatives of the Allied and Associated Powers or before national tribunals. Foreshadowing the notion of crimes against the peace later developed at Nuremberg and Tokyo, the Commission also considered "not strictly war crimes, but acts which provoked the war," such as deliberate violations of the neutrality of Belgium and Luxembourg. Notwithstanding early support for prosecuting German officials for initiating the war, the Commission concluded that acts of aggression should not be the subject of prosecution in light of the lack of legal authority for such a charge and the complexity of undertaking an investigation into the politically charged question of the causes of the war. It reasoned:

The premeditation of a war of aggression, dissimulated under a peaceful pretence, then suddenly declared under false

---

*This latter reference to the "laws of humanity" planted one of the first seeds of the idea that there were crimes against humanity that were punishable separate and apart from conventional war crimes.

> pretexts, is conduct which the public conscience reproves
> and which history will condemn but by reason of the purely
> optional character of the institutions at The Hague for the
> maintenance of peace . . . a war of aggression may not be
> considered as an act directly contrary to positive law, or
> one which can be successfully brought before a tribunal.[9]

The Commission, however, recommended that in the future
"penal sanctions should be provided for such grave outrages
against the elementary principles of international law."[10]

The United States at Annex II advanced four fundamental
reservations to the report's recommendations. First, it objected
to the proposal of creating an international criminal tribunal —
for which, it argued, there was "no precedent, precept, practice, or procedure" — instead of coordinating existing national
military tribunals. Second, it invoked the limitations of jurisdiction when it argued that nations could not legally take part
in the prosecution of crimes committed against the subjects of
other nations. Third, it rejected the notion that any court of law
could prosecute violations of the "laws or principles of humanity," on the ground that such violations were moral rather than
legal breaches and were, as such, nonjusticiable. Fourth, it
argued that to prosecute a head of state outside of his national
jurisdiction would violate basic precepts and privileges of
sovereignty. The Americans indicated their intention not to
participate in any international trial and instead focused
their energies on President Wilson's project for the League
of Nations.

From this point, the potential liability of German and
Ottoman defendants proceeded along separate tracks. The
1919 Treaty of Versailles, ending the war with Germany,
required Germany to accept full responsibility for causing
the war (the so-called war guilt clause), make substantial
territorial concessions, and pay reparations. Most important
for our purposes, Article 227 envisioned the establishment

of an international tribunal composed of representatives of the United States, Great Britain, France, Italy, and Japan to try the former German Emperor, Kaiser Wilhelm II, who was thus singled out for his central role in orchestrating German crimes during the war. In agreeing to this provision, the United States capitulated on its prior position in favor of domestic trials. The envisioned tribunal was to prosecute the Kaiser for "a supreme offense against international morality and the sanctity of treaties" and was to be "guided by the highest motives of international policy, with a view to vindicating the solemn obligations of international undertakings and the validity of international morality."[11] According to Article 228 of the Treaty of Versailles, lesser German defendants were to be tried before the domestic military tribunals of the Allied and Associated Powers. This same provision obligated Germany to hand over "all persons accused of having committed an act in violation of the laws and customs of war, who are specified either by name or by the rank, office or employment which they held under the German authorities." Mixed military tribunals were to prosecute individuals "guilty of criminal acts against the nationals of more than one of the Allied and Associated Powers" pursuant to Article 229. By these terms, the Treaty of Versailles became the first peace treaty to contemplate war crimes trials.

By the time the Versailles Treaty entered into force, six months after the signing of the 1918 general armistice, the Kaiser had fled to the Netherlands, which had remained neutral during the war. The Netherlands refused to extradite him for trial, invoking a long history of providing asylum to political refugees and the double criminality rule, which prevented the Kaiser's extradition to face justice for acts that were not crimes under Dutch law. An American attempt to kidnap the Kaiser was thwarted, and he died in 1941. Article 227 thus remained a dead letter. The Allies never enforced the other penal provisions of the Treaty, either. In the face of continued

Allied equivocation over war crimes trials and fierce objections among the German public to the possible extradition of German nationals, Germany artfully proposed hosting domestic trials before the German Supreme Court in Leipzig. The Allies, desperate to salvage some vestige of the project, agreed. To the extent that cases were brought (out of more than 800 individuals accused of war crimes, including high-level German officials, only 12 proceedings were held), trials proceeded sluggishly against low-level defendants and resulted in acquittals or disproportionately low sentences. Although the Allies protested and then quit the proceedings, they never made good on their threats to further sanction Germany, and no additional cases were pursued.

With respect to the Ottoman Empire, the new Turkish regime — under pressure from the British and perhaps in an effort to head off international trials of its own former leaders — court-martialed in Constantinople an impressive array of once-prominent officials for "crimes against humanity and civilization" and other wartime offenses. Some defendants were tried in absentia because Germany refused to extradite them. The trials provoked a surge of Nationalist backlash, prompting the Turkish government to release a number of important defendants, ostensibly on the ground that there was no case against them. The British took many of these individuals into custody in Malta and elsewhere to prevent their release. As the Turkish civil war heated up, however, the British eventually swapped or released its prisoners, who had been languishing in pretrial detention.

The first treaty of peace with Turkey, the 1920 Treaty of Sèvres, contained accountability provisions mirroring those in the Treaty of Versailles with respect to the right of the Allies to convene military tribunals to prosecute persons guilty of having committed acts in violation of the laws and customs of war. Article 230 also contemplated a tribunal created by the League of Nations to address "the massacres committed during the continuance of the state of war on territory which formed part of the Turkish Empire on August 1, 1914." After the Turkish War of Independence, Mustafa Kemal (a.k.a. Atatürk), who led the Nationalists to victory in the civil war, denounced and refused to ratify the Treaty of Sèvres. Renegotiations produced a successor treaty, the 1923 Treaty of Lausanne, which was silent on the question of international justice or legal account-ability for abuses. To this day, Turkey has never acknowledged responsibility for the campaign against the Armenians and pro-tests diplomatically whenever it is mentioned.

The World War I experiment with international criminal justice thus proved short-lived, a "fiasco" even, according to Henry Morgenthau, Sr., ambassador to the Ottoman Empire from 1913 to 1916. The fragile unity and resolve among the Allies dissipated in the immediate postwar period. Evolving events overtook idealism. In the end, only a handful of indivi-duals were tried, and those who were prosecuted were essen-tially exonerated. This failed history was ever present a mere two decades later as a world war once again ravaged the globe.

The Interwar Period: Efforts to Avert Another World War

"The end of a great war frequently brings a revision of the laws of war in its wake."[12] World War I bore this out. In the tenuous peace during the short interwar period, the international community came together to build institutions to diffuse and settle international disputes and to fill some of the legal lacu-nae that had become so apparent in the post–World War I period. Institutionally, the League of Nations — which fea-tured as its "judicial branch" the precursor to the International Court of Justice, the Permanent Court of International Justice (PCIJ) — announced its goal of providing a global forum for "safeguard[ing] the peace of nations" by resolving inter-national disputes without recourse to war. In 1920, an advisory commission convened in connection with the League of Nations recommended the creation of a permanent international criminal court to have jurisdiction over "crimes constituting a breach of international public order or against the universal law of nations." The proposal, however, was rejected as "premature," and only the PCIJ was created with civil jurisdiction over states.

In response to the new weapons systems deployed during World War I, treaties were drafted regulating or prohibiting the use of various means and methods of war, such as bacteriological agents, poison gas, and submarines, and protecting vulnerable classes of persons, such as POWs and the wounded and sick. The catastrophic war also revived aspects of the just war theory as reflected in the optimistic, if not naive, Kellogg-Briand Pact (or Pact of Paris). The Pact, originally a bilateral treaty between the United States and France that was later opened to global ratification, pledged its members to:

> condemn recourse to war for the solution of international controversies, and renounce it as an instrument of national policy in their relations with one another . . . [and] agree that the settlement or solution of all disputes or conflicts of whatever nature or of whatever origin they may be, which may arise among them, shall never be sought except by pacific means.[13]

Almost immediately after it entered into force, however, the Pact became a nullity, as Japan invaded Manchuria (1931), Italy invaded Ethiopia (1935), and Germany invaded Poland (1939), effectively launching World War II.

World War II: A Return to First Principles

The post–World War II period is nothing less than a watershed moment in the development of ICL. This period heralded the development of two international tribunals for adjudicating international crimes — the International Military Tribunal for the Trial of German Major War Criminals (the IMT or Nuremberg Tribunal) and the International Military Tribunal for the Far East (the IMTFE or Tokyo Tribunal). The Allies established these tribunals to prosecute, respectively, high-level German and Japanese military and civilian authorities whose crimes "had no particular geographic localisation."[14] The Nuremberg Tribunal was established by agreement (the London Agreement of August 8, 1945) among the four victorious Allied Powers: France, the Soviet Union, the United Kingdom, and the United States. By contrast, the Tokyo Tribunal was technically established by a special proclamation issued by the Supreme Allied Commander of the Far East, U.S. General Douglas MacArthur, although with the acquiescence of the other Allied Powers. International judicial proceedings before these institutions were followed by hundreds of trials before military and civilian tribunals in the various zones of occupation throughout Europe and the Pacific theater. As these enforcement efforts were underway, the codification of ICL also began in earnest, with the promulgation of treaties addressing genocide (the 1948 Convention on the Prevention and Punishment of the Crime of Genocide) and war crimes (the four Geneva Conventions of 1949).

That the Allies would adopt a strategy of international criminal justice in the post–World War II period was not a foregone conclusion. For one, the memory of the abject failure of the last effort at international justice following World War I remained fresh. The British and Soviets were more inclined to purge, punish, and, in some cases, simply execute defeated principals without elaborate legal processes. (The devastated French played little role in the initial decision making.) Even Prime Minister Churchill argued in favor of executions for Nazi leaders and summary legal proceedings for the rank and file. In the end, it was pressure from the United States — and in particular from the Secretary of War, Henry Stimson —

that resulted in the adoption of strictly legal processes to adjudge German and Japanese officials accused of violations of international law.

This dramatic change in the U.S. position toward international justice provides one of the most fascinating chapters of the history of ICL. As you will recall, after World War I, the United States was the staunchest opponent of the creation of an international tribunal, considering such an institution to be unprecedented and potentially dangerous. The United States also rejected both the justiciability of crimes against humanity as separate and apart from more traditional war crimes and the notion of a crime of initiating and waging an aggressive war. By the end of World War II, however, the United States had become the champion of trials, domestic and international (even single-handedly establishing the Tokyo Tribunal by executive fiat). The United States also directed the prosecution of crimes against the peace and conspiracy charges.

How can we explain the *volte-face* of the United States? Much may have turned on a key protagonist in this story — Stimson, a lawyer by training. Stimson never wavered in his advocacy that the Nazi defendants should face trials rather than firing squads, a countermajoritarian position when U.S. public opinion at the time strongly favored summary execution or immediate imprisonment. Stimson remained staunchly opposed to alternative proposals that hundreds if not thousands of Nazis be summarily shot, insisting that even the Nazi defendants deserved due process of law in keeping with the best of the American legalistic tradition. Stimson was able to pass the baton to Justice Robert H. Jackson, a Supreme Court Justice (the last one without a law degree) who represented the United States at the Paris Peace Conference and eventually was chief U.S. prosecutor at Nuremberg. Once the Allies arrived at the Paris Peace Conference, the American delegation imposed its postwar strategy on the rest of the Allies, and the Nuremberg Tribunal was established.

The Tribunal convened November 20, 1945 to October 1, 1946. The Tokyo Tribunal (sitting from May 3, 1946 to November 12, 1948) followed closely on its heels.

The subject matter jurisdiction of the two tribunals reflects the ideas being cast about in the post–World War I period. Notwithstanding the original Allies' reticence about criminalizing the resort to war, the Nuremberg and Tokyo Charters at Articles 6(a) and 5(a), respectively, enabled the prosecution for "crimes against the peace," defined as the "planning, preparation, initiation or waging of a war of aggression, or a war in violation of international treaties, agreements or assurances." Prosecutable war crimes, uncontroversially defined in subsection (b), included "murder, ill-treatment or deportation to slave labor or for any other purpose of civilian population of or in occupied territory, murder or ill-treatment of prisoners of war or persons on the seas, killing of hostages, plunder of public or private property, wanton destruction of cities, towns or villages, or devastation not justified by military necessity." The Charter heralded the revival of the concept of crimes against humanity, although little reference was made in the judgment to the crime's World War I ancestry. The crime was defined as "murder, extermination, enslavement, deportation, and other inhumane acts committed against any civilian population, before or during the war, or persecutions on political, racial or religious grounds in execution of or in connection with any crime within the jurisdiction of the Tribunal, whether or not in violation of the domestic law of the country where perpetrated."

Twenty-four Nazi leaders were indicted before the IMT, which was composed of judges from the four Allies. One defendant was too ill to go to trial (Krupp);* one committed

---

*IMT prosecutors attempted to substitute his son Alfried (who ran his family's armaments company during the war) as a defendant, but the judges ruled the substitution came too close to trial. Alfried was later tried in subsequent proceedings for his use of slave labor. As a result of U.S. intervention during the

suicide (Ley); and one was tried and convicted to death in absentia (Bormann). The Tribunal tried the other 21 defendants.[15] Three of those were acquitted (Schacht, von Papen, and Fritzsche); seven were sentenced to prison terms ranging from ten years to life (Hess, Funk, Dönitz, Raeder, von Schirach, Speer, and von Neurath). The other 11 were sentenced to death (Göring, von Rivventrop, Keitel, Kaltenbrunner, Rosenberg, Frank, Frick, Streicher, Saukel, Jodl, and Seyss-Inquart). These defendants were all hung except Göring, who committed suicide hours before he was scheduled to be executed. It has been suggested that he accomplished this with the help of a young American guard who, perhaps unwittingly, smuggled a cyanide pill into Göring's cell.

At the time of Japan's surrender, the Japanese Cabinet launched war crimes trials of Japanese defendants, perhaps thinking that the principle of double jeopardy would prevent subsequent trials by the Allies. Eight accused were tried according to this plan, but all were subsequently retried by the Tokyo Tribunal. The defendants at Tokyo were four former premiers (Hiranuma, Hirota, Koiso, and Tojo), three former foreign ministers (Matsuoka, Shigemitsu, and Togo), four former war ministers (Araki, Hata, Itagaki, and Minami), two former navy ministers (Nagano and Shimada), six former generals (Doihara, Kimura, Matsui, Muto, Sato, and Umezu), two former ambassadors (Oshima and Shiratori), three former economic and financial leaders (Hoshino, Kaya, and Suzuki), one imperial adviser (Kido), one theorist (Okawa), one admiral (Oka), and one colonel (Hashimoto).

The United States, through General MacArthur, exercised far more control and influence over the Tokyo trials than at Nuremberg. Whereas the prosecutions at Nuremberg were led by a multinational team that shared relatively equal power and

---

Cold War, Krupp was eventually released from prison and his property was restored to him.

responsibility, the Tokyo prosecution was led by a single Chief of Counsel from the United States chosen by MacArthur with Associate Counsel from the Allies. The Tribunal itself was composed of judges from newly independent states in addition to representatives of the Allies. All of the decisions of the Tokyo Tribunal were subject to review by MacArthur, although he never exercised this power; there was no provision for review of any of the Nuremberg decisions. In addition, each of the accused at Tokyo had an American defense counsel in addition to one or more Japanese defense counsel. The majority opinion, authored by Judge Webb of Australia, resulted in the sentencing of seven defendants to death by hanging, 16 to life imprisonment, one to 20 years imprisonment, and one to seven years imprisonment.[16] Interestingly, Emperor Hirohito was not indicted or called as a witness by the Tokyo Tribunal, notwithstanding that he was viewed by many as the architect of Japanese imperialism. There is speculation that members of the U.S. government thought the occupation would proceed more smoothly with the emperor in place, albeit with a renunciation of any claims to divinity. By the 1950s, most of the Tokyo defendants sentenced to terms of imprisonment had been paroled. Two defendants returned to high government positions in Japan.

Notwithstanding the importance of the work of the Nuremberg and Tokyo Tribunals, the vast majority of post–World War II prosecutions did not occur before these two international tribunals, but were conducted by the victorious powers in their respective zones of occupation. For example, Allied Control Council Law No. 10, which largely mirrored the terms of the Nuremberg Charter, authorized trials in Germany. The United States hosted 12 key trials, each with a theme and appropriate nickname. The Hostages Trial, for example, involved allegations against German generals leading troops during the Balkans Campaign who were charged with civilian hostage-taking and murder. The RuSHA Trial targeted

14 officials of various SS organizations responsible for the implementation of the Nazi "pure race" program through racial cleansing and resettlement. Defendants included principals from the Rasse- und Siedlungshauptamt (RuSHA) bureau, the office of the Reich Commissioner for the Strengthening of Germanism, the Repatriation Office for Ethnic Germans, and the Lebensborn society. The Einsatzgruppen Trial involved mobile death squads operating primarily behind the frontline in Eastern Europe that indiscriminately targeted Jews, partisans, Roma, disabled persons, and otherwise uncooperative civilians. The Doctors Trial involved medical doctors accused of engaging in human experimentation, and the Justice Case involved German jurists and lawyers held responsible for implementing the Nazi "racial purity" program envisioned by the eugenic laws. The Ministries Trial involved officials of various Reich ministries, who faced charges for atrocities committed both in Germany and in occupied countries during the war. The High Command Trial focused on high-ranking generals and former members of the High Command of Nazi Germany's military forces charged with having participated in planning or facilitating the execution of the war.

Trials proceeded against civilian industrialists as well. For example, the Flick Trial centered on Friedrich Flick and five other high-ranking directors of Flick's group of companies and involved charges of the use of slave labor and plundering. (Flick himself was sentenced to seven years imprisonment. After serving three years, he was released and went on to rebuild his industrial empire. His son was later named one of the richest men in Austria.) The IG Farben Trial concerned the manufacture of Zyklon B, the poison gas used in extermination camps (the other supplier of the gas was the firm Tesch/Stabenow). IG Farben principals were also charged with participating in crimes against the peace, because they had developed processes for synthesizing gasoline and rubber from coal and thereby contributed to Germany's ability to wage war

without access to petroleum resources. Twelve former directors of the Krupp Group were accused of having enabled the
armament of the German military forces and for having used
slave laborers. In total, more than 5,000 trials were held of
German and Japanese POWs accused of committing war
crimes and crimes against humanity.

It is difficult to overstate the significance of the post–World
War II period to the field of ICL. Together, these legal proceedings established many core principles of the field, and
modern tribunals continue to cite these proceedings as persuasive authority. We touch here on the most salient of the
tribunals' contributions. First, the Nuremberg and Tokyo proceedings established that many violations of IHL that had
theretofore given rise only to state responsibility also gave
rise to individual criminal responsibility, even if the relevant
treaty was silent as to criminal penalties. Therefore, when the
Nuremberg defendants argued that they could not legally be
prosecuted for certain acts because they were not technically
crimes under international law at the time the acts were committed, the Tribunal responded that "[c]rimes against international law are committed by men, not by abstract entities,
and only by punishing individuals who commit such crimes can
the provisions of international law be enforced."[17] All of the
post–World War II ICL treaties are premised on this notion of
individual criminal responsibility for breaches. In particular,
it is the cornerstone of the enforcement regime contained in
the four Geneva Conventions of 1949, which with 194 parties
recently became the first treaties to enjoy universal ratification. Each state in the world has now agreed to apprehend
and prosecute, or extradite for prosecution, any individual
found to have committed a "grave breach" of one of the four
Conventions.

Second, the two tribunals established the primacy of international law over domestic law. In many cases, the conduct
for which the accused had been charged was authorized by

domestic law. Indeed, the tribunals' Statutes made clear that crimes against humanity in particular were punishable "whether or not in violation of the domestic law of the country where perpetrated." That international law placed limits on the content of domestic law governing purely domestic affairs was groundbreaking under the prevailing view that international law primarily governed relations between states. The Nuremberg and Tokyo proceedings mark the first time that the international community pierced the veil of sovereignty to hold governmental actors responsible for the mistreatment of their compatriots.

Third, two new crimes officially came into existence with the promulgation of the Nuremberg and Tokyo Charters: crimes against the peace and crimes against humanity. The Allies' prosecutorial strategy focused primarily on the crimes against the peace charge, which the Allies considered the primary justification for punishing individual representatives of the Axis Powers. Jackson, in his opening statement, spoke of aggressive war — not genocide — as the "greatest menace of our times." Indeed, the crimes against humanity allegations appear in parts of the Nuremberg Judgment as mere afterthoughts. Nonetheless, the crimes against humanity charge was revolutionary in piercing the veil of sovereignty and establishing once and for all that international law applied to crimes committed by state actors against their compatriots. The inclusion of both crimes in the Charter was controversial in light of the principle of legality, defined in international law through the maxim *nullum crimen sine lege, nulla poena sine lege*, which dictates that an individual cannot be prosecuted for conduct that was not criminalized at the time the individual acted. This was a primary defense of all the defendants, yet it had no effect on the tribunals. The Nuremberg Tribunal in particular ruled that the defense was inapplicable in light of the obvious wrongfulness of the acts in question. Where the treaties were silent as to the criminality of the prohibited acts therein, the Tribunal found precedent for their prosecution before national tribunals. Accordingly, it argued that the customary international law prohibition of the acts went beyond the conventional one. As discussed in Chapter 5, on the *nullum crimen* defense, these arguments are repeated in modern ICL jurisprudence when judges are faced with new atrocities that do not fit nicely into the framework of existing crimes.

Fourth, although their legacy remains plagued by charges of "victors' justice," the tribunals established clear precedent for the exercise of international penal jurisdiction as distinct from domestic jurisdiction. Indeed, in many respects, this precedent gave rise to a distinct preference for international and multilateral, as opposed to national and unilateral, efforts at international criminal justice. This preference remains compelling today in light of concerns about the potential for abuse and politicization inherent in the practice of universal jurisdiction. Depending on the political will of the international community, international courts can assert a more robust jurisdiction, freed from the limitations that international law and the principle of international comity might place on their domestic counterparts. International tribunals are also able to tap into the existing UN enforcement machinery, such as the Security Council. Notwithstanding this firm foundation for the exercise of international jurisdiction, the international community did not significantly build on this precedent until the post–Cold War period. The mending of entrenched Cold War rivalries created space for the United Nations to revive the promises of the post–World War II era in the face of civil wars in the former Yugoslavia and Sierra Leone, crimes against humanity and genocide in Rwanda and Cambodia, the destruction of East Timor by forces loyal to its former occupier Indonesia, and acts of terrorism in Lebanon. In particular, the Security Council, once paralyzed by East–West obstructionism, could act unanimously without the threat of an automatic veto of one of the permanent five members. These modern international and hybrid tribunals have the blessing of the entire United Nations, either as organs of the Security Council (the Yugoslav and Rwandan tribunals), as the products of treaty negotiations between the state in question and the UN Secretary General (the Special Court for Sierra Leone, the Extraordinary Chambers in the Courts of Cambodia, and the Lebanon tribunal), or as a feature of a UN transitional authority (the East Timor Special Panels).

Fifth, the postwar tribunals confirmed that even high-ranking state officials could be held individually criminally liable for international crimes committed in war. In particular, the IMT proclaimed that "the very essence of the [Nuremberg] Charter is that individuals have international duties which transcend the national obligations of obedience imposed by the individual State."[18] High-ranking state agents thus cannot hide behind state sovereignty when international jurisdiction is at issue. In so holding, the tribunals rejected common law doctrines of head of state and sovereign immunity that might have shielded particular defendants from liability, a result that has been followed by the modern international tribunals in cases involving Yugoslav President Slobodan Milošević, Liberian President Charles Taylor, and Sudanese President Omar al-Bashir. On the flip side of head of state immunity, the post–World War II Tribunals also rejected the claim that individuals implementing superior orders should be exonerated: "That a soldier is ordered to kill or torture in violation of the international law of war has never been recognized as a defense to such acts of brutality, though . . . the order may be urged in mitigation of the punishment."[19]

Sixth, the tribunals convicted civilians and military men as well as private actors — financiers and industrialists — for war crimes and crimes against humanity. State action is not an element of these crimes, although in many situations of mass violence and repression the state is the source of or inspiration for the abuses. Together, this collection of rulings became known as the "Nuremberg principles" and they have shaped the field of ICL ever since.

Post–World War II: The Cold War Freeze

The post–World War II period heralded a wave of optimism about the power of law and judicial institutions to restrain state violence and protect the vulnerable. Just as the ink was drying on the UN Charter and the tribunals' judgments against the major World War II defendants, the Cold War set in, paralyzing efforts to put permanent ICL institutions in place. As a result, for many years, the development of ICL was largely relegated to obscure UN drafting committees, a smattering of domestic proceedings in transitional societies, and the writings of a few dogged academics.

This stagnation did not set in immediately, however. Continuing the typical reactivity of international law, the close of World War II brought about a flurry of drafting endeavors. The international community constructed the United Nations from the ashes of the League of Nations. The lynchpin of its Charter is Article 2(4), which codified a default rule against the use of force subject to two express exceptions — actions undertaken with Security Council approval (Article 42) and measures taken in self-defense (Article 51). It remains an open question whether the historic doctrine of humanitarian intervention survived the passage of the Charter. The Charter forbids the use of force undertaken "against the territorial integrity or political independence of any state." The legality of the use of force to stop atrocities or to otherwise assist people in need is thus an open question, especially in light of the proliferation of human rights treaties.

The immediate postwar era also witnessed the promulgation of the 1948 Genocide Convention[20] and four new Geneva Conventions in 1949 protecting various classes of people in times of war—the wounded, the shipwrecked, POWs, and civilians.[21] These treaties confirmed the new expectation of individual criminal responsibility for international law breaches. The Geneva Conventions, in particular, codified the war crimes recognized at Nuremberg and Tokyo and other proceedings— officially deeming them "grave breaches." The treaties also made such breaches subject to universal criminal jurisdiction, distinguishing them from those breaches that give rise only to state (civil) responsibility. These treaties were followed by other multilateral treaties prohibiting or criminalizing acts of torture, the policy of apartheid, various manifestations of terrorism, war crimes in noninternational armed conflicts, and the international sale and distribution of narcotics. Many of these subsequent treaties contain boilerplate language obliging signatories to either prosecute offenders or extradite them elsewhere for prosecution, regardless of the place of the act's commission or the nationality of the perpetrator or victim (the *aut dedere aut judicare* requirement). This drafting process remains seemingly without end, as international law struggles to keep pace with increasingly destructive and cruel methods of warfare and repression. One of the more recent additions to this pantheon is the 2005 Convention on Disappearances.[22]

In addition to this norm proliferation, members of the international community also tried to build a permanent judicial institution, untainted by the stain of victors' justice, to prosecute international crimes. It was assumed that this work would proceed in parallel with the drafting of substantive law. Indeed, the drafters of the Genocide Convention contemplated the establishment of a permanent international criminal court at Article VI, which provides that individuals charged with committing genocide shall be tried "by a competent tribunal of the State in the territory of which the act was committed, or by such international penal tribunal as may have jurisdiction." Thus, in 1947, the General Assembly requested the International Law Commission (ILC)* to study "the desirability and possibility of establishing an international judicial organ for the trial of persons charged with genocide or other crimes." The ILC was also asked to codify the Nuremberg and Tokyo principles in a Draft Code of Offenses Against the Peace and Security of Mankind that would provide the subject matter jurisdiction of the proposed tribunal.

On other fronts, the international community began the process of building a regime of international human rights that in many respects is the progeny of the crimes against humanity charge at Nuremberg. The groundbreaking Universal Declaration of Human Rights was followed by twin Covenants in 1966 that — reflecting the ideological schisms of the day — protect civil and political rights on one side[23] and economic, social, and cultural rights on the other.[24] Subsequent specialized treaties seek to protect and guarantee equal treatment for racial and ethnic groups, women, children, indigenous people, and the disabled. Over time, states increasingly consented to more robust enforcement regimes in these treaties, granting expert committees the powers to receive reports, monitor human rights practices, accept individual complaints and petitions, recommend reforms and reparations, conduct site visits, and so on. This proliferation of partially overlapping institutions — domestic, regional, and international bodies with varying degrees of adjudicative power — has generated a productive cross-fertilization of norms that is approaching a veritable common law of ICL and international human rights law.

---

*The General Assembly established the ILC that year to promote the progressive development and codification of (primarily) public international law. The ILC is composed of legal experts and played a key role in creating a draft code of international crimes and a draft statute for a permanent international criminal court that served as the starting point for creating the modern ICC.

With the advent of the Cold War, however, work on many of these fronts slowed or stalled. In particular, the project to create a permanent international criminal court hit an impasse, in part because delegates could not agree on a definition of the crime of aggression against the backdrop of United States and Soviet "proxy wars" throughout the developing world. As a result, prior to the establishment in the mid-1990s of the ad hoc criminal tribunals, ICL was characterized by a panoply of articulated rights without judicial institutions in which to launch prosecutions — a rights–remedy gap that characterizes much of public international law.

Notwithstanding the lack of international prosecutions, there was some domestic activity in the form of paradigmatic cases. The most high profile of these is probably the trial of Adolf Eichmann, whose job under the Third Reich was to manage mass deportations from Eastern Europe to brutal ghettos and extermination camps. Following Germany's surrender after World War II, U.S. troops detained Eichmann briefly in an internment camp, although he escaped because he was not recognized. On a false Red Cross passport obtained through the Nazi underground, Eichmann traveled to Argentina where he lived under an assumed name until 1960. That year, Israeli Mossad agents abducted him, causing a major diplomatic rift between Israel and Argentina that went before the UN Security Council. The Council condemned the kidnapping, and ordered Israel to make "appropriate restitution." In Israel, Eichmann was charged with crimes against humanity, war crimes, and "crimes against the Jewish people" under Israel's 1950 Nazi and Nazi Collaborators (Punishment) Law. His primary defense was jurisdictional, arguing that the Israeli courts could not prosecute him under *ex post facto* legislation for acts that he allegedly committed before the State of Israel existed. The Israeli court ruled that it had both universal and passive personality jurisdiction over him.[25] Eichmann did not contest the factual charges against him, but claimed he was just following orders. He was convicted and hanged in 1962.

In 1987, France prosecuted Klaus Barbie — the former head of the Gestapo in Lyon, dubbed the "Butcher of Lyon" — for crimes against humanity committed in connection with his involvement in the deportation of French Jews and partisans during World War II.[26] He had already been prosecuted in absentia for war crimes, but these verdicts lapsed while he was in exile in Bolivia. The crimes against humanity case went forward on the basis of a ruling that the crime carried no statute of limitation. During this trial, he was represented by Jacques Verges, who has subsequently made a name for himself ("the Devil's Advocate") representing high-profile accused war criminals and Holocaust deniers. Verges — an avid anticolonialist — invoked a modified *tu quoque* ("you also") defense by analogizing Barbie's actions to those of France in Algeria during that country's quest for independence. Barbie ultimately died in prison after serving four years of a life sentence.

In the United States, civil suits involving ICL and human rights norms have proceeded under the Alien Tort Statute and related statutes. For example, civil plaintiffs have obtained personal jurisdiction over defendants hailing from the former Yugoslavia, Rwanda, East Timor, the states of the Southern Cone and Central America, the Philippines, and elsewhere. In addition, corporations can also be sued for violating these norms in places where they do business. Although serving important purposes, these tort cases — which occasionally proceed in default — often seem to be a poor substitute for more robust criminal processes and penalties that better reflect the severity of the offenses involved.

Post–Cold War Period: A Renaissance

In the late 1980s, a consortium of Latin American and Caribbean states reinvigorated the project of international criminal justice, primarily because they sought an international mechanism to combat the transnational illicit drug trade. With prompting from the General Assembly, the ILC again turned its attention to drafting a statute for a permanent international criminal court. The ILC completed a draft statute in 1994 that formed the basis for intensified consideration by an Ad Hoc Committee on the Establishment of an International Criminal Court and then a Preparatory Committee on the Establishment of an International Criminal Court.

In the meantime, it appeared that genocide had returned to Europe in the form of deportations, concentration camps, "ethnic cleansing," and mass killings of Bosnian Muslim civilians during the war on the territory of the former Yugoslavia. (To be fair, violations were committed by all three of the immediate parties to the conflict — Bosnian Muslims, Croats, and Serbs — as well as by the former Yugoslavia and recently independent Croatia, which had territorial designs in Bosnia). In the midst of the war, the UN Security Council addressed the conflict in seriatim resolutions. In Resolution 780 adopted on October 6, 1992, the Security Council directed the Secretary General, at the time the Egyptian diplomat Boutros Boutros-Ghali, to establish a Commission of Experts to document violations of international law. As this investigation was ongoing, governments (prominently the United States), and intergovernmental and nongovernmental organizations called for the creation of an ad hoc international tribunal in the Nuremberg tradition to assign individual responsibility for the documented abuses. The interim report of the Commission of Experts echoed these recommendations. In Resolution 808 adopted February 22, 1993, the Security Council unanimously decided "that an international tribunal shall be established for the prosecution of persons responsible for serious violations of international humanitarian law committed in the territory of the former Yugoslavia since 1991." It directed the Secretary General to prepare specific proposals for such a tribunal. In his subsequent report, Boutros-Ghali presented a tribunal blueprint and appended a draft statute setting forth existing international humanitarian and criminal law. Invoking its Chapter VII powers, the Security Council unanimously adopted the draft statute in Resolution 827 on May 25, 1993. The International Criminal Tribunal for Yugoslavia (ICTY) was thus established.

The next year, Rwanda became engulfed in a genocide of colossal proportions. All told, upward of 800,000 Tutsi and moderate Hutu individuals perished within the span of a mere four months—a rate of killing that far exceeded that in the Nazi Holocaust. Having convened a tribunal for the former Yugoslavia, the Security Council could not readily ignore almost a million dead in Rwanda, especially given that the international community had largely stood silent and immobile as the death toll mounted. The Security Council through Resolution 955 thus established the International Criminal Tribunal for Rwanda (ICTR), finding that widespread violations of international law largely within the confines of a single state, although with regional ramifications, constituted a threat to international peace and security within the meaning of Chapter VII of the UN Charter.

As first constructed by the Security Council, the ad hoc tribunals shared an Appeals Chamber and a Chief Prosecutor. South African jurist Richard Goldstone originally held the latter post. Canadian jurist Louise Arbour, who was later chosen to be the UN High Commissioner for Human Rights, next occupied the position. The Security Council then appointed Swiss Prosecutor Carla Del Ponte. From the tribunals' beginning, observers expressed concern that the Rwandan prosecutions were not getting the Chief Prosecutor's full attention. As the Security Council began to contemplate the completion of the tribunals' missions, it split the Office of the Prosecutor into two positions over the objections of Del Ponte. The chief Prosecutor of the ICTR is now Hassan

Bubacar Jallow, a former Solicitor General, Attorney General, Minister of Justice, and Supreme Court Justice of Gambia. In 2007, Del Ponte retired and was replaced by Belgian jurist Serge Brammertz, who was also the chief UN investigator into the death of former Lebanese Prime Minister Rafik Hariri. Later, additional ad hoc tribunals were established by efforts from outside the Security Council to respond to massive crimes committed in Sierra Leone, Cambodia, and East Timor.

The relative success and startup costs of the two ad hoc tribunals served as further inspiration for the drafting of a standing international criminal court. After convening six separate sessions, the Preparatory Committee produced a consolidated draft Statute that served as the basis for comprehensive negotiations at a Diplomatic Conference of Plenipotentiaries on the Establishment of an International Criminal Court held from June 15 to July 17, 1998 in Rome, Italy. A final statute — called the Rome Statute of the International Criminal Court (ICC Statute or Rome Treaty) — was completed and adopted at the Diplomatic Conference, which was attended by delegations from 120 states, multiple observers and intergovernmental organizations, and hundreds of nongovernmental organizations. Only seven states voted against the statute: the United States, China, Israel, Qatar, Libya, Iraq, and Yemen. The ICC entered into force in 2002 with the deposit of the 60th instrument of ratification.

The ICC has jurisdiction over war crimes, crimes against humanity, and genocide as defined by its Statute. Although the crimes against the peace charge was the lynchpin of the Nuremberg indictment and trial, the crime of aggression has eluded modern definition. Drafters of the ICC Statute were unable to come up with a consensus definition of aggression in time for the treaty to be opened for signature, so they punted. Article 5(2) promises that "[t]he Court shall exercise jurisdiction over the crime of aggression once a provision is adopted defining the crime and setting out the conditions under which the Court shall exercise jurisdiction with respect to this crime. Such a provision shall be consistent with the relevant provisions of the Charter of the United Nations." A Working Group continues to seek resolution on issues such as (1) the proper role of the Security Council, the General Assembly, and the International Court of Justice in adjudications of the crime of aggression; and (2) whether the definition should make reference to specific acts that constitute aggression, or be left open for future interpretation by the Court. As of this writing, a Review Conference is to be held by the ICC in 2009–2010 to consider adopting a definition of aggression.

Events from 1994 onward attest that the Nuremberg and Tokyo Tribunals are not mere historical footnotes. Indeed, the modern era promises more than a revival of the Nuremberg legacy. In fact, the international community has built on the promises of that era in significant ways. Key events are the 1998 establishment of a permanent International Criminal Court in The Hague; the 1998 arrest of General Augusto Pinochet of Chile in the United Kingdom in response to an arrest warrant from Spain for him to stand trial for torture, genocide, and other international crimes over which Spain asserts universal jurisdiction; and the 1999 indictment of President Slobodan Milošević, the first against a sitting head of state. Progress toward a more comprehensive system of international justice has not been linear or continuous. Rather, it has featured a number of oversteps and backslides that include the failure of international troops and domestic officials to arrest key indicted war criminals from the Yugoslav war; the in absentia indictment in Belgium of high-level political figures from powerful states, which resulted in an international backlash and a contrite amendment of Belgium's universal jurisdiction law; the failure of the East Timor Special Panels to gain jurisdiction over any defendants of real consequence as a result of Indonesian obstructionism and international neglect; the summary execution of Saddam Hussein after a controversial trial and while important charges remained pending against him; and all the delays, wasted resources, and corrupt functionaries that seem to plague international bureaucracies, no matter how noble their mandate. Most important, perhaps, the tragic events of September 11, 2001, led to the creation of "legal black holes" at Guantánamo and elsewhere where pure power for a time had all but eclipsed law. Yet, the field's movement is inexorably forward, and ICL and justice are undoubtedly here to stay.

~ 2 ~

Sovereignty, Jurisdiction, and Power

Internationalcriminal law (ICL), like all public international law, implicates the principle of state sovereignty.
States have historically resisted scrutiny by international
and foreign tribunals of events within their territory or involving
their nationals as infringements on state sovereignty, especially
when this scrutiny takes the form of criminal investigations
and prosecutions of individuals accused of committing international crimes. Like the parent who insists on disciplining his
or her own child, states often assert the prerogative to decide
whether and how to prosecute their own citizens for crimes they
may have committed. As a result, states often resist exercises of
international or extraterritorial jurisdiction over their nationals
or over events that have occurred within their borders. With the
reemergence of international criminal tribunals on the global
stage and the vitalization of the principle of universal jurisdiction, such exercises of scrutiny are increasingly common. As a
result, the enforcement of ICL has occasioned an erosion of the
principle of state sovereignty — a development that not all
states have accepted quietly.

ICL is now applied, interpreted, and developed through three different types of judicial institutions: domestic, international, and hybrid. Historically, domestic courts were the primary venue for prosecutions of what we would today call international crimes, if they took place at all. Today, international and mixed national–international ("hybrid") tribunals are fast joining domestic courts as adjudicators of ICL. These multilateral institutions have been created by two different means. First, institutions have been created by express state consent, usually through the promulgation of a treaty. Through this model, states agree to subject individuals within their jurisdictions to an international or quasi-international tribunal for prosecution. The International Criminal Court (ICC) and Special Court for Sierra Leone (SCSL) are examples of this approach. Second, institutions have been created through the coercive power of the international community acting collectively; for example, through the auspices of the UN Security Council. The two ad hoc criminal tribunals for Yugoslavia and Rwanda are examples of this approach. Notwithstanding the recent focus on international institutions resulting from these developments, domestic courts remain important fora for ICL development, especially given the increasing acceptance of various forms of extraterritorial jurisdiction.

This chapter provides an overview of the origins of the institutions in which ICL is adjudicated. It also discusses the various jurisdictional frameworks at work with reference to the three types of jurisdiction — prescriptive, adjudicative, and enforcement — and the classic bases for exercising jurisdiction — territoriality, nationality, protectivity, and universality. Finally, it discusses some of the structural limitations imposed by states on these tribunals to cabin their juridical power. The subject matter jurisdiction of the various international and hybrid tribunals is often quite similar. They manifest, however, varying degrees of jurisdictional power over the individuals and events of concern as a result of the different circumstances and power dynamics at play during their formation. This chapter serves as a reminder that although the principle of state sovereignty has been under attack, it remains a potent force in international relations.

CREATURES OF CONSENT

This section discusses the most prominent example of the creation of an international criminal tribunal by consent — the multilateral Rome Treaty that created the ICC. It also discusses the hybrid tribunals that were created by treaty, although the treaties in question were bilateral rather than multilateral. Treaty-based institutions have the advantage of high "buy-in" by participating states. At the same time, there are several weaknesses to this approach. For one, important states may choose not to participate, thus weakening the strength and legitimacy of the tribunal. In addition, as states negotiate the terms of these tribunals' constitutive treaties with the relevant representative of the international community, they may insist on the inclusion of significant structural limitations to control the amount of discretion, independence, and judicial power these institutions can exercise and to ensure some measure of state control over the judicial process. This can result in a significantly weaker institution and potentially one subject to political manipulation.

The International Criminal Court

The ICC illustrates the strengths and weaknesses of the consensual treaty-based approach. The ICC was created by a treaty that was finalized in Rome, Italy in 1998 (often referred to as the Rome Treaty). The treaty came into force on July 1, 2002, after ratification by 60 states. As of this writing, there were 108 state parties to the Rome Treaty. The refusal of three of the five permanent members of the UN Security Council (China, Russia, and the United States) to join the Court, and the aggressive opposition mounted by the United States against the Court, illustrate one of the weaknesses in the consensual approach. In practice, however, it has become clear that the ICC is viewed by some states as a useful institution. At the time of this writing, the ICC prosecutor was pursuing four situations that resulted in indictments. Three of the four cases were brought to the Court by virtue of a referral by the affected state itself. Although each of these three cases has its own peculiarities, together they illustrate a high level of reliance by those states on the ICC to address international crimes committed in their midst.

Drafting the ICC Statute involved juggling a number of moving parts. With respect to each element, states engaged in protracted and multipolar negotiations, with some states and most nongovernmental organizations advocating provisions that would ensure a strong, impartial, and independent institution and others trying to build in significant limitations and checks on the future Court's power at every turn. Two of the most contentious issues to arise during the negotiations for the Rome Treaty concerned the persons over whom and situations over which the Court would have jurisdiction (the so-called preconditions for the exercise of jurisdiction) and how the Court's jurisdiction could be initiated or triggered. Drafters also had to work out a system of resolving jurisdictional conflicts between the future Court and the domestic courts of states that may also have jurisdiction over the events and individuals in question.

Preconditions for the Exercise of Jurisdiction

The Court has jurisdiction over an individual suspected of committing genocide, a crime against humanity, or a war crime if: the act was committed within the territory of a state that is a party to the treaty; or the individual is a national of a state that is a party to the treaty. In other words the preconditions for the Court's assertion of jurisdiction are based on the territorial and active nationality principles of jurisdiction.

These two bases for the assertion of ICC jurisdiction derive from general principles of international law regulating when a state can assert jurisdiction over an individual. Territoriality is the most common, and least controversial, justification for the assertion of jurisdiction. A state may assert jurisdiction over any individual who commits a criminal act within its territory. The Genocide Convention, for example, states that persons charged with genocide shall be tried by a competent tribunal of the state in which the genocide occurred, thus incorporating the territoriality principle. (Interestingly for our purposes, the Genocide Convention also states in the alternative that such a person may be tried before an international tribunal, although no such tribunal existed at the time the Convention was opened for signature.) The territorial principle encompasses two additional situations. First, under the *subjective territorial principle*, a state may assert jurisdiction over acts commenced within the state, but consummated abroad. Second, under the *objective territorial principle*, a state may assert jurisdiction over acts committed abroad that are consummated within the territory of the prosecuting state. A variation of this latter principle — applied most often in the antitrust and securities law contexts — allows a state to regulate acts that cause effects within the state, even if the criminal act itself is committed outside the state.

The nationality justification for the ICC's assertion of jurisdiction is also well established under international law. The ICC's nationality jurisdiction derives from the *active nationality principle*, under which the state of which the alleged perpetrator is a national may assert jurisdiction over that individual's acts wherever they may occur. Under this rationale, a state asserts the right to regulate the activities of its citizens outside of its territory. All the major ICL treaties permit, and in some cases oblige, member states to prosecute nationals who commit international crimes.

The second type of nationality jurisdiction is based on the *passive nationality principle* or the *passive personality principle* of jurisdiction. This principle allows a state to assert jurisdiction over a crime committed against one of its own nationals. In other words, a state may assert jurisdiction based on the nationality of the victim, regardless of the nationality of the offender or where the offense took place. Whereas active nationality is an uncontroversial basis for the assertion of jurisdiction, passive personality jurisdiction has historically received less support from states. Recently, however, passive personality jurisdiction has seen a revival among states that aggressively legislate against acts of terrorism. Such states may criminalize and prosecute acts of terrorism committed against their own citizens anywhere in the world. Notably, the ICC does not have jurisdiction based on the principle of passive nationality; that is to say it does not have jurisdiction over a suspect if the only link to a state party to the Rome Statute is the nationality of the victim.

The Court also does not have jurisdiction based on the principle of universal jurisdiction, although many states supported such a basis for ICC jurisdiction during the negotiations of the Rome Treaty. The principle of universal jurisdiction allows any state to assert jurisdiction over an individual suspected of committing the worst crimes under international law (such as genocide, crimes against humanity, and certain war crimes), even if there is no formal link to the state asserting jurisdiction. (We further discuss the principle of universal jurisdiction later in the context of our consideration of the prosecution of international crimes by national courts.) States supporting an ICC with "universal" jurisdiction argued, for example, that the Court should have the power to assert jurisdiction over any individual in the world suspected of committing genocide or any other international crime giving rise to universal jurisdiction before domestic courts. Drafters of the ICC Statute also rejected a notion of custodial jurisdiction. This would have allowed the Court to proceed whenever the perpetrator was in the custody of a state party, even — potentially — temporarily or forcibly. In addition to expanding the grounds on which the Court could prosecute, custodial jurisdiction would have had the useful side effect of limiting the ability of perpetrators of international crimes to travel abroad to states that had joined the Rome Treaty. Although the ICC's jurisdiction is relatively limited as compared to these failed proposals, the United States and other nations continue to raise concerns about whether nonparties are adequately protected from politically motivated prosecutions. The territorial basis of jurisdiction is particularly troubling to a state like the United States with thousands of troops stationed abroad, many in states that are members of the ICC.

The final jurisdictional regime governing the ICC was part of a "take it or leave it" proposal advanced toward the waning days of the Rome Conference. As it stands, it is only in cases in which the perpetrator hails from a state party or commits crimes on the territory of a state party that the ICC can go forward. In practice, this often amounts to the same state, which constitutes a significant limitation on the ability of the Court to prosecute the commission of international crimes committed worldwide.

One significant exception to these jurisdictional limitations applies to referrals initiated by the UN Security Council to the ICC. The Security Council may refer any matter to the Court for investigation regardless of whether there is a link between the individual or act and a state party. Thus, the Security Council referred the situation in Darfur to the Court, even though the Sudan is not a party to the Treaty and none of the suspects is a national of a state party to the Treaty. The inclusion of a Chapter VII Security Council referral injects an element of coercion into what is otherwise a highly consensual arrangement. In addition to Security Council referrals, states themselves may make ad hoc referrals to the Court pursuant to Article 12(3) for particular crimes that fall within the Court's subject matter jurisdiction. Such referrals are subject to the ICC's jurisdiction limitations, unlike the case of referrals by the Security Council.

Trigger Mechanisms

The Court's jurisdiction may be triggered in one of three ways: (1) by a state party (Article 14), (2) by the Security Council (Article 13(b)), and (3) by the prosecutor acting *propio motu* ("on his or her own motion") (Article 15). Granting the power of referral to a state party was widely accepted. In designing this regime, it was assumed that a state party would refer matters concerning another state party to the Court.* In practice so far, Article 14 has been used for "self-referrals"; that is, situations referred to the Court by the impacted state itself. For example, Uganda invoked Article 14 when it self-referred the "situation concerning the Lord's Resistance Army" to the Court in December 2003. Such self-referrals were not contemplated by the drafters of the Statute, and their legality is likely to be considered by the Court in connection with these cases. It is also unclear to what extent these self-referrals may be revoked by the state in question. For one, it has been argued that the ICC referral has complicated peace negotiations in

---

*The state referral trigger mechanisms is modeled after the state referrals contemplated by the various human rights treaties, which allow state parties to refer another state for investigation to the treaty's enforcement body. In practice, very few states have ever referred another state to one of these institutions. Most matters that come before these institutions arrive through individual petitions. It remains to be seen if the ICC's state referral mechanism will be utilized more frequently.

Uganda, which may cause that state to rethink the propriety of externalizing justice for international crimes occurring there.

Much more contentious during the negotiations was the role of the Security Council in referring matters to the Court and potentially interfering in ongoing proceedings. The United States and other permanent members of the Security Council argued that no situation should be considered by the Court unless the Security Council affirmatively approved. This would mean that any one of the five permanent members of the Security Council, including the United States, could have blocked any investigation or prosecution from going forward by utilizing its veto power. This attempt to circumvent the state consent model was rejected at Rome. Instead, the Security Council may use its Chapter VII powers to refer a matter to the Court (Article 13(b)) or to defer any investigation or prosecution for renewable 12-month terms (Article 16). This means that none of the five permanent members can unilaterally block an investigation or prosecution from going forward. Rather, the permanent members can either block a referral to the Court or block an attempt to defer an investigation or prosecution. As noted earlier, there are no jurisdictional preconditions for the Court to investigate or prosecute a case referred by the Security Council except with respect to the Court's temporal jurisdiction (although even this is not entirely clear from the statute itself).

The power of the prosecutor to initiate an investigation or prosecution *proprio motu* was also a source of disagreement during the Rome Treaty negotiations. As the Treaty stands, the prosecutor may initiate an investigation subject to certain procedural safeguards. These safeguards were introduced at the behest of a number of states, including the United States, that were uncomfortable with vesting the unrestricted power to initiate an investigation with the prosecutor. The prosecutor may initiate an investigation only if he or she can convince a three-judge panel that "there is a reasonable basis to proceed with an investigation, and . . . the case appears to fall within the jurisdiction of the Court" (Article 15(4)). In addition, the prosecutor must defer to an investigation or prosecution by a national authority unless a three-judge panel concludes that such national authorities are unwilling or unable to genuinely investigate the alleged criminal conduct (Article 18).

Admissibility

In addition to requirements of jurisdiction, the ICC is also limited by requirements of admissibility, most clearly set forth in Article 17 of the Rome Treaty. Although the ad hoc tribunals for the former Yugoslavia and Rwanda have primacy over national courts — such that their assertions of jurisdiction take precedence over any attempt by a national court to prosecute a particular individual — the ICC is subject to the reverse regime of complementarity that gives initial primacy to proceedings before domestic courts. According to the principle of complementarity, a cornerstone of the ICC, the Court should not assert jurisdiction over a situation if:

(a) The case is being investigated or prosecuted by a State that has jurisdiction over it, unless the State is unwilling or unable genuinely to carry out the investigation or prosecution;

(b) The case has been investigated by a State that has jurisdiction over it and the State has decided not to prosecute the person concerned, unless the decision resulted from the unwillingness or inability of the State genuinely to prosecute;

(c) The person concerned has already been tried for conduct that is the subject of the complaint, and a trial by the Court is not permitted under article 20, paragraph 3 [referring to the prohibition against being tried for the same offense twice, also known as double jeopardy or *ne bis in idem*];

(d) The case is not of sufficient gravity to justify further action by the Court.

Essentially, the ICC may only hear a case if there is no national court that has initiated a good-faith effort to investigate or prosecute the case.

Although the ICC Statute creates a mechanism for adjudicating admissibility, it provides little guidance on how the Court should interpret terms such as *unwilling* and *unable*. To date, there are no decisions of the Court addressing these provisions, although they are expected in both the Sudan and Ugandan matters. The governments of both countries have established special courts to prosecute those suspected of involvement in the atrocities in Darfur and northern Uganda, respectively. In the Darfur context, the prosecutor has argued that these courts do not meet the requirements of Article 17. Although the Court has not addressed the quality of the proceedings, it did find that the indictments against two Sudanese officials were admissible even though both were under investigation by Sudanese judicial authorities. The court found that the subject matter of the domestic investigations did not include those activities alleged in the international indictment, and thus found the matter admissible.[1] It remains to be seen how credible the Ugandan effort is; the impulse seems to be to shield embattled members of the Lord's Resistance Army from ICC jurisdiction, but not necessarily from domestic prosecution.

Consensual Hybrid Tribunals

Following the establishment of the International Criminal Tribunal for Yugoslavia (ICTY) and the International Criminal Tribunal for Rwanda (ICTR) to address violations of ICL that occurred in Yugoslavia and Rwanda, the international community created a number of tribunals in response to violations committed elsewhere. These newer ad hoc tribunals have been called *hybrid* or *mixed tribunals*, because they are situated within the host state as opposed to being established abroad; are staffed by international and domestic personnel (judges, prosecutors, investigators, defense counsel, and support staff) working in tandem; and apply a mixture of international and domestic law, including local criminal law.

Hybrid tribunals have a number of advantages over purely international and national courts. First, the mix of national and international attributes makes it more likely that the tribunal will be perceived as legitimate by both the domestic and international communities. Second, because they take advantage of a functioning domestic legal system, hybrid tribunals are less likely to have the same startup costs as an ad hoc international tribunal. Third, the use of international law within a partially domestic system may increase the acceptance of international norms within a domestic legal system. This can lead to the incorporation of ICL within national penal codes, further strengthening the effectiveness of these prohibitions and, derivatively, the domestic rule of law. Fourth, because they are located within the host country, hybrid institutions have easier access to evidence and witnesses and are more accessible to both victims and the population of the country in question. Fifth, hybrid tribunals may enable the transfer of legal skills and experience, as local professionals work alongside their international counterparts. These advantages are dependent on the strength and resources of the relevant domestic legal system, and thus may not be borne out in all cases.

Hybrid tribunals also have unique challenges when compared with national or international tribunals. Tensions may arise between staff members from the host country and members of the international staff. Such tensions have arisen, for example, in the Extraordinary Chambers in the Courts of Cambodia (ECCC). The government of the host country may use its influence over the tribunal to try to affect who is investigated or prosecuted, and may withhold financial and other support for domestic political reasons. Lacking a Chapter VII pedigree, these tribunals may have difficulty gaining the cooperation of third-party states that may have custody of defendants or access to important evidence. These problems have led many human rights organizations to argue against the continued use of hybrid tribunals, and to instead argue for the return to purely international tribunals that are free from domestic political pressure and are more likely to apply a consistent interpretation of applicable law to similar conduct.

The creation of the ICC may preclude the establishment of additional ad hoc hybrid or international tribunals. Three situations remain, however, in which such tribunals may be necessary. First, a hybrid or international tribunal would be necessary to prosecute crimes committed prior to the coming into force of the Rome Treaty, as the ICC only has jurisdiction over crimes committed after July 1, 2002 (although as we noted earlier it is not clear if this temporal restriction applies to Security Council referrals to the Court). The tribunal created in Cambodia (the ECCC) to prosecute crimes that occurred from 1975 to 1979 is an example of a hybrid institution engaged in historical justice. Second, an ad hoc tribunal may still be necessary to prosecute crimes committed within the territory of, and by nationals of, states that are not parties to the ICC (unless the UN Security Council refers the matter, as was the case with Darfur in the Sudan). Third, an ad hoc tribunal may be necessary to prosecute criminal acts that are not included within the subject matter jurisdiction of the ICC. The assassination of the former prime minister of Lebanon, Rafik Hariri, does not clearly fit within the subject matter jurisdiction of the ICC. The Security Council thus passed a resolution in 2007 creating the Special Tribunal for Lebanon to investigate and prosecute those responsible for the Hariri assassination and related acts of terrorism. It remains to be seen to what extent the international community is willing to add further hybrid institutions to the modern pantheon.

Some hybrid tribunals are created by consent — usually by virtue of an agreement between the host government and some branch of the United Nations. As we will see later, other hybrid tribunals are also created by a sovereign power, either at the global level, by the United Nations, or by the nation-state itself.

The hybrid tribunals established for Sierra Leone and Cambodia were created by an agreement between the United Nations and the country at issue. Hybrid tribunals created by this consensual model tend to be *specialized* tribunals that are either embedded within (Cambodia) or independent from (Sierra Leone) the domestic court system. The ECCC, established to prosecute surviving members of the Khmer Rouge, was the product of over a decade of negotiations between the United Nations and the Cambodian government. Throughout these negotiations, the Cambodian government pushed for a tribunal controlled by Cambodians. The United Nations, along with most of the international human rights community, pushed for a tribunal controlled by "internationals" — that is, individuals appointed by the United Nations. The resulting body is a tribunal with a complex dual structure that embodies and, some might argue, exacerbates tensions between the two sets of personnel. The majority of the judges are appointed by the Cambodian government, but decisions of the Court require a supermajority, effectively requiring the vote of at least one "international" judge for the will of the majority of Cambodian judges to become a decision of the court. In addition, the Office of the Prosecutor is a dual one; there are two co-prosecutors, one appointed by the United Nations and the other by the Cambodian government. Disagreements between the co-prosecutors are resolved by a panel of ECCC judges. These divisions between UN and Cambodian government personnel exist throughout the structure of the ECCC, including among the defense counsel, who appear to have collectively adopted the one "international" and one "national" counsel model even though this is not required by the agreement establishing the ECCC. Although this is an awkward and unwieldy structure seemingly designed to promote gridlock, as of this writing the Court is up and running and, so far, there have been no major public disagreements between the coprosecutors or among the UN-appointed and Cambodian-appointed judges.

Although also created by an agreement between the United Nations and the country at issue, the SCSL is markedly different in its structure. Unlike the ECCC, the SCSL is not a part of the domestic legal system. Rather, the SCSL operates wholly separate from the Sierra Leonean court system. The majority of the judges are "internationals," and the government of Sierra Leone used some of its appointments to select non–Sierra Leoneans for key posts. Having just emerged from a brutal civil war, the Sierra Leoneans were much more pliant negotiating partners than their Cambodian counterparts, whose views about the ECCC vacillated over time. Attitudes among Cambodian political elites toward the ECCC ranged from outright hostility (with the ECCC seen as a threat to their domestic political power) to greedy support (with the ECCC seen as a source of badly needed hard currency).

The emergence of these hybrid tribunals has given rise to the question of when a hybrid tribunal ceases to be an international tribunal. The determination of whether a judicial body is a domestic or an international court has some practical ramifications with respect to a number of legal doctrines. For example, a domestic court may be bound by a statute of limitation or an amnesty law enacted by the local legislature, whereas an international court would not.[2] In addition, domestic courts may be bound by certain immunity doctrines — such as sovereign immunity or head of state immunity — by virtue of the sovereign equality of states and the imperatives of international comity.

In two key decisions emerging from the SCSL, one concerning the constitutionality of the Court[3] and the other addressing the argument that former Liberian President Charles Taylor should enjoy head of state immunity,[4] the Special Court embraced an international identity. It based its ruling on the following factors: (1) its provenance (a treaty negotiated by the UN Secretary General between Sierra Leone and the UN General Assembly that was initiated and approved by the UN Security Council), (2) domestic ratification legislation asserting that the Court is not part of the Sierra Leonean judiciary, (3) its independent legal personality and ability to enter into agreements with states, (4) its enjoyment of the privileges and immunities of an international institution, and (5) its subject matter jurisdiction (mostly, although not exclusively, international crimes). This question is likely to receive sustained attention by the ECCC, because those Chambers are more firmly embedded in the domestic judicial system and, as noted earlier, are governed by a majority of Cambodian jurists (who nonetheless need the vote of an international judge to prevail). This issue may come up when defendants being prosecuted for crimes committed during the Khmer Rouge era attempt to assert domestic statutes of limitation, amnesties, and pardons as bars to prosecution.

CREATURES OF COERCION

The second way in which international tribunals are created is through the exercise of a sovereign power — either international (usually the UN Security Council) or domestic (the nation-state itself). The latter is not controversial, as it is consistent with the idea that states retain the power to determine how, if at all, to engage with international law. The former is more controversial, as it involves the use of coercive power that may result in institutions that do not reflect the priorities or preferences of interested and implicated states.

Nuremberg and Tokyo

The first international criminal tribunals ever formed—the Nuremberg and Tokyo Tribunals—were created by the exercise of global sovereign power. The four victorious powers—France, the Soviet Union, the United Kingdom, and the United States—established the Nuremberg Tribunal pursuant to the London Agreement of August 8, 1945. By contrast, the United States established the Tokyo Tribunal through a special proclamation issued by the Supreme Allied Commander of the Far East, U.S. General Douglas MacArthur, with the acquiescence of the other Allied states. Thus, although the Nuremberg Tribunal was created by a treaty, the four states involved in its creation essentially dictated the terms of the new institution and imposed them on the rest of the international community. In addition to being created by a small number of states, these two tribunals are unique among their peers in being established by victorious powers after a military defeat.

The Ad Hoc International Tribunals

Almost 50 years would pass before the appearance of another set of international criminal tribunals—the ICTY and ICTR. These ad hoc tribunals were also created by a global sovereign, but unlike their predecessors they were not established following a military victory. Rather, they were created by the UN Security Council under the authority of the UN Charter. The Security Council created the ICTY—its official name is the International Tribunal for the Prosecution of Persons Responsible for Serious Violations of International Humanitarian Law Committed in the Territory of the Former

Yugoslavia Since 1991 — in response to the violent breakup of Yugoslavia. Between the end of World War II and 1991, the Republic of Yugoslavia was a federation of six republics (Slovenia, Croatia, Bosnia-Herzegovina, Serbia, Montenegro, and Macedonia) and two autonomous units (Vojvodina and Kosovo). The federation broke apart in 1991 and 1992 when Slovenia, Croatia, Macedonia, and then Bosnia-Herzegovina declared their independence, resulting in an extremely violent conflict that generated photographs evocative of the Nazi concentration camps, horrific victim accounts of the creation of rape camps, and the newly coined practice of ethnic cleansing that many equated with genocide.

In the face of inactivity by the international community in response to mass atrocities reminiscent of World War II, the UN Security Council initiated a process that resulted in the creation of the ICTY. The Security Council created the ICTY under its Chapter VII powers, which empower the Council to pass resolutions binding on all states in response to breaches of the peace, threats to the peace, or acts of aggression. Why would the Security Council create the tribunal using its sovereign powers rather than initiating a treaty-based consensual method of formation? At least three explanations suggest themselves. First, it was clear at the time that the Federal Republic of Yugoslavia and its constituent breakaway republics would not agree to subject their citizens to the jurisdiction of an international criminal tribunal. Thus, one of the advantages of Security Council action under Chapter VII is that it can trump the unwillingness of the affected state(s) to hold individuals accountable for crimes committed within their jurisdiction, including by their nationals. Recall that the ICC can only exercise jurisdiction over the nationals of nonparties who commit crimes on the territories of nonparties via Security Council referral. Thus, even in the most consent-based tribunal, one sees the exertion of global sovereign power by the Security Council.

The second reason the ICTY was created by the Security Council and not by treaty is time. Drafting, negotiating, and encouraging states to ratify a treaty takes far more time than Security Council action. The Rome Treaty took a number of years to negotiate, and four years passed between the conclusion of the drafting of the treaty and the ratification by enough states to bring it into force. Because the ICTY was created to address an ongoing conflict in the hope of exerting a deterrent effect, any significant delay in its creation was unacceptable to its proponents and would have undermined one of its central purposes. Third, there was a need on the part of the members of the Security Council, particularly the major military powers, to appear to be doing something in the face of the first mass atrocities in Europe since the Nazi Holocaust. Politically, the United States and Europe were unwilling to commit much in the way of military troops to end the ethnic cleansing and other international crimes committed in the former Yugoslavia. Creating the ICTY gave the Security Council and its members a concrete response to these atrocities to which they could point. This third explanation raises the question of whether the creation of the ICTY was enough. In other words, should the United Nations, Security Council, or states acting through the North Atlantic Treaty Organization (NATO) or another regional body have done more at the time to address the atrocities in the former Yugoslavia?

As the first such tribunal to be established since the post–World War II tribunals, the ICTY was faced with a number of unprecedented legal questions. The first defendant prosecuted before the Tribunal, Dusko Tadić, challenged the legality of the Tribunal's establishment by the Security Council. The Trial Chamber dismissed this challenge, reasoning that it did not have the power to ascertain its own legitimacy. The Appeals Chamber also dismissed Tadić's challenge, but differed with the Trial Chamber and held that it did have the power to evaluate its own legitimacy. In this, its first decision, the Appeals Chamber held that the Security Council had the authority to create an international criminal tribunal under its Chapter VII powers even though the UN Charter does not list judicial institutions as among the available Chapter VII responses.[5]

The ICTY has subject matter jurisdiction over the following crimes, which are defined in its statute: war crimes, crimes against humanity, and genocide. The temporal jurisdiction begins on January 1, 1991 and is open-ended. Thus, NATO became subject to the jurisdiction of the ICTY when it intervened militarily in 1999 to repel the military forces of Yugoslavia that were attacking the Kosovar minority population. In response to requests that she investigate allegations of violations committed by the NATO forces, the ICTY Prosecutor established a committee to advise her on whether there was enough evidence to initiate an investigation against NATO soldiers. The committee looked at a number of specific incidents and concluded that the applicable law was insufficiently developed and that there was insufficient evidence of wrongdoing to warrant a more formal investigation. Needless to say, this conclusion generated significant criticism.

The UN Security Council created a second tribunal under its Chapter VII powers in response to the 1994 genocide in Rwanda, the ICTR—formally known by the rambling moniker, the International Criminal Tribunal for the Prosecution of Persons Responsible for Genocide and Other Serious Violations of International Humanitarian Law Committed in the Territory of Rwanda and Rwandan Citizens Responsible for Genocide and Other Such Violations Committed in the Territory of Neighbouring States, between 1 January 1994 and 31 December 1994. The ICTR differs from the ICTY in that the former was created in response to an internal conflict and genocide that was largely over by the time the Tribunal was created, whereas the latter was created in response to an international conflict that was ongoing at the time the Tribunal was created. Although questions have been raised by some commentators about the use of the Security Council Chapter

VII powers to address what was mostly an internal conflict, such a challenge was not brought before the Tribunal itself. The ICTR has jurisdiction over the same crimes as the ICTY (war crimes, crimes against humanity, and genocide), although the definitions and scope of some of these crimes differ between the ICTY and ICTR. Unlike the ICTY, the ICTR's temporal jurisdiction is not open-ended, but instead only covers acts committed during the calendar year of 1994.

Both the ICTY and ICTR are ad hoc tribunals, limited to a specific country, a specific set of crimes, and a specific time period. Both are subsidiary organs of the United Nations. Because they were intended to be temporary courts, they are now in the process of winding down their affairs. The Security Council announced a "completion strategy" in Security Council Resolution 1503, pursuant to which both the ICTY and ICTR are supposed to conclude their trial work by 2008, although at the time of this writing the deadline had passed, and both tribunals still had a number of outstanding cases. To facilitate their closing, the tribunals are each directed to transfer some of their cases to appropriate and competent national jurisdictions for prosecution. The ICTY in particular is to defer prosecution of middle-level or lower defendants to local courts to focus the last few years of operation on those most responsible for abuses at the leadership level.

Imposed Hybrid Tribunals

As noted earlier, hybrid tribunals have been created by both of the methods we highlight here: by consent and by sovereign power. As compared with the ECCC and the SCSL, which were created by treaty, the hybrid judicial systems established in Kosovo and East Timor were created by UN transitional authorities essentially holding these territories' sovereignty in trust in an immediate postconflict situation. In both cases, there was concern that the domestic court system was either unable or unwilling to address adequately and impartially the violations of criminal law (both domestic and international) committed in these territories. In Kosovo, the UN Mission in Kosovo (UNMIK) appointed (without consultation with the local authorities) international judges and prosecutors to work with their local counterparts within the Kosovo judicial system. This move was in reaction to complaints that the domestic legal system was not impartial. Initially, international judges did not constitute a majority of the judges hearing a particular case, but UNMIK eventually established special tribunals consisting of three judges, the majority of whom were international. Cases may be referred to these special tribunals either by the United Nations, the prosecutor, the accused, or defense counsel.

In East Timor, the Security Council created the United Nations Transitional Administration in East Timor (UNTAET) to administer the executive, legislative, and judicial functions of the country and bring to justice those responsible for international human rights violations committed following that country's independence referendum. Pursuant to this mandate, UNTAET created "Special Panels with Exclusive Jurisdiction over Serious Criminal Offenses" within the district courts and courts of appeals in Dili, East Timor. Prosecutions were conducted by a Serious Crimes Unit (SCU), composed almost entirely of international staff. The existing court management serviced the Special Panels, presided over by a majority of international judges. The Special Panels had jurisdiction over crimes — including war crimes, crimes against humanity, and genocide — committed in East Timor since 1975. They were to operate until May 2005, but the Security Council, by Resolution 1543, extended their operation for a year to organize evidence for continued East Timorese prosecutions, if pursued. As with Kosovo, the United Nations created these panels unilaterally without significant negotiations with the local government.

The vast majority of perpetrators resided in Indonesia and were thus effectively out of reach of the Special Panels. Although technically outside the Special Court's mandate, the Special Panels issued many indictments for individuals residing in Indonesia, including General Wiranto, once the head of the Indonesian armed forces. In total, after 55 trials, 84 defendants were convicted and four were acquitted. Few of these defendants can be described as leaders or individuals with significant command authority. As of this writing, more than 300 indictees remain at large.

DOMESTIC LEGAL SYSTEMS

Historically, domestic courts (both civilian and military) have been the venue in which most international crimes have been prosecuted — if they have been prosecuted at all. Even with the proliferation of international and hybrid tribunals, and particularly with the creation of the ICC, domestic courts will continue to develop, and implement, ICL. In fact, the ICC's complementarity principle envisions a central role for domestic courts in the enforcement of ICL. In the process of ratifying the ICC Statute, states have begun actively codifying ICL to harmonize their domestic penal codes with the ICC Statute and, presumably, to enable them to preempt any assertion of jurisdiction by the ICC. Thus, many states have passed legislation that for the first time criminalizes the major international crimes. In many cases, these statutes allow for the assertion of extraterritorial forms of criminal jurisdiction.

Civilian Courts

As discussed previously, international law recognizes four bases by which a state may assert jurisdiction: territoriality, nationality, protectivity, and universality. Domestic prosecutions for international crimes have proceeded on the basis of territoriality and nationality jurisdiction, which were discussed earlier in connection with the ICC's jurisdictional preconditions. The protective principle of jurisdiction permits a state to assert jurisdiction over acts that threaten the integrity and interests of the state. Although the protective principle could be interpreted quite broadly to encompass anything that a state deems in its vital interest, it has traditionally been limited to a narrow range of activities such as counterfeiting, espionage, falsification of government documents, perjury before a consular official, or violations of immigration or customs laws. The protective principle thus justifies the criminalization of activities that violate the integrity of core governmental functions.

The last basis of jurisdiction, universality, is the one most relevant to ICL, and thus one to which we devote more discussion. Under the universality principle, a state may assert jurisdiction over an offender regardless of the nationality of the offender or victim, the place of commission of the wrongful act, or any other link to the state asserting jurisdiction. The universality principle, often referred to as universal jurisdiction, asserts that there are certain acts that are so heinous, and that so violate the integrity of the international community, that any state may prosecute or otherwise assert jurisdiction over an individual suspected of committing them.

Universal jurisdiction arose out of the growth of piracy in eighteenth- and nineteenth-century Europe and North America. Pirates were often effectively stateless and committed their crimes on the high seas (although attacks on flagships often triggered territorial jurisdiction). Consequently, it was at times difficult for states to assert jurisdiction over pirates under any of the traditional principles of jurisdiction. Pirates were referred to as *hostis humani generis* ("enemies of all humankind"). Under the then novel theory of universal jurisdiction, any state could prosecute a pirate even if that state or its citizens had not been harmed.

Those responsible for violations of the most serious provisions of ICL today join pirates as "enemies of all humankind." Although there is some debate about which specific violations trigger universal jurisdiction, it is generally accepted that the following offenses do: slavery, genocide, war crimes, crimes against humanity, and torture. Universal jurisdiction over these offenses exists as a function of treaty or customary international law. Treaty obligations may render the exercise of universal jurisdiction mandatory, at least where an offender is found on national territory and is not extradited. Universal jurisdiction is generally considered permissive under customary international law, but several academics have cogently argued for a "duty to prosecute" grave international crimes.

There is general agreement that a state may invoke the universality principle to prosecute or otherwise hold accountable an individual accused when that individual is found on the prosecuting state's territory (in effect, a form of custodial jurisdiction). By contrast, there is less agreement on whether the universality principle allows a state to apprehend or otherwise seek the extradition of a suspect who is physically present outside of its own territory. Some argue that universal jurisdiction is conditional on the presence of the accused within the territorial jurisdiction of the state asserting jurisdiction. In other words, these commentators would argue that a state could not prosecute an individual in absentia, even if the prosecution was for one of the limited crimes subject to the universality principle. Treaties that embody the *aut dedere aut judicare* principle (extradite or prosecute) presume the custody of the accused and accordingly may permit the exercise of universal jurisdiction only where that condition precedent is satisfied.

Although there is some evidence to support this argument, we do not think that the issue is clearly decided as a matter of international law. Some states, particularly those with a civil law legal system, allow criminal prosecution of individuals in absentia. Given that such prosecutions do not evidently violate international law, it is not clear why such prosecutions for violations of the worst crimes under international law would not also be consistent with international law. In states that allow in absentia prosecutions, prosecutions pursuant to universal jurisdiction could proceed under the same terms as ordinary in absentia prosecutions. States that disallow in absentia prosecutions would have to discontinue the criminal proceedings at a certain point as directed by the relevant domestic rules in the event they are not able to obtain the custody of the accused through extradition, negotiation, abduction, or other means. Depending on when this point is reached, however, significant progress may be made toward investigating and publicizing the commission of international crimes.

Three judges of the International Court of Justice (ICJ) in *dicta*, as well as some prominent commentators, have argued that in absentia universal jurisdiction is permitted.[6] The question was raised when Belgium issued an arrest warrant against Abdulaye Yerodia Ndombasi, the Minister of Foreign Affairs of the Democratic Republic of the Congo (DRC), pursuant to an indictment alleging serious violations of international humanitarian law (IHL) committed against the Tutsi population prior to his becoming foreign minister. The DRC brought suit against Belgium before the ICJ claiming that the issuance of the arrest warrant violated the immunities from criminal process afforded to incumbent foreign ministers. As the pleadings evolved, the case eventually centered on the question of immunity, the majority of the court finding that incumbent foreign ministers were immune from the criminal jurisdiction of other states (but not from the jurisdiction of an international criminal tribunal with proper jurisdiction over the defendant). The majority limited its analysis to the question of immunity without addressing the question of whether international law would otherwise allow Belgium to assert such jurisdiction absent such immunity.

A minority of the Court, however, felt that the question of jurisdiction was antecedent and thus had to be answered before reaching the question of immunity. They concluded that international law does allow assertions of universal jurisdiction like that asserted by Belgium, including assertions of jurisdiction over an individual not physically present within that state's territory (in absentia). Three of the judges wrote extensively on the legality of universal jurisdiction, and laid down the following conditions for a state to assert universal jurisdiction in absentia: (1) the national state of the accused must be given an opportunity to act on the allegations; (2) the prosecution must be initiated by a prosecutor or *juge d'instruction* who is independent from control by the rest of the government; (3) special circumstances must exist to justify the assertion of jurisdiction, such as a request by the victims for the initiation of such a case; and (4) such jurisdiction must only be asserted over the most heinous crimes.

By contrast, a prominent ICL expert and former President of the ICTY, Antonio Cassese, argues that although such assertions of jurisdiction may be desirable, they are not at the moment permitted under international law.[7] Professor Cassese's position was effectively adopted by Judge Ranjeva of the ICJ, who in a declaration stated that customary international law only recognized universal jurisdiction for maritime piracy, and that conventional law only provides for universal jurisdiction by national courts in a limited number of circumstances. Judge Reczek took an even more skeptical view of universal jurisdiction, in effect arguing that a state could only exert such jurisdiction if there was some connection to the forum state. In contrast, Judge Van den Wyngaert asserted that universal jurisdiction is permitted under international law by both national and international tribunals without any link to the forum state, thus going further than any of the other dissenters. As this brief summary of the opinions makes clear, the position of universal jurisdiction under international law is uncertain and in flux.

Despite this uncertainty, a number of states in the last decade have asserted universal jurisdiction over major international crimes. The Spanish attempt to prosecute former Chilean dictator Augusto Pinochet and the Senegalese prosecution of the former Chadian dictator Hissène Habré were both justified at least in part by the universality principle. The *Habré* case raises a question of competing assertions of universal jurisdiction, as prosecutions were initiated in both Belgium and Senegal. Habré was overthrown in 1990 and fled to Senegal. A Chadian Truth Commission concluded that Habré was responsible for systematic torture and the murder of more than 40,000 people during his dictatorship. Victims of his atrocities initiated a criminal prosecution in Senegal, but the Senegalese court dismissed the case, reasoning that Senegal had not incorporated ICL into its domestic law, so that the Senegalese courts did not have jurisdiction. The victims then pushed for the initiation of proceedings against Habré in Belgium under that country's universal jurisdiction law. Pursuant to an extradition request by Belgium, the Senegalese authorities arrested Habré in 2005. The Senegalese court ordered the release of Habré, arguing that pursuant to the *Yerodia* case Habré was entitled to immunity from Belgian jurisdiction. Under pressure from the international community, including many African states, Senegal rearrested Habré and submitted the question of his immunity to the African Union. The African Union convened a panel of eminent African jurists who concluded that Senegal should amend its laws and assert jurisdiction over Habré for the alleged crimes he committed. The case is currently pending in Senegal.

As a policy matter, universal jurisdiction is not without its concerns and detractors. Many of the more successful assertions of universal jurisdiction have been by northern developed countries against officials from southern developing countries. In many cases, the accused comes from a state that was a colony of the state asserting jurisdiction, thus raising the specter of neo-colonialism. There are exceptions, including the *Habré* case and several proceedings against U.S., Chinese, and Israeli officials that have been, and are being, pursued in Belgium, Germany, and Spain (although most cases against individuals from more powerful countries have been dismissed or are only in preliminary in absentia proceedings). Even in the *Habré* case, however, Senegal was pushed to assert jurisdiction in part because of the assertion of jurisdiction by Belgium. More generally, some express unease at placing the decision of whom to prosecute with individual nation-state authorities, for fear that only officials from politically unpopular or weak states will be targeted, and officials from powerful states will enjoy a de facto immunity. Moreover, many argue that universal jurisdiction threatens to create judicial chaos, as foreign officials become incapable of travelling to states with universal jurisdiction laws on the books.

Domestic Military Courts

In addition to trials before regularly constituted civilian courts, courts martial and military commissions can exercise jurisdiction over violations of IHL. Courts martial are military courts that prosecute members of the armed forces subject to military law, including the law of armed conflict. Courts martial may also be employed to prosecute enemy prisoners of war (POWs) for war crimes, individuals subject to martial law, or belligerents within occupied territory. In the United States, for example, trials by courts martial are governed by the Manual for Courts-Martial (MCM), prescribed by executive order, which contains the procedural and evidentiary rules for courts martial as well as the Uniform Code of Military Justice (UCMJ). Some of the military offenses within the UCMJ have domestic law analogs, whereas others are specific to the military (e.g., the crimes of dereliction of duty or conduct unbecoming an officer).

Although military commissions have become associated with the modern "war on terror," they are not a new phenomenon. Indeed, throughout history, the United States and other nations have utilized military commissions to prosecute individuals for violations of the laws of war. Military commissions were born of military necessity. They have been constituted when the civilian courts are either unavailable or impractical, or in the context of martial law or belligerent occupation. For example, the United States prosecuted saboteurs and war criminals before military commissions during and following World War II. At that time, the U.S. Supreme Court issued several rulings confirming that military commissions can lawfully prosecute enemy belligerents for violations of the law of armed conflict.[8] Historically, although military commissions have not been governed by statute, they were conducted largely according to the procedural rules then governing courts martial. In such proceedings, the international law of armed conflict has been held to be incorporated, in effect as "military common law," to be applied by the commission.

The 1949 Geneva Conventions require that POWs on trial for war crimes be prosecuted under the same procedures that would apply to the prosecuting army's own members ("the parity principle"). In *Hamdan v. Rumsfeld*,[9] the U.S. Supreme Court cited the safeguards embodied in the Geneva Conventions (as well as the UCMJ) to invalidate the military commissions established to prosecute individuals detained at Guantánamo Bay. A plurality opinion also reasoned that the charged offense, conspiracy to violate the law of armed conflict, was not a cognizable violation of international law and therefore could not be tried by military commission. Most recently, the U.S. Supreme Court extended the line of cases involving military commissions and held for the first time that those individuals detained at Guantánamo Bay were entitled to challenge their detention in U.S. federal courts under the constitutionally protected ancient writ of *habeas corpus*.[10]

EXTRADITION, TRANSFER, RENDITION, AND ABDUCTION

Although a number of domestic systems allow in absentia criminal trials, many do not; nor do the existing international and hybrid tribunals. As a result, the exercise of international and domestic jurisdiction is often dependent on the ability of the tribunal to obtain custody of the accused. This is an area in which domestic legal systems become crucially important in transferring individuals from their custody to another jurisdiction, such as another state's legal system or an international tribunal. This is also an area in which one sees assertions of state sovereignty and the use of coercive powers (sometimes rising to the level of international abduction) as states alternatively resist and acquiesce in requests for such transfers.

In most transnational cases, an act of extradition operates to transfer an accused between nation states. *Extradition* is the process by which one state (the requested state) transfers to the custody of another state (the requesting state) an individual wanted for trial in the requesting state. Extradition is usually governed by a web of bilateral treaties, although the European system has a multilateral treaty governing extradition within Europe. Extradition often provides an example of cooperation among states in the enforcement of ICL, but states continue to assert their sovereign prerogative not to extradite someone if (1) the act for which the requesting state wants to prosecute the individual is not a crime in the requested state (the so-called double criminality rule); (2) the act for which the requesting state wants to prosecute the individual is a political act (the political offense exception); (3) the individual is a national of the requested state; and (4) humanitarian reasons or concern about the lack of due process in the requesting state counsel against extraditing the individual. Each of these exceptions to extradition is premised on powers reserved to the requested state, and there are obvious situations in which the requested state benefits from either sending or refusing to send an accused individual to the requesting state. These exceptions are also designed to benefit and protect the individual accused. For example, in allowing Augusto Pinochet to return to Chile rather than be extradited to Spain, where he was wanted for violations of ICL committed in Chile, the United Kingdom cited humanitarian concerns arising from Pinochet's age and health. At the same time, the Chilean government made it quite clear to the United Kingdom that it did not want Pinochet sent to Spain. The inevitable diplomatic friction that would have been created by extraditing Pinochet to stand trial was undoubtedly a factor in the decision of the U.K. government to return him to Chile. These means to resist extradition thus may hinder the furtherance of international justice.

When an international tribunal requests that a state hand over a suspect for prosecution, we speak of "transfer" or "surrender" and not extradition. Extradition is the term used to describe the horizontal relationship between the two states involved in the transfer of an accused. Although these are different processes, many of the doctrines and procedures that are applicable to extradition proceedings have been adapted to the context of surrender proceedings involving international tribunals. With respect to the two original ad hoc tribunals, states are obligated to transfer a suspect if the tribunal so requests by virtue of the tribunals' statutes and their Chapter VII provenance. This coercive obligation establishes the primacy of the ad hoc tribunals' jurisdiction over domestic courts. Theoretically, any state that refused to cooperate would be subject to sanction by the UN Security Council. A similar obligation exists under the Rome Treaty, whereby state parties are required to cooperate with the ICC to make suspects available to the Court. Unlike the ad hoc tribunals, the Court lacks any ability to coerce states to cooperate; rather, the obligation to cooperate is one accepted by states on ratification of the Rome Treaty. This obligation exists only if an interested state does not decide to investigate or prosecute the individual under the Court's complementarity regime.

Security Council backing does not necessarily guarantee state compliance, even from a permanent member of the Security Council. Early in the life of the ICTR, the tribunal requested the United States to transfer a suspect, Elizaphan Ntakirutimana, for prosecution. Ntakirutimana sued the U.S. government in a U.S. federal court to halt his transfer to the ICTR. The various judges hearing the case took the position that the U.S. government needed to submit evidence that would establish probable cause that Ntakirutimana was guilty of the acts alleged by the ICTR prosecutor. The U.S. courts eventually found that the evidence did support such a probable cause finding, and Ntakirutimana was transferred to the ICTR. Critics of this approach argued that under the authority of the Security Council, the United States was obligated to transfer the suspect immediately on request. In fact, Article 28 of the ICTR Statute is clear that all states must cooperate in the investigation and prosecution of accused persons and "shall comply without undue delay with any request for assistance" issued by a Trial Chamber, including for "the arrest or detention of persons [or] the surrender or the transfer of the accused." Further, Rule 58 of the ICTR's Rules of Procedure and Evidence state that these obligations "shall prevail over any legal impediment to the surrender or transfer of the accused to the Tribunal which may exist under the national law or extradition treaties of the State concerned." That said, the U.S. Surrender Agreements with the ad hoc tribunals, which were implemented with a provision tacked onto the National Defense and Authorization Act[11] with little Congressional discussion, do contemplate at Article 2(3) that the United States would conduct some sort of judicial hearing before surrendering an individual to the Tribunal:

> A request for surrender of a person who is sought for prosecution shall also be supported by copies of the warrant of arrest and of the indictment and by information sufficient to establish there is a reasonable basis to believe that the person sought has committed the violation or violations for which surrender is requested.[12]

The United States is the only state to undertake such a treaty to effectuate transfers.[13] This example illustrates the tensions among furthering international justice, respecting state sovereignty, and ensuring the rights of criminal suspects.

More controversially, individuals may be abducted to bring them within international or domestic custody. For example, the Israeli government abducted Adolf Eichmann to transfer him from Argentina to Israel, where he was prosecuted, convicted, and executed for his involvement in the Nazi Holocaust. The UN Security Council condemned the abduction, but only required that Israel pay appropriate reparation to Argentina. The United States has more controversially resorted to abduction, both to bring suspects into the United States to be tried criminally, as well as to detain individuals in offshore prisons for interrogation. The U.S. Supreme Court in a series of opinions has found that a U.S. court has personal jurisdiction over an individual even if he was abducted and forcibly brought into U.S. territory,[14] and that such an abduction (at least where the individual was transferred to lawful custody within 12 hours) does not violate a clear and universal rule of international human rights law that would give rise to a civil claim for relief on the part of the person abducted.[15] The ICTY essentially adopted this so-called *male captus, bene detentus* doctrine (which states that an improper capture can nonetheless result in valid detention) in a case in which private parties abducted the accused and brought him into the custody of the multinational force in Bosnia.[16] The Trial Chamber did contemplate, however, that there may be a legal impediment to jurisdiction if the accused had been very seriously mistreated before being handed over to the Tribunal or if Tribunal staff played a part in the abduction.[17]

Even more controversial is the U.S. practice of *rendering* individuals to third states (for purposes of taking advantage of aggressive interrogation techniques employed by that third state that in some cases rise to the level of torture), or to U.S. facilities outside of the territory of the United States. European states have initiated suits in absentia against Central Intelligence Agency operatives involved in such renderings, although as of this writing no judgments have been reached. Numerous international human rights bodies, including the Committee Against Torture and the Human Rights Committee, have concluded that such renditions violate the Convention Against Torture[18] and the International Covenant on Civil and Political Rights,[19] respectively. The international community continues to grapple with how to evaluate the legal implications of these assertions of state power. In particular, whereas abductions for the purpose of prosecuting an individual for an international crime (the Eichmann example) may be more palatable, those committed for the purposes of detention with no trial, or detention with interrogation or torture, raise more acute concerns.

CONCLUSION

As should be apparent, a high degree of jurisdictional redundancy characterizes the ICL system, as ICL norms are codified and adjudicated in both the international and domestic contexts. In addition, these jurisdictional regimes are created by very different types of processes — some cooperative, some more coercive. In some circumstances, international tribunals exercise primacy over domestic tribunals that may also have jurisdiction over the crimes in question (such as the state in whose territory the crimes were committed). In the case of the ICC, by contrast, international jurisdiction is complementary to domestic jurisdiction such that if a domestic court is prosecuting a particular crime, the ICC should stay its hand. Much uncertainty surrounds how this principle of complementarity is to be adjudicated. Indeed, important rulings are likely to be released in the midst of your course on ICL. Furthermore, there are no firm rules governing how competing exercises of jurisdiction are to be resolved between these institutions or whether and how future jurisdictional regimes should be created at the international level. As you review the materials in your primary text, consider whether the forum in question is likely to be the most impartial, fair, and robust or whether the case would have been better pursued elsewhere.

⮑ 3 ⮐

The Making of International Criminal Law

F undamental to any legal system are processes, doctrines, and conventions concerning the development of the applicable substantive rules. How law is developed, and where one looks to determine the applicable rules, is particularly important for a system of law that imposes criminal liability on individuals. Criminal law may result in the deprivation of an individual's fundamental right to liberty through incarceration, and — in some domestic jurisdictions — the ultimate penalty of execution. *Nullum crimen sine lege* (NCSL), a fundamental principle of justice that applies to all criminal law systems, requires that the penal law be clear and easily ascertained, and thus provide adequate notice to individuals that certain conduct may result in criminal liability. It is thus important to master the sources of international criminal law (ICL). We discuss the uneasy relationship between ICL and NCSL in its own chapter (Chapter 5).

As we will see, like in public international law generally there is a core set of rules concerning sources of ICL over which there is little controversy. These rules derive from Article 38 of the Statute of the International Court of Justice (ICJ), which most agree is a definitive articulation of the primary sources of public international law. Article 38 lists treaties, customary international law, and general principles of law as primary sources, and judicial decisions and the writings of publicists as subsidiary sources. This article operates very much like a "choice of law" provision for the ICJ. In certain situations, however, ICL tribunals establish their own rules with respect to sources of law. For example, the Rome Treaty creating the International Criminal Court (ICC) at Article 21 sets forth a hierarchical set of sources applicable to the ICC that deviates from Article 38 by, among other things, deemphasizing general principles of law.

Certain traditional sources of public international law may sit uncomfortably in a system of penal law. Given the grave consequences of criminal liability, there may be greater concern for the rights of criminal defendants where there is significant uncertainty about the applicable law or where the applicable law is not easily ascertainable. Thus, source of law doctrines that are relatively uncontroversial in the context of most fields of public international law may evince more controversy in the criminal context. Codified rules, such as those found in treaties, are the least troubling; rules that derive from customary international law or from general principles of justice are more susceptible to uncertainty, and raise special concerns with respect to ICL.

In ICL, there is a recurring tension between a requirement of justice that the law be certain and explicit, as embodied in the doctrine of NCSL, and the concern that the more rigid we make our doctrine of sources the more likely we are to provide those responsible for some of the worst atrocities known to humankind with a technical defense to avoid criminal liability. This tension was evident at the birth of the modern ICL regime in the post–World War II period, when individuals were prosecuted for the novel offenses of crimes against humanity and crimes against the peace. A strict application of the principle of NCSL to these offenses at Nuremberg would have limited the ability of the Allies to hold the Nazi high command accountable for aggressive war and most of the crimes of the Holocaust. As we will see, this tension between wanting to keep the law flexible enough to adapt to the seemingly endless innovations of criminal activity without violating the fundamental rights of those accused of such atrocities is still present today. The dilemma is summed up by Professor Alain Pellet, who, in criticizing the decision to include in the Rome Treaty detailed definitions of the crimes within the jurisdiction of the ICC, noted:

> by freezing [international law] in a sometimes daring but often inadequate and regressive text, the authors of the Statute have limited the chances of making the Court an efficient instrument in the struggle against the crimes it is supposed to repress. . . . Unfortunately men's criminal imagination appears unlimited and, by enclosing the definition of the crimes in narrow, punctilious formulations, they have forbidden the judges in advance to suppress future malevolent inventions of the human spirit.[1]

Despite Pellet's characterization of the ICC Statute, the applicable sources laid out in Article 21 contemplate moving outside the specific definitions in the Treaty if criminal activity is not clearly proscribed. Thus, under Article 21 the Court is to apply first the definition of crimes found in the Statute and in the Elements of Crimes and Rules of Procedure and Evidence. Second, the Court is to look, "where appropriate, [to] applicable treaties and the principles and rules of international law, including the established principles of the international law of armed conflict." According to this provision, if treaties external to the ICC more clearly criminalize activity than the Rome Treaty, then the Court may rely on those outside sources for interpretive guidance. In addition, where neither the

Statute nor applicable treaties provide a clear rule of decision, the Court may look to general principles of law derived from the national legal systems of the world, so long as such principles are not in conflict with either the Statute or international law. This expansive grant of authority to the Court is tempered by a provision in the same Article 21 that states that the application and interpretation of the enumerated sources of law must be consistent with "internationally recognized human rights." As the principle of NCSL is considered a fundamental principle of human rights, and is contained in all the omnibus human rights treaties, this last provision provides a significant counterweight to the seemingly expansive grant provided in the other subsections of Article 21. The possibility of amending the Rome Treaty to account for the evolution of ICL remains open, as envisioned by Article 121 of the Treaty.

TREATIES

Treaties are the least controversial source of international law, and the one that domestically trained lawyers find the easiest to grasp. The law of treaties — the body of rules that governs the formation, interpretation, implementation, and termination of treaties — is itself codified in a series of treaties, most importantly the 1969 Vienna Convention on the Law of Treaties.[2] Although a little over 100 states have ratified the Vienna Convention, there is general consensus that the provisions of the Convention have risen to the level of customary international law, which is to say that the treaty sets forth a legal regime that is binding on all states, not just those that have joined the Convention.

ICL is a field replete with treaty law. In fact, the field of international humanitarian law (IHL), also called the law of armed conflict, is one of the earliest subjects of international treaty law, and is today one of the most codified areas of international law. The Geneva Conventions of 1949 enjoy the unique distinction of being the only treaties — as of this writing — that have been ratified by every state in the world. Treaties establishing international crimes arguably provide adequate fair notice to nationals of treaty members, and thus pose fewer problems with respect to the NCSL principle than other sources of ICL.

Treaties come in two basic types. Bilateral treaties are entered into between two states, or between a state and another entity, usually an international organization. Multilateral treaties are open for ratification to a large number of states and often to all states in the world. Regional treaties, such as the American Convention on Human Rights, are multilateral treaties but are restricted with respect to the states that may ratify them. Some analogize bilateral treaties to contracts and multilateral treaties to legislation. As with many such analogies, these comparisons often confuse as much as they assist. Contract principles such as offer, acceptance, and the intent of the parties apply to bilateral treaties, but they apply equally to multilateral treaties. By the same token, whereas multilateral treaties are often legislative in nature — setting down general principles of applicable law and creating a legal regime binding on all members — bilateral treaties may also embody such law-making provisions (extradition treaties, for example), and multilateral treaties, as we shall see, are significantly different in their formation and operation than domestic legislation. Multilateral treaties are a primary building block of ICL. Bilateral treaties do play a lesser, although still important, role in some aspects of ICL; for example, extradition treaties govern the procedures by which a suspect may be transferred from one jurisdiction to another.

States generally first *sign* and then *ratify* a treaty. Signature alone of a treaty indicates a state's acceptance of the terms of the treaty and its intent to ratify, accept, or approve the treaty. Although a state is usually not legally bound by the terms of a treaty it has only signed (unless the state so agrees), a signatory state may not violate the object and purpose of a treaty. There is broad agreement that signature has the effect of creating such an obligation on the part of a state; there is little consensus on the content of this obligation or on the consequences of its violation.

A state becomes an official party to a treaty, and thus fully bound by its terms, upon ratification. (A state may also *accede* to a treaty that has already entered into force; this has the same effect as ratification.) It is important to distinguish between two types of ratification procedures — those required as a matter of international law and those required as a matter of domestic law. Internationally, ratification is usually effectuated by the state depositing a document indicating its intent to be bound by the treaty with an official depository, such as the UN Secretary General. Domestically, ratification may require compliance with procedures set forth in that state's constitution or applicable legislation. In the United States, for example, the President may only ratify a treaty after receiving the advice and consent of the Senate.

Many human rights treaties, including those that permit or impose criminal liability, are often ratified with reservations. A *reservation* is a declaration that purports to alter the legal effect of a treaty provision with respect to that state. A state may agree to ratify a treaty conditional on the ability to attach reservations. On ratifying the International Covenant on Civil and Political Rights (ICCPR), for example, the United States attached a reservation with respect to Article 20, which prohibits, among other things, hate speech. The U.S. reservation states that Article 20 does not apply to the U.S. to the extent that it conflicts with the right of free speech and association protected by the U.S. Constitution and other U.S. law. A treaty may, by its terms, forbid the use of reservations. The Rome Treaty, for example, disallows reservations. Where reservations are permitted, states may not attach reservations that violate the object and purpose of the treaty — imposing the same test, and raising the same interpretative and remedial questions, as the obligation undertaken by a state upon signing a treaty.

There is very little jurisprudence on what constitutes the object and purpose of a treaty. The most authoritative treatment of the issue involves reservations to the 1948 Genocide Convention. In 1951, the ICJ issued an Advisory Opinion on the question of reservations to the Genocide Convention.[3] On ratification, many states had attached reservations to Article IX of the Convention, which vests jurisdiction in the ICJ over disputes relating to the "interpretation, application or fulfillment" of the treaty "including those relating to the responsibility of a State for genocide." The ICJ stated in its advisory opinion that the question of whether a reserving state was a party to a treaty was determined by the compatibility of that state's reservation with the object and purpose of the treaty, and not by the assent of other member states to the reservation. The ICJ pointedly did not opine on whether the specific reservations at issue were in fact consistent with the object and purpose of the Genocide Convention.

The effect of a reservation that is not compatible with the object and purpose of a treaty is unclear. The Human Rights Committee (the body created by the ICCPR) has stated in a general comment that an unacceptable reservation to the ICCPR will be null and void, and that the treaty will be binding on the ratifying state without the effect of the reservation.[4] This is somewhat problematic, as in most cases states agree to ratify a treaty conditional on the acceptance of their asserted reservation. If the reservation is null and void, the underlying provision applies to the ratifying state despite that state's clear intent not to be bound by that provision. Thus, many states, including the United States, formally indicated their disagreement with this approach of the Committee to reservations.

In addition to reservations, the United States and other nations may attach "understandings" and "declarations" to a treaty. *Understandings* are meant to clarify, but not alter, the legal meaning or effect of a provision. A *declaration* is normally used to indicate a state's agreement to a particular optional part of a treaty — for example, allowing other state parties to bring complaints alleging a violation of the state's obligations under the treaty (as provided under Article 41(1) of the ICCPR). Collectively, reservations, understandings, and declarations are often referred to as RUDs. Notwithstanding the label a state attaches to a declaration or understanding, if the intent of the provision is to alter the legal effect of a treaty provision, then the declaration or understanding is treated as a reservation.

According to the Vienna Convention, treaty interpretation is based on the plain language of its terms in their context. Thus, a treaty clause is to be interpreted based on its "ordinary meaning . . . in [its] context and in the light of [the treaty's] object and purpose" (Article 31(1)). The overall approach is to discern the intent of the state parties. For context, the Convention directs us to the following: (1) the preamble and any annexes to the treaty; (2) other written agreements related to the treaty, either entered into among the state parties or accepted by others as related to the treaty; (3) any subsequent agreements concerning the interpretation or application of the treaty; (4) any subsequent practice of the parties concerning the application of the treaty that reflects agreement among the parties concerning the treaty's interpretation; and (5) any applicable rules of international law that apply to the parties (see Article 31(2)-(3)). In addition to this contextual guidance, as noted earlier, it is generally accepted at the international level that treaties are to be treated as living documents. In other words, they are to be interpreted in the context of the time in which they are being applied, and not as they would have been interpreted at the time of their drafting. Compare this to U.S. constitutional law, where "originalists" argue that the U.S. Constitution should be interpreted as it would have been at the time of its drafting without taking into account subsequent cultural, legal, and political developments.

In addition to the primary means of treaty interpretation, the Vienna Convention lists the treaty's *travaux préparatoires* (drafting history) as a supplementary means of interpretation where a textual interpretation leads to ambiguity, obscurity, or unreasonable results (Article 32). All ICL treaties have published drafting histories that can be useful to understanding the intentions of the parties, the meaning of particular treaty terms, and the reach of the treaty. These records are particularly valuable in historical justice cases adjudicating crimes committed well in the past, because they provide evidence of the state of ICL at the time historical abuses occurred. The ICC Statute in particular has generated a small library of works aimed at explaining the origins and meanings of its many provisions.[5]

A tension often arises, however, in effectuating the apparent intentions of treaty drafters—primarily states that may engage in political compromises to protect themselves from any potential treaty liability—and the higher purposes of a treaty, which may undermine sovereign interests. Some scholars have raised the question of whether the basic canons of treaty law should be modified in the case of international human rights treaties, given the fact that the beneficiaries of such treaties tend to be individuals and not states. The argument is that because such treaties are meant to benefit individuals directly, they should be interpreted with that purpose in mind. This argues for a mode of interpretation less focused on the intentions of the state parties (which may be to protect state sovereignty) and more on the overall or articulated purpose of the treaty, as may be gleaned from its preamble, for example. Similar arguments have been raised with respect to ICL treaties, although as noted earlier, the fact that ICL treaties may be applied in the penal context raises special concerns with respect to the principle of NCSL and the imperative of specificity in criminal law.

An example of a tribunal taking a purposive approach to treaty interpretation is the International Criminal Tribunal for Yugoslavia's (ICTY's) interpretation of the term "national" found in the 1949 Geneva Conventions. Article 4 of the Fourth Geneva Convention protecting civilians defines the class of people it protects as "those who, at a given moment and in any manner whatsoever, find themselves, in case of a conflict or occupation, in the hands of a Party to the conflict or Occupying Power *of which they are not nationals.*"[6] The ICTY was faced with the prosecution of members of one ethnicity (Bosnian Muslims) for violations committed against individuals of the same nationality but of different ethnicity (Bosnian Serbs). The defendants challenged the prosecution, arguing that because all of the parties were of the same Bosnian nationality, the Geneva Conventions did not apply, citing Article 4. The Appeals Chamber rejected this argument, noting that the object and purpose of the Geneva Conventions is to protect civilians who are captured by a party to which they owed no allegiance and that owes them no duties of protection based on citizenship. The fact that the parties to the conflict in the former Yugoslavia divided along ethnicity rather than nationality should not, the court reasoned, result in the inapplicability of the Geneva Conventions.[7] In this way, the ICTY ignored the plain text of the treaty and instead resorted to its object and purpose to redefine a key term that was the lynchpin of the Conventions' grave breaches regime.

It is tempting to rely exclusively on treaties when looking for ICL because they provide a concrete text with which to work. These treaties, however, rarely mirror comprehensive criminal codes in their specificity, scope, or depth. As a result, courts and litigants engaged in the enforcement of ICL often look to customary international law as another important source of applicable law.

CUSTOMARY INTERNATIONAL LAW

Customary international law is a second major source of public international law, and is consequently an important source of ICL. Customary international law consists of two elements: collective state practice undertaken out of a sense of legal obligation. This formula thus comprises an objective element (state practice) and a subjective element (*opinio iuris* or *juris*). State conduct undertaken out of convenience or habit in and of itself does not constitute customary international law. Such conduct must be carried out with the perception that it is or should be required by law. Inaction may also constitute practice. As the Restatement (Third) of Foreign Relations Law states at comment b to § 102: "[i]naction may constitute state practice, as when a state acquiesces in acts of another state that affect its legal rights." Some scholars and jurists give more emphasis to the objective element, arguing that one can imply the subjective element if there is near-universal practice. Others focus more on the subjective element, arguing that normative and aspirational statements in themselves can create law, even in the face of contrary or inconsistent state practice. This latter position becomes more defensible to the extent one can argue that such statements themselves constitute state practice.

Customary international law, being premised on state conduct, reflects the general international law principle of state consent. Thus, according to a doctrine that remains controversial, states may "opt out" of a rule of customary international law if they become *persistent objectors* as the rule is being formed and when it is applied. A state persistently objects by making clear that it does not agree with an emerging rule of customary international law. More than silence is required to become a persistent objector. For example, the United States has consistently and continuously made clear its objection to the emergence of a rule prohibiting capital punishment under international law. The U.S. objection has manifested itself through the continued legalization of capital punishment under domestic law and clear official statements opposing any suggestion that capital punishment is now prohibited under international human rights law. Such statements appear, for example, in reservations the United States has attached to international treaties restricting or prohibiting the use of capital punishment.

The one major exception to this general rule of state consent concerns *peremptory norms* of international law (so-called *jus cogens*), from which no state may opt out. The prohibitions against some of the worst crimes under international law — such as slavery, genocide, and crimes against humanity — constitute *jus cogens* ("compelling law"). Unlike customary international law, states my not opt out of a *jus cogens* rule. Rules of *jus cogens* occupy an uneasy place in an international legal system that emphasizes positive law-making and state consent. They are the clearest manifestation of the natural law origins of international law.

As should be clear, confusion may arise concerning state action that conflicts with a rule of customary international law: Is the state objecting to an emerging rule or violating an existing rule? In the alternative, is the nonconforming conduct indicative of a weakening or evolution of the rule or the lack of a customary rule altogether? The key, of course, is whether the rule in question is emerging or established, a determination that is difficult to make, as the date at which an emerging rule of customary international law "crystallizes" is often unclear. A focus on articulations of *opinio juris* — what states say they believe the rule to be — can also be of assistance.

Although ICL is increasingly codified, customary international law remains an important source of applicable rules. Throughout your course, consider the role that customary international law plays in the cases in your primary text. It is possible to envision customary international law being used in four primary ways: (1) as the source of a substantive rule criminalizing certain acts; (2) to fill gaps in a treaty-created prohibition; (3) as a guide to interpreting an otherwise applicable rule of law; and (4) as confirmation that certain activity was criminalized at the time it was committed where an applicable treaty prohibition is silent as to the existence of individual criminal responsibility.

With respect to the first option, even though the existing international tribunals impose criminal liability pursuant to their constitutive statutes, they often invoke customary international law. For example, when the Security Council created the ICTY, it indicated that the Tribunal would only prosecute those crimes prohibited by customary international law or by a treaty applicable to the former Yugoslavia. Article 3 of the ICTY Statute accordingly grants jurisdiction over "violations of the laws or customs of war" and contains an open-ended list of war crimes (drawn from the 1909 Hague Convention). The ICTY has used Article 3 to import the customary international law of war crimes into the subject matter jurisdiction of the ICTY. This direct application of customary international law is in marked contrast to domestic courts, which rarely apply customary international law directly in penal proceedings. U.S. courts, for example, have applied customary international law to impose *civil* liability on individuals who have violated international criminal law (under the Alien Tort Statute), but have not used customary international law to impose *criminal* liability.

With respect to the second option, customary international law is used to supplement and fill lacunae in treaty law, for example to establish the elements of an offense defined in a statute or treaty. In the *Čelebići* case before the ICTY, defendants moved for the dismissal of the counts that alleged the commission of "wilfully causing great suffering or serious injury to body or health," "inhuman treatment," and "cruel treatment" on the ground that they were not defined with sufficient specificity under international law to serve as the basis for a criminal prosecution.[8] In rejecting the defense and convicting the defendants, an ICTY Trial Chamber added content to its Statute by relying on the Geneva Conventions' drafting history, the discussions within human rights institutions concerning analogous provisions in human rights treaties addressed to state parties and giving rise to state responsibility in their breach, and the overarching principles animating IHL.

Third, customary international law can be used as a guide to interpretation. Thus, the ICTY has held that unless the contrary intent is clear from the text of a treaty, the presumption is that the provisions of a treaty are meant to be consistent with customary international law.[9] This interpretive doctrine is similar to that adopted in the United States with respect to international law, where the presumption is that unless the contrary intent is clearly expressed by Congress, statutes are to be interpreted so as not to conflict with international law.[10]

Fourth, many treaties prohibit specific conduct, but do not clearly render that conduct criminal by mandating the imposition of individual penal responsibility in the event of a breach. The ICTY looked to customary international law to conclude that violations of common Article 3 of the 1949 Geneva Conventions gave rise to individual criminal responsibility, even though that provision is silent as to applicable remedies and implies only the civil responsibility of state parties to the treaty.[11] A more controversial use of customary international law to confirm an ICL prohibition can be seen in the decision involving child recruitment brought before the Special Court for Sierra Leone.[12] The Statute of the Special Court asserted criminal jurisdiction over child recruitment committed during the conflict in Sierra Leone. The question facing the Special Court was whether child recruitment was criminalized by 1996 when the acts subject to the prosecution were committed. The majority cited national rules governing the minimum age of conscription, the drafting history of the ICC Statute, and human rights treaties aimed at prohibiting the recruitment and enlistment of child soldiers for support of the existence of a customary penal rule in 1996. Judge Robertson (United Kingdom) in dissent disagreed, finding that there was not enough evidence to support the assertion that child recruitment had been criminalized by the time the majority asserted. He argued that the crime of enlisting or using child soldiers did not fully crystallize until the 1998 promulgation of the ICC Statute, which clearly lists such conduct as a war crime. Judge Robertson took issue with the majority for conflating abhorrent conduct with criminal conduct, arguing that "it is precisely when the acts are abhorrent and deeply shocking that the principle of legality must be most stringently applied, to ensure that the defendant is not convicted out of disgust rather than evidence, or of a non-existent crime."[13] Given that Sierra Leonean law did not prohibit child recruitment, Judge Robertson argued that there was no way for the embattled defendants to reasonably ascertain, through competent legal advice, that they were committing a crime when they enlisted and recruited child soldiers. He concluded that, however "inconvenient" the result, NCSL compelled the dismissal of the challenged charge.

GENERAL PRINCIPLES OF LAW

The third source of international law identified in Article 38 of the ICJ Statute, general principles of law, is the least developed of the three. Article 38 refers to "general principles of law recognized by civilized nations." The modifier "civilized nations" has been effectively dropped as an arcane, and even offensive, qualification. Instead, the term "general principles of law" is interpreted to refer to general principles found in the major legal systems of the world. The ICTY Appeals Chamber, for example, identified three groupings of states in discussing general principles of law concerned with the availability of duress in a prosecution for war crimes and crimes against humanity: (1) civil law systems; (2) common law systems; and (3) the "criminal law of other states," under which they grouped Japan, China, Morocco, Somalia, and Ethiopia.[14] In practice, however, judges mostly look at common law and civil law systems to discern applicable rules. It is important not to confuse general principles of law with customary international law, although sometimes the evidence used to prove the one may also prove the other. Customary international law requires *opinio juris* — a requirement not found in general principles of law — and customary international law consists of rules that states adopt as rules of international law. General principles of law, on the other hand, consist of commonalities found in different legal systems that are not necessarily thought of by the states adopting or relying on them as international law.

One of the earliest references in the field of ICL to the applicability of general principles of law is found at Nuremberg in justifying the inclusion of crimes against humanity as a crime within that tribunal's jurisdiction. The prosecutors at Nuremberg argued that crimes against humanity constitute, "in the last analysis, nothing less than the preparation for political ends and in a systematic manner, of common law crimes such as theft, looting, ill treatment, enslavement, murders, and assassinations, crimes that are provided for and punishable under the penal laws of all civilized states."[15] Today, general principles of law encompass those principles that are common to most criminal legal systems and those principles considered inherent to the international legal system or to any system of criminal justice. The first concept incorporates an expressly comparative law approach; the second is deduced from the overall object and purpose of ICL.

General principles of law have been used to define the elements of the constitutive acts of crimes against humanity and war crimes, such as murder or rape, that are common to domestic legal systems. The question before the ICTY Trial

Chamber in the *Furundžija* case, for example, concerned the definition of rape under international law. Furundžija had been charged with rape as a war crime for forcing a woman to engage in oral sex. The law of the former Yugoslavia treated such conduct as sexual assault — a lesser crime — rather than rape. The Tribunal surveyed the definition of rape found in many national legal systems and discerned a trend toward broadening the definition of rape to include acts previously classified as less serious offenses. Supplementing its more empirical and comparative approach, the Trial Chamber also referred to the object and purpose of humanitarian law and human rights law (to protect and promote human dignity) to find that the charged conduct at issue constituted rape under ICL.[16]

There are times when no clear or consensus rule can be discerned from the world's legal systems. In such situations, international criminal tribunals will take a more teleological (purposive) approach to discern an applicable rule. As just noted, the Trial Chamber in *Furundžija* adopted a teleological approach to confirm the rule it derived from looking at a wide range of national legal systems. As another example, the ICTY had to determine how to address situations of concurrent convictions for the same underlying conduct. Domestic law, as it turned out, dealt with this situation in a variety of ways, and no clear trend was apparent. The Trial Chamber then resorted to international practice and the object and purpose of ICL, stating: "Faced with this discrepancy in municipal legal systems, the Trial Chamber considers that a fair solution can be derived both from the object and purpose of the provisions of the Statute and from 'the general principles of justice applied by jurists and practiced by military courts' referred to by the International Military Tribunal at Nuremberg."[17]

Whereas the ad hoc ICL tribunals have drawn on general principles of law as a source of law, Article 21 of the Statute of the ICC makes clear that such general principles are a tertiary source of law for that court. The primary sources of law are the Court's Statute, its Elements of Crimes, and its Rules of Procedure and Evidence. Secondarily, the Court is to apply, "where appropriate, applicable treaties and the principles and rules of international law." It is presumed that the "rules of international law" include customary international law, although the precise term is not used. Finally, the Court is empowered to look at "general principles of law derived by the Court from national laws of legal systems of the world."

JUDICIAL DECISIONS

International law generally does not recognize the doctrine of *stare decisis*. Although trial chambers (the courts of first instance) must follow the rulings of their corresponding appellate chambers, they need not necessarily following their own prior rulings or the rulings of their sister chambers. Moreover, judicial decisions are not formally binding across international criminal tribunals. Thus, the different ICL systems are not bound by each other's precedent except insofar as the ICTY and the International Criminal Tribunal for Rwanda (ICTR) share an Appeals Chamber. Likewise, most domestic tribunals are not bound, as a formal matter, to the rulings of international tribunals and vice versa. A notable exception appears in the Statute of the Special Court for Sierra Leone, which provides at Article 20(3) that "[t]he judges of the Appeals Chamber of the Special Court shall be guided by the decisions of the Appeals Chamber of the International Tribunals for the former Yugoslavia and for Rwanda." The international system is thus more akin to a civil, rather than common, law system. Civil law systems eschew the rigid version of *stare decisis* on the ground that it is for the legislature, and not the courts, to make law. That said, even civil law systems privilege uniformity and predictability in judicial pronouncements, and some systems recognize that legal rulings can become binding "jurisprudence" if they are followed on a sufficient number of occasions.

Despite the fact that *stare decisis* is not formally recognized in ICL,[18] both the ad hoc international criminal tribunals and the ICC draw heavily on their previous jurisprudence for identifying rules of decision. Thus, under the ICC Statute, the Court "*may* apply principles and rules of law as interpreted in its previous decisions" (Article 21(2), emphasis added). The ICTY and ICTR regularly cite to their earlier decisions for general principles of law, thus creating a consistent and coherent jurisprudence. Indeed, judicial decisions are regularly cited by ICL tribunals as persuasive authority, and some would be forgiven for mistaking these citations as operating like formal precedent in a common law system.

ICL tribunals also look to domestic court decisions as a source of ICL. With the more frequent assertion by states of universal jurisdiction over international crimes (for example, the cases against Pinochet of Chile and Habré of Chad), domestic courts are becoming a richer source of ICL jurisprudence. Such decisions are, of course, not binding on international tribunals, but they can be used in a number of ways. First, domestic decisions interpreting ICL may be used as persuasive authority. Second, such decisions are a rich source of general principles of law, which provide an independent source of international law as noted earlier. Third, such decisions provide evidence of state practice and *opinio juris*, and thus can be used as evidence of an emerging or existing principle of customary international law.

THE WORKS OF SCHOLARS

Article 38 of the ICJ Statute also lists "the teachings of the most highly qualified publicists of the various nations" as a subsidiary means for the determination of rules of international law.

Although your law professor may argue otherwise, the works of legal scholars are not law per se. Nonetheless, courts may rely on legal scholarship to identify applicable rules of law, especially rules of customary international law or general principles of law that require significant comparative research to identify and catalog applicable state practice, domestic law, and evidence of *opinio juris*. The U.S. Supreme Court has confirmed the value of "the works of jurists and commentators who by years of labor, research and experience, have made themselves peculiarly well acquainted with the subjects of which they treat. Such works are resorted to by judicial tribunals, not for the speculation of their authors concerning what the law ought to be, but for trustworthy evidence of what the law really is."[19]

"SOFT LAW"

The resolutions, declarations, statements, and records of multilateral bodies — such as the UN General Assembly, the International Law Commission, or the Committee Against Torture — do not fit squarely in the sources schema contained in the ICJ or ICC Statutes. Indeed, according to the UN Charter, General Assembly resolutions do not have the force of law; they are merely recommendatory. Nongovernmental bodies, such as the International Law Commission or the International Committee of the Red Cross, do not play any formal role in law generation under the traditional understanding of how international law is made. And yet, nongovernmental organizations are now intimately involved in efforts to codify international crimes and create institutions for their prosecution.

Although such pronouncements are not law per se, they can provide another source of legal principles, especially when they have received unanimous approbation. Accordingly, such "soft law" has been relied on by ICL tribunals, either as evidence of state practice, *opinio juris*, or both, or as embodying general principles of law. For example, the tribunal in the *Justice Case*, prosecuting Nazi jurists within the U.S. zone of occupation following the conclusion of the Nuremberg proceedings, noted the importance of General Assembly Resolution 96(I) declaring genocide to be an international crime as an expression of an already developed international prohibition of genocide. In this regard, it stated: "The General Assembly is not an international legislature, but it is the most authoritative organ in existence for the interpretation of world opinion. Its recognition of genocide as an international crime is persuasive evidence of the fact."[20]

CONCLUSION

ICL litigants and jurists regularly make use of the multiplicity of sources of international law set forth in Article 38 of the ICJ Statute — multilateral treaties, international custom, general principles of law, judicial decisions, and even the writings of publicists — to identify applicable rules of decision and to resolve interpretive questions. Indeed, jurists seem quite comfortable cobbling together the applicable law from these various sources, notwithstanding that no one source may provide all the necessary ingredients to address the legal question at hand.

International tribunals frequently start with the relevant state's treaty obligations to determine the rules to which defendants were bound at the time in question. Beyond treaty law, courts adjudicating ICL also resort to customary international law, especially when there is no complete rule of decision available in an applicable treaty. Indeed, in many cases, customary international law appears to "come to the rescue" where treaty provisions are either silent as to a particular issue (e.g., whether conduct constitutes a prosecutable crime), ambiguous or incomplete in application (e.g., with regard to the elements of a crime that must be proven by a prosecutor to secure a conviction), or even when they are more constrained in their articulation of a legal principle. Although purporting to apply customary international law, international criminal tribunals are not always rigorous about applying the traditional customary international law formula. At times, tribunals are content to look at what states say and overlook what states actually do.

As you review the cases in your primary text, pay particular attention to the way in which the litigants and the judges identify the applicable law and consider to what extent the methodology employed is consistent with your understanding of the formal rules governing international law sources. In addition, consider to what extent ICL has adapted the traditional hierarchy of sources set forth in Article 38 of the Statute of the ICJ. To the extent that tribunals are departing from the standard sources doctrine, query why they have done so and whether the results remain legitimate under the circumstances.

∽ 4 ∼

The Internationalization of Crimes

This chapter is concerned with the question of how acts that would otherwise constitute domestic crimes may also be considered international crimes. Many international crimes actually encompass a constellation of individual crimes. Some of these predicate crimes are unique to international criminal law (ICL) or international humanitarian law (IHL), such as the crime of perfidy — making someone believe an individual is entitled to protected status under the law of war. Other predicate crimes have domestic law analogs in the familiar crimes of assault, mayhem, and murder. These domestic crimes are considered international crimes when certain attendant circumstances are present. As a matter of definitional structure, these attendant circumstances usually appear in the *chapeau** of the crime's definition.

A major challenge to developing and codifying the field of ICL has been to identify these attendant circumstances to

---

*Chapeau ("hat") elements are circumstantial elements that apply uniformly to a subsequent list of prohibited acts.

fully distinguish international crimes from domestic ones. For example, what attributes make an act of murder a crime against humanity, a war crime, or genocide? A clear demarcation of what crimes fall within international jurisdiction is important, not only for academic or doctrinal reasons. For one, the complete collapse of the distinction between international and domestic crimes would be worrisome to states. It would occasion the ceding of a high degree of jurisdictional sovereignty, as international crimes are often subject to international and extraterritorial jurisdiction. These concerns could result in the withdrawal of support for, and consent to, the regime of ICL, which would be a major reversal of global policy trends. The distinction between international and ordinary crimes also carries certain expressive implications—calling the imprisonment of an individual the crime against humanity of unlawful detention carries greater stigma than a mere kidnapping or false imprisonment allegation. Preserving a notion of international crimes protects them from the semantic inflation that might result if every abhorrent act were designated an international crime. Notwithstanding the importance of retaining a distinction between international and domestic crimes, no grand analytic theory for this process has been identified. Instead, several different approaches are apparent in distinguishing these two bodies of penal law. Keep these approaches in mind as you study the various substantive crimes in your course.

THE JURISDICTIONAL APPROACH

A primary, and facile, explanation for differentiating between international and domestic crimes is jurisdictional: International crimes are those crimes that are prosecuted before international tribunals or pursuant to extraordinary jurisdictional forms. There is no doubt that the distinction between international crimes and "ordinary" crimes has jurisdictional implications. For example, when an act rises to the level of an international crime it may be prosecuted before an international tribunal if one exists with jurisdiction over the act. Additionally, such an act may be subject to certain extraordinary forms of extraterritorial jurisdiction by states with no tangible nexus to the crime with respect to the nationality of the perpetrator or victim or the place of commission. The authorization to exercise extraterritorial jurisdiction may be a function of customary international law or a treaty obligation. This jurisdictional explanation, however, raises a chicken-and-egg problem: Are international crimes dubbed international because they can be, or are, prosecuted before international tribunals, or are these crimes prosecuted before international tribunals because they are international crimes?

THE INTER-NATIONAL APPROACH

The second approach we call the "inter-national" approach. Put simply, this approach defines as international crimes those crimes that transcend national boundaries and thus involve the interests of more than one state. The relevant transnational dimensions may relate to the nationality of the participants or the place, or places, where the crime was committed. Historically, IHL only recognized war crimes as capable of being committed against nationals of an opposing belligerent in an international armed conflict. The positive law addressing non-international armed conflicts (which include, but are not limited to, classic civil wars that pit compatriots against each other) does not include any penal component. It is only through the jurisprudence of the modern ICL tribunals that a notion of war crimes outside of international armed conflict is now fully recognized.

Although not requiring proof of the existence of an armed conflict, the crime of aggression, as currently conceptualized, does require some transnational element; there is no notion in international law of exclusively internal acts of aggression. This inter-national approach does not account for all international crimes, however. Although the definition of genocide and certain definitions of crimes against humanity recognize nationality as a ground for repression, both crimes can be committed within the borders of a single state, even absent any cross-border effect. Indeed, crimes against humanity emerged as a new international crime at Nuremberg precisely to reach conduct that would not constitute war crimes because the victim and the perpetrator shared the same nationality.

THE IDENTITY APPROACH

Other approaches to delineating international from domestic crimes focus on the identities of the perpetrators or victims. A third approach we call the "state perpetrator" approach. State action — shown either by way of a governmental policy or through the conduct of state actors enjoying the protection or authorization of a state — has often been cited as a potential defining element of international crimes. Some historical definitions of crimes against humanity included a state action requirement, although contemporary definitions are more catholic in prohibiting action instigated or directed by any organization or group as well as by an official government. Such a limitation was specifically rejected in the case of genocide, as Article IV of the Genocide Convention makes clear that genocide may be committed by private actors with no state involvement.

Although the definitions of crimes against humanity in the statutes of the ad hoc tribunals do not include reference to state action, this limitation has partially snuck back into the definition in the Statute of the International Criminal Court (ICC) in Article 7(2)(a). That article defines the term "attack against any civilian population" as a course of conduct "involving the multiple commission of acts . . . against any civilian population, pursuant to or in furtherance of a State or organizational policy to commit such attack." It remains to be seen what showing will satisfy the requirement of an "organizational policy" before the ICC. In addition, the ICC's draft definition of aggression is currently formulated in terms of state action: It must be shown that a state committed an act of aggression as defined by the ICC Statute. If such a showing is made, then individuals who knowingly and intentionally order or otherwise participate actively in the act of aggression can be prosecuted for their contributions thereto. Current drafts of the crime of aggression do not recognize the possibility of non-state (or substate) actors committing aggression. Thus, acts of aggression trigger ICC jurisdiction *only* if they are committed by a state actor.

This focus on the state as perpetrator reflects the pragmatic consideration that crimes committed by, or at the behest of, a state will not be adequately or uniformly punished within the applicable domestic criminal systems and so must be penalized and prosecuted at the international level. Indeed, ICL developed in part because states were unwilling (or unable) to prosecute breaches of international law committed by state agents, often pursuant to a state policy. The abortive Leipzig Trials at the close of World War I provide an apt example of the way in which states can institutionalize impunity through inaction and sham proceedings. Concerns about limiting international jurisdiction to those crimes that are the least likely to be pursued by an individual state partially explains the absence in the ICC Statute of several crimes that are the subject of well-subscribed-to multilateral treaties — such as terrorism crimes, drug trafficking, and counterfeiting. The ICC's drafters assumed that such crimes are likely to be aggressively prosecuted in domestic proceedings as they are usually committed by non-state actors and threaten sovereign values.

A fourth, and inverse, approach for defining a crime as international may be called the "protected group" approach.

Many international crimes involve group-based repression. The collective nature of these crimes may serve to enhance their egregiousness and the culpability of the perpetrator, especially where groups are targeted on the basis of "suspect" classifications like race or ethnicity. Most saliently, the crimes of genocide and persecution (an enumerated crime against humanity) require that the victim be targeted on the basis of his or her membership in a particular group or on discriminatory grounds. This approach does not explain all crimes defined as international, as acts other than persecution can constitute crimes against humanity if they are committed in the context of a widespread or systematic attack against any sort of civilian population, however defined. Interestingly in its first case, the International Criminal Tribunal for the former Yugoslavia (ICTY) attempted to narrow the definition of crimes against humanity by requiring discriminatory intent for all of its constituent acts.[1] This ruling was overturned on appeal[2] on the ground that discriminatory intent is required for the crime of persecution only.*

The definition of war crimes within the Geneva Conventions also incorporates this group-based approach. The penal provisions of the Geneva Conventions are implicated only when the victims fall within one of various categories of "protected person." The Fourth Geneva Convention, for example, recognizes certain acts (so-called grave breaches) as war crimes only when they are committed against individuals who are not protected by the other three Conventions (addressing the

---

*The Statute of the International Criminal Tribunal for Rwanda is an exception to this approach. That statute requires a showing of discriminatory intent (recognizing national, political, racial, or religious grounds) for all crimes against humanity, not just persecution. In that statute, persecution as a crime against humanity may only be committed on narrower (political, racial, and religious) grounds. This peculiar discrepancy is probably a drafting oversight, or an effort to conform the statute to the reality of the violence in Rwanda, rather than an attempt to modify the definition of crimes against humanity under international law.

wounded, the shipwrecked, and prisoners of war), but who are of a nationality different than that of the perpetrators. Specifically, protected persons are those persons who find themselves "at a given moment and in any manner whatsoever . . . in the hands of a Party to the conflict or Occupying Power of which they are not nationals."[3]

The need to prove a nationality distinction between victim and perpetrator has relaxed in the modern jurisprudence. In a case involving individuals of different group identity (Serb and Muslim) but of the same nationality (Bosnian), the ICTY Appeals Chamber held that a key purpose of the Geneva Conventions is to protect victims who are "different" from the perpetrators, and thus interpreted "nationality" to include ethnicity and other forms of group identification even when the individuals were all of the same formal nationality. The ICTY Appeals Chamber thus effectively redefined "protected persons" in terms of the party to the conflict with which the victims had "substantial relations more than . . . formal bonds" of citizenship.[4]

THE POLICY APPROACH

Related to the state action requirement, and as a fifth approach, certain definitions of international crimes include a policy element as a way to distinguish international crimes from domestic ones. In addition to including a gravity threshold, Article 8 of the ICC Statute concerning war crimes also suggests a preference for prosecuting crimes "in particular" when committed "as part of a plan or policy. . . ." With respect to crimes against humanity, the ICC Statute defines "attack" as including a state or organizational policy to commit the attack. The ICC definition of crimes against humanity thus seems to require proof of a policy by virtue of the operative definition of "attack." The customary international law definition of crimes against humanity, by contrast, does not appear to have such a requirement, although proof of a policy is often valuable as an evidentiary matter.

THE NEXUS TO ARMED CONFLICT APPROACH

The sixth approach we call the "nexus" approach. Under this theory, a crime becomes international because of its relationship to an event with international implications, such as an armed conflict. This bootstrapping is nicely illustrated with the definition of crimes against humanity adopted by the World War II tribunals. Much of the Nazi Holocaust involved acts that, traditionally, would not have implicated international law. The Holocaust primarily (although not exclusively) involved perpetrators and victims of the same nationality or of allied nationality, and occurred within the territorial jurisdiction of the state of which those individuals were nationals. The Allies conceived of the charge of crimes against humanity to encompass the crimes of the Holocaust. They gave a nod to then-existing international law by requiring that acts prosecuted as crimes against humanity have a nexus to another crime within the jurisdiction of the Tribunal, namely either crimes against peace (that is, aggression) or war crimes. As a result of this definition of crimes against humanity, the Nuremberg Tribunal expressly refused to prosecute individuals for acts that occurred prior to September 1, 1939, the year in which Germany launched World War II by invading Poland. It is now well settled that crimes against humanity are entirely autonomous from, and may be prosecuted absent, a state of war, although it is unclear exactly when this development occurred. When subsequent definitions of crimes against humanity were drafted, drafters struggled with identifying internationalizing elements to replace the so-called war nexus.

The less radical version of the nexus approach is illustrated with war crimes, which require as a threshold element some link to an armed conflict, either international or noninternational. Internal disturbances, riots, and the like, which exhibit either an inadequate degree of intensity or whose opposing parties are insufficiently organized, do not trigger IHL and, by extension, the war crimes prohibitions. By contrast, where a state of armed conflict exists, either international or noninternational, crimes committed in connection therewith can be classified as war crimes. The law continues to grapple with exactly what sort of nexus between the crimes and the armed conflict is required — for example, is mere temporality enough, or must the acts be committed as part of, or in furtherance of, the armed conflict? Although the international tribunals have made clear that such a nexus is required, they have not clearly defined what relationship is required; rather, they speak of the acts being "closely related to"[5] or exhibiting an "obvious link with"[6] the armed conflict. By contrast and somewhat counterintuitively, the crime of aggression, which remains under diplomatic discussion vis-à-vis the ICC, can under most draft definitions be committed absent a full-scale armed conflict. Nonetheless, the *actus reus* of the crime — which will likely include some combination of invasion, attack, occupation, bombardment, blockade, and so on — often leads to, or occurs in connection with, armed conflict.

THE GLOBAL STABILITY APPROACH

The seventh approach we call the "global stability" approach. A crime rises to the level of international concern because of its effect on international public order and its ability to jeopardize the peace and security of the international community as a whole (recognizing, of course, that the international community is far from monolithic). Violent acts of aggression, efforts to exterminate entire populations, and even the large-scale commission of war crimes can destabilize entire regions and lead to international armed conflict, thus justifying a collective and coordinated penal response. This is true where the immediate effects are exclusively internal. Indeed, early definitions of crimes against humanity drafted by the International Law Commission in its effort to promulgate a Draft Code of Offences Against the Peace and Security of Mankind used terms such as "widespread," "massive," or "systematic" to modify the *actus reus* of the crime and distinguish international crimes from their domestic counterparts. An early commentator at the end of the Nuremberg and Tokyo proceedings justified the internationalization of those prosecutions as follows:

> As a rule systematic mass action, particularly if it was authoritative, was necessary to transform common crime, punishable under municipal law, into a crime against humanity, which thus became also a concern of international law. Only crimes which either by their magnitude and savagery or by their large number or by the fact that a similar pattern was applied at different times and places endangered the international community or shocked the conscience of mankind, warranted intervention by States other than that on whose territory the crimes had been committed, or whose subjects had been their victims.[7]

THE DIGNITY APPROACH

This quotation also suggests an eighth approach to defining international crimes that we call the "dignity of humanity" approach. A crime becomes of international concern if it exceeds a minimum threshold with respect to its gravity, or if it otherwise violates certain fundamental values of the global community. Such crimes are considered to be of international concern even if they do not formally transcend any international borders and even if they do not immediately threaten the stability of the international community. Rather, because of their enormity, such crimes are of concern to all of humanity, and not just to the immediate victims or even a single polity. In other words, such crimes "signal a larger constituency."[8] This concept was expressed in the Moscow Declaration, in which the United States, the United Kingdom, and the Soviet Union first articulated their two-part prosecutorial strategy for Nazi officers and party members: trials in the *locus delicti* for lower level defendants and some sort of joint prosecution of those individuals whose offenses had no particular geographical location. More recently, Article 1 of the ICC Statute limits the exercise of jurisdiction to "the most serious crimes of international concern."[9] Likewise, the war crimes provision (Article 8) contains threshold language focusing the jurisdiction of the Court with respect to war crimes "in particular" when they are committed "as part of a large-scale commission of such crimes."

Under this approach, the principle of universal jurisdiction can be conceptualized as the delegation of jurisdictional authority to any state that is able to obtain jurisdiction over a *hostis humani generis* — enemy of all humankind. This idea is also contained in the very lexicon of one of the central ICL crimes: the crime against humanity. Thus, genocide or crimes against humanity committed exclusively within the territorial jurisdiction of one state now clearly trigger the ICL regime.

Defining a crime as international because of its gravity does, however, present certain challenges. Using a concept of gravity to identify international crimes is somewhat subjective where harm caused by criminal action may be incommensurable. In addition, gravity alone may not be sufficient to exclude domestic crimes, which can be horrific in their effects. In any case, most modern definitions of international crimes allow for the prosecution of single or isolated criminal acts, so long as they are committed within the context required by the definition of the offense. To prosecute an individual for crimes against humanity, for example, the criminal act must have been committed within the context of a widespread or systematic attack against a civilian population with knowledge of the attack. These threshold concepts of "widespread" and "systematic" now modify the attendant attack rather than the constitutive offense, the effects of which may be more modest in their impact. The prohibition against war crimes requires only the existence of an armed conflict, and a single war crime can constitute an international crime, even absent any serious impact. Even with the crime of genocide, a single act of violence against a protected group may constitute genocide at a theoretical level. As such, threshold provisions like those in Articles 1 and 8 of the ICC Statute are more jurisdictional than definitional.

THE *MENS REA* APPROACH

A ninth, and final, approach to delineating international crimes focuses on the motive or intent of the perpetrator. For example, the definition of crimes against humanity contains two *mens rea* elements. The first is the *mens rea* element associated with the constitutive crime, such as intent to kill with respect to murder. The second is found in the definition's *chapeau* and requires a showing that the individual knew that the act of intentional murder was part of a widespread or systematic attack against a civilian population. (See Article 7(1) of the ICC Statute.) This second-order *mens rea* element helps to internationalize the crime by connecting the act to a larger campaign of violence or persecution.

Terrorism crimes are also often defined in terms of the perpetrator's subjective motive in committing the crime, with motive being defined as the reason that people engage in crime.

Many terrorism definitions focus on the perpetrator's goal of terrorizing the civilian population; coercing or inducing a government to do or abstain from doing some act; disrupting public services; or otherwise achieving some political, military, ethnic, ideological, or religious goal. Criminal acts that do not involve these particular motives are not prosecutable as acts of terrorism. This reliance on motive as an internationalizing element is somewhat unique in the penal law, as most offenses do not include motive as a substantive element of the crime.

CONCLUSION

In the end, one is left with the impression that the different international crimes have been designated as such for different reasons. This heterogeneity in many ways reflects the fact that ICL has historically evolved along disparate strands that are only today converging in a handful of centralized institutions, most notably the ICC, and in the world's domestic penal codes. In general, the *chapeau* of each crime's definition is where one often finds clues to a justification for internationalization. For war crimes, the key overarching element is the existence of an armed conflict. Crimes against humanity exist where there is a widespread or systematic attack against a civilian population. The unifying theme for the crime of genocide is the targeting of a protected group. Both crimes against humanity and genocide also include second-order *mens rea* elements that apply to the attendant circumstances rather than to the enumerated crimes. As a result of these additional elements, the prosecution of an international crime requires the introduction of evidence that satisfies more elements than would normally be required for a domestic prosecution. This, in turn, contributes to the length and complexity of modern international trials.

~ 5 ~

The Principle of Legality in International Criminal Law

A s a species of criminal law, international criminal law (ICL) implicates the principle of legality (*nullum crimen sine lege*, or NCSL).* NCSL asserts in essence the *ex post facto* prohibition — conduct must be criminalized and penalties fixed in advance of any criminal prosecution. NCSL is supplemented by two corollary legislative and interpretive principles compelling criminal statutes to be drafted with precision (the principle of specificity) and interpreted in favor of the accused (the rule of lenity). The principle of NCSL serves two key purposes: It ensures that individuals have fair notice of prescribed conduct so they can rationally adjust their behavior to avoid sanction, and it protects the

---

*Although not unknown in ancient Roman or Greek law, the NCSL principle experienced a resurgence in the Enlightenment period, when the prevailing political ideology was one of reaction against oppressive government and judicial arbitrariness. German jurist Paul Johann Anselm Ritter Von Feuerbach (1775–1833) is credited with coining the maxim.

citizenry from arbitrary state action in the face of ambiguities and gaps in the law. NCSL thus embodies an essential element of the rule of law by speaking to the very legitimacy of a legal rule and providing a check on the power of government over individuals.

The principle of legality finds expression in a number of human rights treaties. Some human rights instruments express the concept as an absolute prohibition. For example, the Universal Declaration of Human Rights states unequivocally at Article 11(2) that "[n]o one shall be held guilty of any penal offense on account of any act or omission which did not constitute a penal offense, under national or international law, at the time it was committed." The International Covenant on Civil and Political Rights builds on this prohibition with the admonition at Article 15 that "[n]or shall a heavier penalty be imposed than the one that was applicable at the time when the criminal offense was committed. If, subsequent to the commission of the offense, provision is made by law for the imposition of the lighter penalty, the offender shall benefit thereby." This provision goes on, however, to emphasize that the principle is satisfied where the act is criminalized at the international level: "Nothing in this article shall prejudice the trial and punishment of any person for any act or omission which, at the time when it was committed, was criminal according to the general principles of law recognized by the community of nations."

Although the principle of NCSL appears in all of the omnibus human rights treaties (albeit in slightly different formulations), the International Criminal Court (ICC) is the only ICL tribunal whose constitutive statute contains an express articulation of the NCSL principle. Specifically, the ICC Statute provides at Article 24(2) that: "[i]n the event of a change in the law applicable to a given case prior to a final judgement, the law more favourable to the person being investigated, prosecuted or convicted shall apply." Likewise, the principle of strict construction and the rule of lenity are specifically mandated at Article 22(2), which states: "The definition of a crime shall be strictly construed and shall not be extended by analogy. In case of ambiguity, the definition shall be interpreted in favour of the person being investigated, prosecuted or convicted."

Despite its absence in the majority of ICL statutes, the dictates of the principle of NCSL are acutely relevant, and particularly compelling, in the field of ICL. Indeed, the principle of NCSL goes to the very heart of how international crimes are developed, interpreted, and applied. Yet, even today—as ICL is at its peak in terms of codification and available precedent—defendants regularly argue that the acts for which they are being prosecuted were not criminal at the time they acted. This is largely because international, and to a certain extent domestic, courts are seen to be actively engaged in applying new ICL norms to past conduct and engaging in a full-scale—if unacknowledged—refashioning of ICL through their jurisprudence. Along the way, courts are updating and expanding historical treaties and prohibitions, upsetting arrangements carefully negotiated between states, rejecting political compromises made by states during multilateral drafting conferences, and adding content to vaguely worded provisions that were conceived more as retrospective condemnations of past horrors than as codes for prospective penal enforcement. Although ICL tribunals may achieve substantive justice with these outcomes, they also risk undermining the legitimacy of ICL as a field of criminal law by violating the human rights of criminal defendants appearing before them.

Why is the NCSL defense so ubiquitous in ICL? Have the ICL tribunals adequately protected the interests served by the principle of NCSL in proceedings before them? Because of the importance of these questions to the field of ICL, this book devotes a chapter to the recurring themes, analytical claims, and arguments employed by ICL tribunals to address the dictates of NCSL. As you read the primary texts in your course, consider whether the opinions adhere to the principle of legality as you understand it, or whether ICL judges have compromised the fundamental rights embodied in the principle of NCSL in their efforts to ensure accountability and advance the law.

NCSL IN INTERNATIONAL CRIMINAL LAW

First, we address the question of why the defense of NCSL is so ubiquitous in ICL. For one, the ICL being applied by today's tribunals is an incomplete and rapidly evolving area of law. Although adjudication and codification have proceeded at an aggressive pace since the end of the Cold War, there are still large gaps in positive law. Many of the primary sources of ICL rules, especially those dealing with the law of armed conflict, originated in an era in which war was waged differently. This has led skeptics to critique such treaties as being outmoded and even "quaint." Modern tribunals must apply these antiquated provisions in the context of modern belligerency. The international system lacks a standing world legislature that can fill interstices and lacunae, modernize ancient prohibitions, or fix faulty formulations. In the domestic arena, there is the expectation that the legislature will rectify problems in the law if they are revealed through the exoneration of individuals who committed bad acts. The only way ICL treaties can be amended is through the sporadic and sluggish multilateral treaty drafting process. Indeed, states are loath to renegotiate existing treaties, not only because of the transaction costs inherent in such endeavors, but also because of the confusion wrought in trying to keep track of which states have ratified which version of a treaty, although occasionally new protocols do emerge to update earlier efforts.

Modern tribunals are also asked to interpret treaties that were drafted without the precision we now expect from modern penal codes. The crimes themselves are rarely drafted in terms of the basic elements of criminal law — *mens rea*, *actus reus*, attendant circumstances, and so on. This is due, in part, to the fact that most treaty drafting is done by diplomats lacking technical drafting skills (rather than specialists in comparative criminal law) who are working in the context of political, and often politicized, multilateral negotiations. Moreover, it was not necessarily envisioned that ICL treaty provisions would be applied directly as rules of decision in criminal prosecutions. Rather, it was expected that states would incorporate the general prohibitions contained in these treaties into their domestic penal codes and then apply these presumably more precise criminal definitions in their own courts when they had custody of an accused. The establishment of the international criminal tribunals has, for the first time, forced the direct applicability of these provisions.

Many international treaties are open-textured, such as those prescribing the war crimes of "willfully causing great suffering," committing "inhumane and degrading treatment or punishment," or causing the destruction of property "not justified by military necessity." This is at times by design, as drafters indicated that it would be impossible to envision every type of conduct that deserved prohibition or where drafters sought to establish a general standard against which particular actions would be judged. In other circumstances, these pockets of vagueness reflect the concerted ambiguity that results from difficult interstate negotiations in which certain states have been known to jealously guard the prerogatives of state sovereignty. It is thus left to the courts to add content to these provisions. This is so even though domestic principles of statutory construction would often counsel against courts filling deliberate omissions in legislation. Although the ICC Statute, with its Elements of

Crimes, better approximates the penal code ideal, key terms remain undefined even in that Treaty, such as the definitions of protected groups in the genocide provision.

In the absence of an applicable treaty provision, modern criminal tribunals are asked to glean genuine international custom from divergent state conduct and self-serving rhetoric. Finding the relevant state practice at the time a defendant acted may be a challenge where domestic codification was incomplete and domestic prosecutions episodic. On the international plane, the adjudication of ICL is decentralized. Since the establishment of the International Criminal Tribunal for the Former Yugoslavia (ICTY), the first modern ad hoc tribunal, additional international, hybrid, and domestic fora have proliferated that are not, as a technical matter, generally bound by the precedent generated by sister courts. Many courts must essentially start from scratch in identifying the applicable law.

At the time the ad hoc tribunals began their work, ICL was thus characterized by a certain degree of systemic indeterminacy. It was difficult to identify positive law, and what law existed was incomplete. Moreover, states were not inclined to develop new rules or clarify the old ones. These circumstances generated a temptation toward judicial legislation to avoid situations of *non liquet* ("it is not clear") that would exonerate a defendant who has allegedly committed heinous acts. How the ICL tribunals have justified this approach is the topic of the rest of this chapter.

RESPONSES TO NCSL DEFENSES

The Applicability of *Nullum Crimen Sine Lege* in International Criminal Law

A recurring argument in the face of the defense of NCSL is that the principle simply does not apply in ICL to the same force and effect as it does in the domestic penal order. This argument has several facets to it. One facet of this argument is apparent in defenses raised during the Nuremberg and Tokyo proceedings. Judge Cassese, for example, has opined that in the postwar period, "[t]he strict legal prohibition of *ex post facto* law had not yet found expression in international law."[1] Even now, 50 years later, one ICTY Trial Chamber reasoned "[i]t is not certain to what extent [the principle of legality and its components] have been admitted as part of international legal practice, separate and apart from the existence of the national legal system. This is essentially because of the different methods of criminalisation of conduct in national and international criminal justice systems."[2]

Jurists explain the absence of a rigorous manifestation of NCSL in ICL with reference to the difference between international and national legal processes. They note in particular that because the states approach the NCSL principle somewhat differently, no precise or even strict formulation of the principle has emerged that would be applicable to international courts. By this reasoning, international tribunals may relax the notion of NCSL in their proceedings, in contradistinction to domestic courts that remain constrained by their own particular constitutional, statutory, or treaty obligations with respect to the principle. The principle's frequent invocation by modern international criminal tribunals suggests that this position is overstated. Although none of the statutes of the ad hoc tribunals specifically contains the NCSL principle, tribunals generally accept the applicability of the principle and the values it protects to proceedings before them. Most international courts thus treat NCSL as a general principle of law.

A different facet of this argument about the limited applicability of NCSL in ICL is premised on characterizing NCSL as a flexible principle of justice that can yield to competing imperatives. Convicting a defendant in breach of the principle of NCSL is one form of injustice. Allowing "loopholes" in the law to exonerate an accused who caused serious harm or acted immorally results in an injustice of an altogether different, perhaps more profound, kind. By subordinating the principle of NCSL to a vision of substantive justice, tribunals have determined that the former injustice is less problematic than the latter. Thus, in explaining the outcome at Nuremberg, one commentator—himself an ICL judge—noted that, at the time, "the *nullum crimen sine lege* principle could be regarded as a moral maxim destined to yield to superior exigencies whenever it would have been contrary to justice not to hold persons accountable for appalling atrocities."[3]

In the alternative, it is argued that NCSL is not a principle of justice but of policy, easily overridden where inexpedient in application. Thus, courts balance considerations of the rights of the accused against the needs of the international community for security, accountability, and the preservation of world order. Most important in this line of reasoning, perhaps, has been the belief that a vigorous system of international justice will create a more robust system of deterrence that will prevent such abuses in the future. International courts are confronted with the need to strike the right balance between these two sets of imperatives.

Acts as *Malum in Se*

Jurists also tend to deemphasize NCSL in the face of an act that is *malum in se* — inherently bad or "wrong in itself." NCSL was at the heart of the defendants' defense before the Nuremberg and Tokyo Tribunals following World War II, particularly with respect to the novel charge of crimes against the peace (the crime of aggression in today's lexicon). The Nuremberg Tribunal rejected the NCSL defense based on the notion that it is not unfair to prosecute individuals for conduct that is *malum in se*:

> To assert that it is unjust to punish those who in defiance of treaties and assurances have attacked neighboring states without warning is obviously untrue, for in such circumstances the attacker must know that he is doing wrong, and so far from it being unjust to punish him, it would be unjust if his wrong were allowed to go unpunished.[4]

In other words, it was argued, no innocents were ensnared at Nuremberg. Formal notice of the penal consequences of such conduct is deemed unnecessary when the acts in question shock the collective conscience of the international community and when it would be unjust to exonerate responsible individuals. This rhetoric retains contemporary currency. As one ICTY Trial Chamber argued, "[t]he purpose of this principle [NCSL] is to prevent the prosecution and punishment of an individual for acts which he reasonably believed to be lawful at the time of their commission. It strains credibility to contend that the accused would not recognize the criminal nature of the acts alleged in the Indictment."[5]

These statements, which elide the morally wrong and the legally criminal, invoke the natural law tradition found in all of public international law. This tradition is particularly cogent in ICL, which has as its origins the belief that the law must conform to a universal transnational morality and conception of justice. Because such moral rules are considered universally and intrinsically knowable in advance, prior articulation and actual notice are deemed unnecessary. Courts adjudicating serious violations of ICL thus envision themselves as operating in a realm of greater moral certainty that, it is argued, justifies overlooking a strict application of NCSL. It is perhaps not surprising that jurists would resort to ideas of natural law in the face of atrocity, when a desire to ensure the confluence of law and morality is likely to be at its strongest. In this way, tribunals appear compelled to respond to innovations in atrocity where positive law is silent.

This reasoning is most palatable when applied to heinous conduct that, for whatever reason, falls outside of positive law. Tribunals limited to adjudicating only the most "serious" of ICL violations can perhaps more easily execute this leap from *contra bonos mores* ("against good morals") to prosecutable crime. This move is increasingly difficult with respect to acts that are morally contested.

Illegality = Criminality

In his dissenting opinion in *Norman*,[6] Judge Robertson made the point that the recruitment of child soldiers by states may have been prohibited by international law, but it did not yet rise to the level of an international crime. NCSL defenses are frequently asserted in situations in which there is a norm governing state behavior that does not, on its face, govern individual behavior or render such behavior subject to penal consequences. Many historical ICL and international humanitarian law (IHL) treaties are silent as to individual criminal responsibility precisely because they were drafted at a time when the international community only conceived of collective (state) responsibility for breaches. This meant that injured states could resort to reprisals or seek reparations from responsible states in the event of a breach. Nonetheless, starting with the Nuremberg Tribunal, modern tribunals quite easily equate the international condemnation of a practice with its criminalization.

At Nuremberg, for example, the Tribunal argued that because the Kellogg-Briand Pact and various bilateral treaties of neutrality and nonaggression prohibited the acts of aggression undertaken by Germany, the defendants' conduct was unquestionably "wrong" and thus punishable. It reasoned that the Pact with its "solemn renunciation of war as an instrument of national policy necessarily involves the proposition that such a war is illegal in international law; and that those who plan and wage such a war, with its inevitable and terrible consequences, are committing a crime in so doing."[7] In so arguing, the Tribunal transformed a treaty devoted to the regulation of state conduct (providing as a sanction that the state in question would "be denied the benefits furnished by" the Pact and thus render itself vulnerable to reprisals and claims for reparations) into one regulating individual conduct. By this reasoning, the treaty's renunciation of war *ipso facto* rendered war unlawful under general international law, and the illegality of war under general international law *ipso facto* rendered the pursuit of war a crime under international law. The Tribunal concluded, "On this view of the case alone, it would appear that the maxim [NCSL] has no application to the present facts."[8] In this way, the launching of aggressive war in Europe became an international crime over and above a breach of a contractual obligation.

Before the ICTY, defendant Dusko Tadić contested, among other things, the legality of the charges against him under Article 3 of the ICTY Statute ("The Laws and Customs of War"). His argument was based on the premise that the conflict in the former Yugoslavia was a civil — rather than international — war. He contended (accurately) that neither the 1949 Geneva Conventions nor the 1907 Hague Convention regulated noninternational armed conflicts in any detail and, to the extent that they did, any such rules did not give rise to individual criminal responsibility. In upholding the Article 3 charges against Tadić, the Appeals Chamber identified four factors that must be met for an offense to be charged as a violation of Article 3 of the ICTY Statute:

> (a) the act must infringe a rule of IHL;
> (b) the rule must be customary in nature or, if contained in a treaty, the treaty must be applicable;

(c) the violation must be "serious," which is to say the rule must protect "important values" and "the breach must involve grave consequences for the victim;" and

(d) the violation must entail, under customary or conventional law, individual criminal responsibility.[9]

With respect to the applicability of individual criminal responsibility, point (d), the Appeals Chamber noted that the Nuremberg Tribunal had concluded that individual criminal responsibility could exist in the absence of an explicit treaty provision to that effect. The Appeals Chamber surveyed state practice — in the form of national prosecutions, military manuals, and legislation criminalizing IHL violations in internal conflict — to conclude that although common Article 3 and Protocol II are silent as to criminal enforcement, certain breaches of the law of armed conflict committed in noninternational armed conflicts nonetheless constitute international crimes as a matter of customary international law.

Tribunals justify the elision of illegality into criminality with three strands of argument. One postulates that a treaty's silence as to the penal consequences of a breach does not mean treaty breaches are not crimes. This position is articulated even where sister treaties expressly provide for criminal penalties such that a strict application of the *a contrario* principle would dictate the opposite result. When forced to explain these treaty silences, tribunals reason that states intended to leave details of enforcement to state parties and the international community rather than mandate any particular enforcement regime. This approach disregards an obvious counterexplanation that drafting states made a deliberate choice *not* to criminalize such behavior and instead leave enforcement at the level of state responsibility only. The second strand of this argument concedes the lack of criminalization, but argues that the application of such laws is only marginally retroactive insofar as they prescribe penal consequences rather than collective responsibility. This, it is argued, does not invoke a full-fledged *ex post facto* problem. Third, it is argued that assigning individual rather than collective responsibility is a more progressive and fair form of enforcement, even where the applicable law is silent as to such sanctions.

Notice Anywhere Is Notice Everywhere

In filling gaps in positive law, jurists often make use of the multiplicity of sources of international law set forth in Article 38 of the International Court of Justice (ICJ) Statute: multilateral treaties, international custom, "the general principles of law recognized by civilized nations," and (as subsidiary means) judicial decisions and the writings of publicists. These disparate sources of law may articulate different or even contradictory standards with respect to the same subject matter, and international law has only rudimentary rules for reconciling competing sources of authority. Tribunals have ruled that so long as a defendant has notice of prohibited conduct in one of these various sources of law, then the principle of NCSL is satisfied and the prosecution can proceed.

Courts adjudicating ICL often resort to customary international law in particular when an otherwise applicable treaty is silent, ambiguous, or more constrained in its articulation of a legal principle. The *Scilingo* case[10] before the Spanish *Audiencia Nacional*, a national court with special jurisdiction over international crimes, provides a good example of this reasoning. Adolfo Scilingo was prosecuted for his complicity in crimes committed during the reign of the Argentine military *junta*. Although the investigating judge had charged him with terrorism, torture, and genocide — three crimes that had long existed in the Spanish *Codigo Penal* — the Audiencia Nacional (the court of first instance) convicted him of crimes against humanity, which had only been codified in Spanish law in 2004, well after the acts of which Scilingo was accused. The

Audiencia rejected the defendant's argument that the prosecution was *ex post facto*, reasoning that crimes against humanity were prohibited by customary international law at the time of the events in question. The court ruled that the *jus cogens* and *erga omnes* nature of the customary international law prohibition against crimes against humanity was implicitly incorporated into, and thus directly applicable in, the Spanish domestic legal system. The court also cited analogous provisions in Argentine domestic law, which it ruled were sufficient to put the defendant on notice of potential penalties for his conduct. This ruling is significant, because the Spanish Constitution specifically incorporates the principle of legality in several places.

On appeal, the *Tribunal Supremo* (Supreme Court) upheld the conviction, but rejected the Audiencia's reasoning.[11] In particular, it ruled that customary international law was not directly applicable within the Spanish system. Instead, it ruled that it could substitute a conviction for the well-established domestic crimes of murder and illegal detention. That Spanish law did not provide universal jurisdiction over such crimes was of no moment, because given the context in which Scilingo committed his crimes — in furtherance of a state-sponsored policy to eradicate subversion — they constituted crimes against humanity under ICL and thus were subject to universal jurisdiction. Crimes against humanity thus did not provide the appropriate substantive charge against the defendant, but the fact that the acts in question constituted crimes against humanity gave the Spanish courts universal jurisdiction over them as a matter of customary international law. The Supreme Court then sentenced Scilingo based on the Spanish penal code, which was more lenient than the Argentine code, because the former provided maximum penalties for the crimes in question. Given the NCSL provisions in the Spanish Constitution, this judgment will inevitably be appealed to the *Tribunal Constitucional* (the Constitutional Court).

In looking to customary international law to "fill gaps" in positive law, courts are not rigorous about applying the traditional customary international law formula, which requires a showing of state practice coupled with *opinio juris*. Rather, courts seem willing to overlook or discount contrary state practice and focus on articulations of *opinio juris* as found in the pronouncements of states and other institutions, including nongovernmental or intergovernmental organizations. Courts may also "double count" discursive practices as both *usus* (practice) and *opinio juris*. Although this untethering of *opinio juris* from state practice is part of much public international law reasoning, it is particularly common in ICL, where the disjunction between the two elements is often so wide.

Tribunals will also cite applicable domestic law as a source of advance notice that certain conduct is prohibited. Many international crimes have domestic analogs with definitions that differ only in that they lack the *chapeau* elements that internationalize such crimes and render them prosecutable before an international tribunal. For example, an act of murder becomes a crime against humanity when it is committed in the context of a widespread and systematic attack against a civilian population with knowledge of that attack. In this way, domestic crimes serve as predicate acts for their international analogs. Tribunals have reasoned that the prohibition in domestic law of the predicate acts can provide notice of the wrongfulness and criminality of the underlying conduct. Courts have reasoned that if an act is criminal under domestic law, there is no NCSL problem where the act is simply prosecuted under an international law analog.

Even academic scholarship has been found to provide some notice to defendants. The German case against Nikola Jorgić marked one of the first universal jurisdiction cases to be brought and the first German prosecution for genocide since ratification of the Genocide Convention in 1954. Jorgić had fled to Germany after the war in the former Yugoslavia.

German officials later charged him with participating in assaults and massacres of Bosnian civilians in his home region of Doboj. Jurisdiction in Germany was premised on Article 6 of the German Code incorporating universal jurisdiction. The crime of genocide is defined in Article 220a of the German Criminal Code identical to the Genocide Convention definition. Nonetheless, the German Constitutional Court expanded the notion of genocide to include cultural genocide, which was specifically excluded from the Genocide Convention. It reasoned that the intent to destroy the group "includes the annihilation of a group as a social unit with its special qualities, uniqueness and its feeling of togetherness, not exclusively their physical-biological annihilation."[12] Citing a General Assembly resolution equating ethnic cleansing in the former Yugoslavia with genocide, the German court held that prohibited acts could include destroying or looting houses or buildings of importance to the group or the expulsion of members of the group. The court reasoned that the prohibition against genocide protects legal interests that "lie[] beyond the individual, namely the social existence of a group." This, it noted, "has a broader meaning than physical-biological annihilation."[13] The court concluded that this interpretation was "within the margins of the possible interpretation of the international law elements of the crime of genocide."[14] In so ruling, the court rejected contrary language in the *Krstić* case before the ICTY, which rejected the criminality of cultural genocide.[15] Jorgić was convicted of genocide and sentenced to life imprisonment.

Jorgić challenged his prosecution and conviction before the European Court of Human Rights (ECHR),[16] claiming that his prosecution violated several provisions of the European Convention for the Protection of Human Rights and Fundamental Freedoms including his right to be free from *ex post facto* prosecution (Article 7). With regard to the latter claim, Jorgić argued that the German courts had expansively construed the genocide prohibition beyond the contours of positive law. The ECHR ruled that the German courts' interpretation was both in keeping with the "essence of the offense" and could reasonably have been foreseen at the material time by the applicant with the assistance of counsel. The ECHR determined that several aspects of the *actus reus* of genocide do not require the physical or biological destruction of the group, so the German court's interpretation found support in the text of the law. In addition, the ECHR determined that Jorgić could have foreseen the more expansive interpretation of the provision, especially given the degree of uncertainty in the law on this point, and in light of the work of several German scholars advancing such an interpretation. Thus, the ECHR determined that the German courts enjoyed discretion under the European Convention to adopt the interpretation of the genocide prohibition that they saw fit.

So long as notice is available to the defendant from some source of law, and not even necessarily one binding on the defendant at the time he acted, tribunals have found no breach of the NCSL principle. Tribunals thus assume defendants' ability to undertake virtually global legal research to determine the scope and content of ICL and insist that "ignorance of ICL is no excuse." So long as the defendant could reasonably ascertain in advance that the particular conduct is prohibited, perhaps even with the help of counsel, the NCSL principle is satisfied. This is especially true with respect to individuals to whom ICL is directly addressed — soldiers and statesmen.

The Object and Purpose of ICL

NCSL defenses often arise in situations in which tribunals must add content to vaguely worded prohibitions. To do so, tribunals will often look to the object and purpose of the relevant treaty or larger body of law. This approach is well established within the jurisprudence of the various human rights institutions, which quite self-consciously interpret their constitutive treaties as "living" instruments that must adapt to modern needs to advance fundamental human rights. As these institutions see it, the goal of human rights treaty regimes is not to enforce reciprocal obligations adopted by contracting states *inter se*, but to create and sustain a protective public order applicable to all those within the *espace juridique* of signatory states.

International criminal tribunals have adopted a similar approach, endeavoring to effectuate the object and purpose of ICL and IHL in interpreting substantive norms. At least in the realm of IHL, a teleological approach is also permitted, if not mandated, by the Martens Clause, a familiar component of many IHL treaties. This clause provides:

> Until a more complete code of the laws of war is issued, the High Contracting Parties think it right to declare that in cases not included in the Regulations adopted by them, populations and belligerents remain under the protection and empire of the principles of international law, as they result from the usages established between civilized nations, from the laws of humanity and the requirements of the public conscience.

The clause suggests a reservoir of uncodified law applicable in armed conflict. It allows courts to go beyond the written text and refer not only to customary international law ("the usages established between civilized nations") but also to the moral bases of humanitarian obligations by making reference "to pre-juridical principles [and] to the sentiments of humanity."[17] As such, the Martens Clause also provides a principle of interpretation that is in keeping with the principles of humanity and moral standards. The clause, however, was drafted at a time when individual criminal responsibility—with its attendant concerns with adhering to the principle of legality—was not yet established as an expected response to treaty breaches.

In *Prosecutor v. Hadžihasanović*, the defendants argued that IHL did not allow superiors to be prosecuted for the acts of their subordinates in internal armed conflicts, primarily because Protocol I, applicable in international conflicts, is the first and only IHL treaty to set out the elements of the superior responsibility doctrine.[18] Taking an expansive teleological approach, the Trial Chamber relied on the *Tadić* decision referenced earlier to rule that the defendants could be prosecuted under the superior responsibility doctrine in an internal armed conflict. To start, it looked to the object and purpose of the Security Council in creating the ICTY. It cited statements made by states during the drafting of the ICTY Statute assuming that the doctrine of command responsibility would be applicable before the Tribunal without reference to the nature of the conflict, although this survey revealed that no state specifically argued for, or acknowledged, the applicability of the doctrine in noninternational armed conflicts. The Trial Chamber then went further to examine the object and purpose of IHL writ large, separate and apart from the intentions of particular members of the Security Council, which it identified as the "regulat[ion of] the means and methods of warfare and [the protection of] persons not actively participating in armed conflict from harm" and the "respect for human dignity."[19] The Trial Chamber invoked the Martens Clause, contained in Protocol II governing noninternational armed conflict, as inspiration to consider the fundamental principles underlying IHL. The Chamber noted that the doctrine of superior responsibility promotes two such principles: the existence of individual criminal responsibility for violations, even where treaties are silent on enforcement, and the principle of responsible command.

The precise framing of the overarching object and purpose of ICL has contributed to the tribunals' more relaxed approach to the dictates of the strict version of NCSL. A fundamental assumption underpinning the principle of legality is that it will deter crime by ensuring fair notice of proscribed conduct. This assumes known — or knowable — law and rational actors who will structure their conduct to avoid anticipated censure. To date, deterrence has not been a primary motivation of existing ICL tribunals. Many modern tribunals were established (or have asserted jurisdiction) after the horrific events in question; the ICC, and to some extent the ICTY, are exceptions. Being *ex post*, these tribunals were unable to exert any deterrent effect on defendants within their personal jurisdiction and had to settle for contributing to the general deterrence of future perpetrators. Even scholars devoted to the field doubt whether ICL can achieve deterrence under contemporary circumstances where international justice remains sporadic and random and cannot yet create consistent expectations of capture and punishment. Until legal censure is more certain, the narratives that explain why seemingly ordinary people do evil things in the context of war or state-sponsored repression — because they are beset by prejudices, intoxicated by power, manipulated by elites, terrified into submission by superior orders or threats of retaliation for their inaction, or caught up in a maelstrom of violence — likely will overwhelm any cost-benefit analysis in which individual perpetrators may engage.

Where deterrence is deemphasized, other goals of criminology — retribution, the incapacitation of perpetrators, the rehabilitation of victims, and the public condemnation of injurious behavior — become more salient. These goals (and retribution in particular) are advanced where the strict dictates of NCSL are overlooked. Although we may decry retribution as a primitive and unenlightened motivation for criminal law, its enduring potency cannot be denied. Anti-impunity is often cited as a key object and purpose of ICL. In the face of centuries, if not millennia, of impunity for what we now consider human rights atrocities, retributive impulses may exceed concerns for the strict adherence to the legality principle as courts are unwilling to let bad behavior continue to go unpunished. In ICL, where the problem historically has been chronic under-enforcement of the law, there is still little concern for over-deterrence and a concomitant willingness to overlook legalisms that would lead to impunity in an effort to jumpstart a system of greater accountability.

CONCLUSION

Innovative judges and expansive interpretations are not unique or endemic to ICL. Although the codification of ICL will probably never be complete, the rate of change is slowing significantly. Early cases addressed important open areas in legal doctrine. Today's cases address issues that are more nuanced, involving the resolution of more micro-inconsistencies and the filling in of increasingly smaller gaps in the law. As a result, there is less and less space for judges to build on the ICL edifice. Although there will always be a need to elucidate hazy points and adapt to changing circumstances through the progressive development of the law through judicial law-making, like any maturing system of law the next phase of the evolution of ICL will happen at the outer edges of doctrine, where the implications of new ideas are perhaps less dramatic.

As the Yugoslav and Rwandan Tribunals implement their Completion Strategies and the work of the Special Court for Sierra Leone winds down, international prosecutions will increasingly proceed before the ICC, unless the international community creates more ad hoc and hybrid courts. The ICC is governed by a robustly worded NCSL provision that not only prohibits the retroactive application of law, but also mandates strict construction in favor of defendants. As the jurisdiction of the Court is expressly proscriptive, these provisions will likely be most relevant where amendments to the statute are made, such as with the anticipated addition of the definition of the crime of aggression, or the less likely addition of the crimes of terrorism or drug trafficking. That said, there are "legality deficits" within the statute, as many crimes remain vaguely or sparingly worded. As the ICC begins to issue substantive decisions and judgments, the new Court will undoubtedly be faced with the pressure to innovate. It remains to be seen to what extent the NCSL provisions will truly cabin the ability of the Court to adopt expansive or novel interpretations to crimes within its jurisdiction.

Given all this, it is tempting to conclude that the dilemma posed by the NCSL principle in ICL has a relatively short shelf life. To a certain degree, it does. Nonetheless, areas remain in which innovation is possible and will be tempting. For example, the Extraordinary Chambers in the Courts of Cambodia will have to determine the state of ICL in the 1975–1979 period, when the Khmer Rouge were in power. Many developments in ICL most relevant to the Khmer Rouge era are the result of the work of the two ad hoc tribunals in the late 1990s. This includes the almost complete convergence of the law on war crimes relevant to internal and international armed conflicts, the official abandonment of the war nexus for crimes against humanity, and the adoption of the subjective approach to protected group identity and membership for genocide. Likewise, the contemplated subject matter jurisdiction for the ad hoc tribunal envisioned for Lebanon includes crimes of terrorism, for which there is no omnibus international definition.

Where the defense of NCSL will retain great currency going forward will be in domestic proceedings, especially where courts adjudicating historical justice cases must decide what law to apply to events that preceded the ICL renaissance. In connection with their ratification of the ICC Statute, states are increasingly incorporating international crimes into their domestic penal codes. Such crimes are often subject to universal jurisdiction, granting domestic courts an expansive extraterritorial reach. As was the case in *Scilingo*, there will undoubtedly be additional efforts to apply these new statutes to conduct that predates codification. Such retroactive justice is enabled by the trend among national courts and legislatures to extend, toll, or abolish altogether statutes of limitation for international crimes. The NCSL dilemma also remains relevant for idiosyncratic or expansive interpretations of established law, as seen in the *Jorgić* case.

The line of cases discussed in this chapter reveals a series of interpretive devices and rhetorical moves employed by criminal tribunals to — at a minimum — fill lacunae and interstices within positive law and — at a maximum — extend the reach of ICL beyond what extant positive law provides. In many of the decisions, tribunals have departed from, expanded on, or rejected outright rules carefully negotiated by states during treaty drafting processes. This has the potential to upset the "constitutional" balance — if it can be called that — between states and the adjudicative institutions they create in the international system. As you review the cases in your ICL text, be conscious of the arguments tribunals are using as they interpret or expand extant treaty language and consider the legitimacy of the case outcomes along the two key dimensions of respect for state sovereignty and the rights of defendants.

part II

Intersections

In this part, we shift gears to consider the core international crimes — war crimes, crimes against the peace or aggression, crimes against humanity, and genocide — alongside the primary international criminal law (ICL) defenses and forms of responsibility. This part focuses on crimes within the jurisdiction of the International Criminal Court (ICC) and other international, or quasi-international, tribunals. The terrorism crimes are addressed as stand-alone crimes because they are closely related to the core crimes and are the subject of active prosecution by states under extraterritorial forms of jurisdiction. In addition, the international crime of torture (which is also an enumerated war crime and crime against humanity) is discussed with reference to the defense of necessity. Largely excluded from this part are other transnational crimes — such as money laundering, trafficking in people and narcotics, and international arms dealing — on the theory that such crimes are primarily (but not exclusively) defined by domestic law and prosecuted before domestic tribunals. Some of these transnational crimes were originally contemplated within the subject matter jurisdiction of the ICC. Indeed, Trinidad and Tobago first proposed reopening discussions on a permanent international criminal court after years of Cold War quiescence because they wanted an international forum to prosecute transnational drug crimes that were overwhelming certain smaller states. As negotiations for the ICC progressed, however, these crimes fell away and states focused on the core crimes.

As the following chapters indicate, the elements of international law offenses overlap considerably. For one, a single act may implicate multiple international crimes. For example, an act of murder can constitute a war crime (when a protected person is intentionally killed within the context of an armed conflict), a crime against humanity (when a person is intentionally killed within the context of a widespread or systematic attack against a civilian population), or an act of genocide (when a member of a protected group is killed with the specific intent to destroy that person's group, in whole or in part). Similarly, consider the multiple counts the following event could generate: A protected person from a minority ethnic group is intentionally killed using a prohibited weapon in the context of the bombardment of an undefended town involving excessive force out of proportion to any military advantage. The person killed could be considered the victim of multiple crimes. In addition, a perpetrator involved in this assault may be indicted under several theories of liability: for committing, ordering, inciting, instigating, permitting, failing to prevent or punish, and being complicit in the international crimes committed.

The overlap of international crimes raises multiple questions about the administration of justice. These include questions about how a prosecutor should charge defendants whose conduct implicates multiple prohibitions, how a tribunal should construct its verdict in light of multiple and overlapping counts in an indictment, and how a defendant should be sentenced where multiple crimes are proven. Resolving these questions of charging and sentencing may hinge on whether the crimes charged constitute lesser included offenses of each other. The international criminal tribunals have largely adopted the approach articulated by the U.S. Supreme Court in *Blockburger v. United States*, 284 U.S. 299, 304 (1932):

> The applicable rule is that where the same act or transaction constitutes a violation of two distinct statutory provisions, the test to be applied to determine whether there are two offences or only one, is whether each provision requires proof of an additional fact which the other does not.

The test thus requires a determination of whether each offense contains an element not required by the other. If so, the crime that is fully encompassed is a lesser included offense of the crime containing the additional element. As you review these materials, it is also worth considering whether the ICC may prosecute crimes that were purposefully excluded from its subject matter jurisdiction, such as terrorism crimes, where the acts can also be characterized as war crimes or crimes against humanity.

∽ 6 ∾

The Legal Regulation of Armed Conflict

As discussed in more detail in Chapter 1, the law of armed conflict, also called the law of war, has historically encompassed two main foci: *jus ad bellum* and *jus in bello*. The former addresses the legality of going to war and historically took the form of theological and then secular "just war" theories; the latter concedes the *de facto* existence of war and seeks to regulate belligerent conduct within it. Although some of the world's greatest minds grappled with establishing standards for determining when states had the right to go to war, by the late nineteenth century, the right to wage war began to be viewed as an attribute of state sovereignty. Further development of the *jus ad bellum* was all but eclipsed by prolific developments in *jus in bello*. Nonetheless, these two approaches to regulating warfare converged in the charters of the World War II international tribunals, which prosecuted violations of both bodies of law as crimes giving rise to individual criminal responsibility.

In the postwar period, violations of *jus ad bellum* (referred to as "crimes against the peace" at Nuremberg and Tokyo) all but disappeared from the pantheon of international criminal law (ICL). Instead, Article 2(4) of the UN Charter addressed states — rather than individuals — and prohibited the "threat or use of force against the territorial integrity or political independence of any state, or in any other manner inconsistent with the Purposes of the United Nations." Under the Charter regime, breaches of this provision give rise to state responsibility, rather than individual criminal responsibility.

Contemporary international law now views the conceptual distinction between the *jus ad bellum* and the *jus in bello* as axiomatic: The legal evaluation of the conduct of hostilities is an inquiry entirely independent of the legal evaluation of the lawfulness of the resort to armed force. Accordingly, a just (or lawful) war may be fought unlawfully, and an unjust (or unlawful) war may be fought lawfully. Under the *jus in bello*, by consequence, all parties are treated equally, regardless of who initiated the armed conflict and their reasons for doing so. Indeed, the International Committee of the Red Cross (ICRC) remains strictly agnostic about the cause(s) of any armed conflicts in which it operates while strictly scrutinizing their consequences. That said, there is an intuitive appeal to the position, still advocated by some, that any act of armed force committed within the context of an unlawful war should *ipso facto* be treated as a war crime. In addition, many groups fighting against what they consider to be oppressive, racist, or occupier states have argued that any act committed in furtherance of a just war must itself also be deemed just and lawful.

Although crimes against the peace merit only a short chapter in the annals of ICL, the idea that the resort to war itself is a criminal act has proven to be more than mere history. The *jus ad bellum* and *jus in bello* have reunited in the Statute of the International Criminal Court (ICC), although the full scope of the crime of aggression — the modern lexicon for crimes against the peace — has yet to be determined. This chapter briefly traces some high points in the development of the penal components of these two bodies of law. It then presents the basic framework for understanding the contemporary law of aggression and then war crimes, noting areas in the law that remain in flux. Underlying this chapter is a rich legacy of legal rules aimed at the regulation of hostilities that belies the claim by Cicero that *silent enim leges inter arma* — the laws are silent among those at war.

JUS AD BELLUM

The Original Crime of Aggression

The Charters for both the Nuremberg and Tokyo Tribunals contained the charge of "crimes against the peace" alongside the charges of war crimes and crimes against humanity. The postwar architects of international justice defined crimes against the peace somewhat tautologically at Article 6(a) as "planning, preparation, initiation or waging of a war of aggression, or a war in violation of international treaties, agreements or assurances."[1] In addition, the Charters allowed for the prosecution of individuals for "participation in a common plan or conspiracy" to commit aggression. Count One of the Nuremberg Indictment charged all the defendants with conspiring to commit crimes against the peace. Count Two charged all but five defendants with committing crimes against the peace. All but four defendants were charged with war crimes in Count Three.

Although the World War II defendants did not submit to the equally novel crimes against humanity charge without objection, the crimes against the peace charge was the most controversial element of the Charters at the time. Both sets of defendants argued that the concept of crimes against the peace violated the principle of legality, because war had never before been criminalized in international law, so the prohibition against crimes against the peace in the two Charters was, in effect, ex post facto legislation. As is discussed more fully in

Chapter 5 on the defense of *nullum crimen sine lege*, the tribunals ruled that the proven acts of aggression were unlawful, and thus criminal, under extant treaties and customary norms, although none of these sources expressly provided for criminal penalties in the event of a breach.

The crime of aggression was the centerpiece of the Nuremberg Trial, which was to be "the Trial to end all wars." Indeed, a majority of the Nuremberg Tribunal's judgment consists of describing the aggressive acts of Germany, including the invasions of (*inter alia*) Poland, Austria, Czechoslovakia, and Belgium in violation of the Kellogg–Briand Pact, various bilateral treaties and assurances of nonaggression, and declarations of neutrality. In its final judgment, the Nuremberg Tribunal reasoned that belligerency was the proximate cause of all the other crimes alleged: "[t]o initiate a war of aggression, therefore, is not only an international crime; it is the supreme international crime differing only from other war crimes in that it contains within itself the accumulated evil of the whole."[2] Given the importance of this crime in the postwar period, it is noteworthy that none of the statutes of the contemporary ad hoc tribunals contains the crime of aggression, even though it would have arguably been relevant in the conflicts in the former Yugoslavia, East Timor, and Sierra Leone.

The post-war tribunals laid the foundation for the recognition of the crime of aggression. As peace descended on the globe, states immediately turned to the creation of the United Nations, an institution primarily concerned with the maintenance of peace and security. Article 2(4) of the UN Charter, quoted earlier, sets forth a presumption against the use of force internationally. The UN Security Council bears the primary responsibility for maintaining international peace, through identifying threats to the peace and acts of aggression (Article 39) and deciding on measures, including the use of armed force, in response (Articles 41 and 42).[3] The Charter recognizes only two scenarios in which the use of force by a state is

potentially lawful: in response to Security Council authorization and in self-defense (Article 51).* In addition, the Responsibility to Protect initiative of the United Nations raises
questions about the lawfulness of humanitarian intervention
where such an intervention is not employed against the
territorial integrity or political independence of a state, but
in defense of individuals in need.[4] All these Charter provisions
address potential state responsibility for acts of aggression, not
individual criminal responsibility. Collectively, they significantly weaken von Clausewitz's claim that "war is a mere con-
tinuation of policy by other means"[5] by largely invalidating war
as a valid policy choice.

In the postwar period, the international community failed
to draft a comprehensive treaty setting forth the elements of
the crime of aggression as it did with genocide and war crimes.
In taking up the proposal for establishing a permanent international criminal court, the International Law Commission
(ILC) promulgated a Draft Code of Crimes Against the
Peace and Security of Mankind that was to provide the substantive law to be adjudicated before the proposed court. Early
versions of the Draft Code designated the crime of aggression
as a crime against the peace and security at Article 2 and
defined the crime as:

> (1) Any act of aggression, including the employment by
> the authorities of a State of armed force against another State
> for any purpose other than national or collective self-defence

---

*Article 51 reads: "Nothing in the present Charter shall impair the inherent
right of individual or collective self-defence if an armed attack occurs against a
Member of the United Nations, until the Security Council has taken measures
necessary to maintain international peace and security. Measures taken by Members in the exercise of this right of self-defence shall be immediately reported to
the Security Council and shall not in any way affect the authority and responsibility of the Security Council under the present Charter to take at any time such
action as it deems necessary in order to maintain or restore international peace
and security." The conditions under which states may claim preemptive or antic-
ipatory self-defense remain contested under international law.

or in pursuance of a decision or recommendation of a competent organ of the United Nations.

(2) Any threat by the authorities of a State to resort to an act of aggression against another State.[6]

In 1954, the Draft Code project went into quiescence, not to be fully revived until the 1990s.

In 1974, the UN General Assembly unanimously passed Resolution 3314 to "guide" the Security Council in determining the occurrence of aggression in the exercise of its Chapter VII power.[7] Article 1 provides that aggression is the "use of armed force by a State against the sovereignty, territorial integrity or political independence of another State, or in any other manner inconsistent with the Charter of the United Nations." The resolution contains in Article 3 a nonexhaustive list of acts comprising aggression, regardless of the existence of a declaration of war, that includes:

(a) The invasion or attack by the armed forces of a State of the territory of another State, or any military occupation, however temporary, resulting from such invasion or attack, or any annexation by the use of force of the territory of another State or part thereof;

(b) Bombardment by the armed forces of a State against the territory of another State or the use of any weapons by a State against the territory of another State;

(c) The blockade of the ports or coasts of a State by the armed forces of another State;

(d) An attack by the armed forces of a State on the land, sea or air forces, or marine and air fleets of another State;

(e) The use of armed forces of one State which are within the territory of another State with the agreement of the receiving State, in contravention of the conditions provided for in the agreement or any extension of their presence in such territory beyond the termination of the agreement;

(f) The action of a State in allowing its territory, which it has placed at the disposal of another State, to be used by that other State for perpetrating an act of aggression against a third State;

    (g) The sending by or on behalf of a State of armed bands, groups, irregulars or mercenaries, which carry out acts of armed force against another State of such gravity as to amount to the acts listed above, or its substantial involvement therein.[8]

The resolution at Article 5(2) states that a "war of aggression is a crime against international peace," but the remainder of the resolution is geared toward state, rather than individual, responsibility. Notwithstanding this consensus definition of aggression, only a few states have incorporated the crime of aggression into their penal codes.[9] Nonetheless, when the international community again turned to the drafting of a statute for a permanent international criminal court in the 1990s, many state delegates argued for the revival of the crime of aggression in keeping with the Nuremberg and Tokyo legacy.

The Modern Crime of Aggression

Article 5(1) of the ICC Statute lists the crime of aggression as a crime over which the ICC has jurisdiction. Delegates to the Rome Conference, however, were unable to agree on the crime's definition or on any applicable jurisdictional preconditions. Accordingly, Article 5(2) promises that the Court "shall exercise jurisdiction over the crime of aggression once a provision is adopted in accordance with articles 121 and 123 defining the crime and setting out the conditions under which the Court shall exercise jurisdiction with respect to this crime. Such a provision shall be consistent with the relevant provisions of the Charter of the United Nations." Resolution F of the Final Act of the Rome Conference requested that the Preparatory Commission prepare proposals for a provision on aggression to be presented to the Assembly of State Parties. The anticipated provision is to be considered at the first Review Conference, to be held in 2009 or 2010.[10] Thus, the Court cannot exercise jurisdiction over the crime of aggression until this Committee completes its work and a definition of aggression is approved by a two-thirds majority of the Assembly of State Parties and ratified by seven-eighths of the State Parties.

In 2002, the Assembly of State Parties adopted a resolution that established a Special Working Group on the Crime of Aggression, with Ambassador Christian Wenaweser of Liechtenstein now serving as chair, to continue to work on a proposed amendment to the ICC Statute.[11] The group is open to all states, including non-State Parties. Two main issues facing the Special Working Group are defining the crime in terms of individual conduct, which requires coordination with the General Principles set forth in Part 3 of the Rome Treaty, and identifying any preconditions for the exercise of jurisdiction.

Defining the Crime of Aggression

The definition of the crime of aggression has several elements that have eluded drafters. These include elements addressing issues of personal jurisdiction, *actus reus, mens rea*, applicable forms of responsibility, and the necessity to show state action. Although much remains in flux, the crime of aggression is currently formulated in terms of state action: It must be shown that a state committed an act of aggression as defined by the statute. If such a showing is made, then individuals who knowingly and intentionally ordered or otherwise participated actively in the act of aggression can be prosecuted for their contributions thereto. The draft amendment to the ICC's Elements of Crimes for the crime of aggression has not been significantly amended since 2002. At that time, the proposed amendment included the following elements for the crime of aggression:

1. The perpetrator was in a position effectively to exercise control over or to direct the political or military action of the State which committed an act of aggression as defined by element 5.

2. The perpetrator was knowingly in that position.
3. The perpetrator ordered or participated actively in the planning, preparation or execution of the act of aggression.
4. The perpetrator committed element 3 with intent and knowledge.
5. An act of aggression, that is to say an act referred to in United Nations General Assembly resolution 3314, was committed by the State.
6. The perpetrator knew the actions of the State amounted to an act of aggression.
7. The act of aggression, by its character, gravity, and scale constituted a flagrant violation of the Charter of the United Nations.
8. The perpetrator had intent and knowledge with respect to element 7.

A preliminary challenge facing drafters has been to determine who in a military or civilian hierarchy may be charged with the crime of aggression. Early in the discussions, delegates proposed that the crime of aggression should be chargeable only against individuals in leadership positions rather than against the rank and file. According to current formulations of the "leadership clause," the defendant must be in a "position effectively to exercise control over or to direct the political or military action of a State."[12]

A second area of discussion has concerned the actions of the relevant state to which the defendant was connected. This has been framed as a circumstance element of the crime of aggression on the theory that aggression can only be committed through the collective act of a state by harnessing the state's war-making machinery.* Delegates have debated whether this provision should include a generic definition of aggression or

---

*Most definitions of aggression do not consider the possibility of aggression being committed by non- or substate groups, and few argue that it should. *But see*

an enumerated list along the lines of, and perhaps identical to, Articles 1 and 3 in G.A. Resolution 3314. To date, the preferred approach has been the combination of a generic *chapeau* followed by a nonexhaustive list of specific acts mirroring the structure of the crimes against humanity article in the ICC Statute. In this regard, the terms of Resolution 3314 have exerted a strong pull, especially among the African and Arab states, with delegates resisting efforts to either amend its list of aggressive acts or exclude reference to the resolution altogether. In addition, delegates have debated whether to include language limiting the jurisdiction of the Court to "flagrant" or "manifest" acts of aggression in violation of the UN Charter. Some states have argued that such a threshold is inherent to Article 1 of the ICC Statute, which limits the Court to considering "the most serious crimes of international concern."

A third open question concerns the nature of the defendant's participation in the act of aggression. Delegates have adopted two approaches — the so-called differentiated approach applies all forms of responsibility in Article 25(3) to the crime of aggression except for subparagraph (f) addressing attempt. Article 25(3) sets forth various forms of responsibility applicable to all crimes within the jurisdiction of the ICC: committing a crime; ordering, soliciting, or inducing a crime; aiding or abetting a crime; or contributing to the commission of a crime through a group acting with a common

---

Antonio Cassese, *On Some Problematical Aspects of the Crime of Aggression*, 20 Leiden J. Int'l L. 841, 846 (2007) ("[t]here is . . . no logical or legal obstacle to rules on aggression also criminalizing aggressive acts by non-state entities (such as terrorist armed groups, organized insurgents, liberation movements, and the like) against a state. . . . If the purpose of the relevant international rules is to protect the world community from serious breaches of the peace, one fails to see why individuals operating for non-state entities should be immune from criminal liability for aggressive conduct.").

purpose.* The "differentiated" draft text reads as follows (with contested and alternative language indicated by parentheses): "that person (leads) (directs) (organizes and/or directs) (engages in) the planning, preparation, initiation or execution of an act of aggression/armed attack." Alternatively, the so-called monist approach considers the various forms of commission outlined in Article 25(3) to be inapplicable to the crime of aggression and allows for prosecution only where the defendant has "order[ed] or participate[d] actively in the planning, preparation, initiation or execution of an act of aggression/armed attack." Some delegates also took the position that Article 28 addressing superior responsibility does not apply to the crime of aggression.

Preconditions for the Exercise of Jurisdiction

The placeholder text in Article 5(2) of the ICC Statute provides that any future definition of aggression in the ICC Statute "shall be consistent with the relevant provisions of the Charter of the United Nations." This seemingly innocuous phrase pinpoints one of the most highly contentious issues of defining the crime of aggression: what role the Security Council or other UN bodies will play in determining the existence of a sovereign act of aggression as a prerequisite to the ICC's jurisdiction over a case against a responsible individual. Many states have argued that a prior determination that an act of aggression by a state has occurred is crucial before the Court should proceed with an individual prosecution to prevent the politicization of the Court. They also point to limitations on the Court's jurisdiction and its institutional competency, arguing that the Court is charged with determining individual criminal responsibility and not state responsibility.

---

*Incitement is relevant only for the crime of genocide pursuant to Article 23(e).

This raises the question, who should make such a prior determination. Most states assume that any determination should be made by the Security Council, given its singular role in the UN system in addressing breaches of the peace.* The ILC, for example, recommended in Article 23 of its Draft Code that the Security Council must first declare that an act of aggression occurred by a state before the ICC could exercise jurisdiction over the crime. Not surprisingly, this approach was strongly supported by the permanent members of the Security Council (China, France, Russia, the United Kingdom, and the United States). Although the UN Charter does not explicitly state that *only* the Security Council may make that determination, proponents of an exclusive role for the Security Council argue that UN practice, in light of the logic and structure of the Charter, dictates this result. Additionally, these states argue that an absence of a Security Council determination will make it difficult to find an individual liable, because the perpetrator can raise the lack of Security Council action as proof that his or her nation did not commit an act of aggression.

Other delegates have argued that Article 39 of the UN Charter gives only primary, but not exclusive, authority to the Security Council to determine the existence of an act of aggression. These delegates argue that the Court should be able to proceed where a prior determination by the General Assembly or even the International Court of Justice (ICJ) has been made. Advocates of a broader approach point to Articles 10, 12, and 14, which all allow the UN General Assembly to consider and make recommendations about any matters within

---

*Article 39 of the UN Charter provides that "the Security Council shall determine the existence of any threat to the peace, breach of the peace, or act of aggression and shall make recommendations, or decide what measures shall be taken in accordance with Articles 41 and 42, to maintain or restore international peace and security."

the scope of the Charter,* and Articles 36 and 65 of the Statute of the ICJ, which extend the Court's advisory** and contentious jurisdiction to disputes under international law or the Charter. There is precedent for General Assembly determinations that states have engaged in acts of aggression and for ICJ determinations that states have used force in violation of Article 2(4) of the Charter,[13] although the latter is not necessarily the equivalent of a finding that such states committed acts of aggression. Proponents of a nonexclusive role for the Security Council argue that if the Security Council has exclusive power to determine whether a sovereign act of aggression occurred, it may paralyze the Court if the Council is unwilling or unable to make the predicate determination. Furthermore, they argue that the veto power may enable the agents of permanent members or their friends and allies to be shielded from prosecution. They also note that the Security

---

*General Assembly Resolution 377, the so-called Uniting for Peace Resolution, purports to empower the General Assembly to implement "collective measures" (including the use of force) when the Security Council cannot reach consensus in the face of an apparent act of aggression, breach of the peace, or threat to the peace. *See* U.N. Doc. No. A/Res/377 (V) A (Nov. 3, 1950). The United States proposed Resolution 377 shortly after the commencement of the Korean War following the exercise of a Russian veto in the Security Council. The General Assembly has invoked the Resolution ten times since 1950 (for example, after Egypt nationalized the Suez Canal, provoking an English/French occupation). Because it allows for the exercise of military force, it seems that the resolution would *a fortiori* allow for a declaration that a state has engaged in an act of aggression.

**The ICJ's advisory opinions generally involve questions of law rather than fact, so it is not clear if the ICJ could contribute in the necessary way to an ICC prosecution in an advisory capacity. Utilizing the contentious jurisdiction of the Court would require the initiation of a case by a state (presumably the victim of the act of aggression) against the putative perpetrator state. In addition, at the moment, Article 119 of the Rome Statute only allows the ICJ to make determinations in disputes between State Parties as to the interpretation of the Rome Statute. Such intervention is allowed only after the dispute between State Parties has been referred to the ICJ by the Assembly of State Parties. This provision may need to be amended if some more active role of the ICJ is contemplated by the aggression provisions (for example, if the ICC could trigger the ICJ's advisory jurisdiction).

Council has no power to determine the existence of past acts of aggression, absent immediate threat, whereas the General Assembly and ICJ are bound by no temporal limitations. Finally, it is argued that a political determination could impede the development of precedent and customary international law.

Other states have argued that a prior determination of state aggression is not necessary at all, notwithstanding the language of Article 5(2). The concern is that any formal precondition might hinder the Court's ability to take cognizance of international crimes within its jurisdiction and lead to inconsistent outcomes. Requiring a determination about aggression before the Court can act may even go so far as to undermine the legitimacy of the Court by making its work dependent on determinations by the political, and potentially politicized, branches of the United Nations. To make the case that the ICC Statute is already adequately "consistent" with the Charter provisions, proponents of a more autonomous Court point to Article 13 of the ICC Statute, which allows the Security Council to refer situations to the Court even if none of the relevant states has ratified the treaty, and Article 16, which allows the Security Council to request (subject to indefinite renewal) the Court to defer an investigation for 12 months in a Chapter VII resolution.*

In any case, there is wide agreement that to protect a defendant's due process rights, any prior determination by another legal or political entity that an act of aggression had occurred could not be binding on the Court. Thus, the Court would be empowered to reexamine the existence of an act of aggression

---

*Article 16 provides that "No investigation or prosecution may be commenced or proceeded with under this Statute for a period of 12 months after the Security Council, in a resolution adopted under Chapter VII of the Charter of the United Nations, has requested the Court to that effect; that request may be renewed by the Council under the same conditions."

by the relevant state, and defendants would be able to refute the determination before the Court. This also ensures that the prosecution remains subject to the penal burden of proof, beyond a reasonable doubt, which is likely more rigorous than that required by any other UN institution in determining state responsibility for acts of aggression.

Including the Crime of Aggression in the ICC Statute

Notwithstanding the ICC's placeholder provision and this intense work to reach a consensus definition of aggression, deep divisions remain among states and nongovernmental organizations as to whether the ICC should exercise jurisdiction over the crime of aggression at all. The primary objection to its inclusion is that the crime of aggression threatens to indelibly politicize the Court, even if—or especially if—other UN bodies contribute to the determination that a state has committed an act of aggression. Under certain proposals, for example, a Security Council decision not to make a determination of aggression on purely political grounds would effectively bar the ICC from considering the matter. As a judicial body, it is argued, the Court should not be dependent on any political determination involving crimes within its jurisdiction. It is further argued that aggression is a crime of state that is by definition committed against another state, rather than the crime of an individual that is committed against other individuals. Thus, only collective, rather than individual, culpability should be considered, and because the ICC only has jurisdiction over individuals, it is an inappropriate forum for apportioning such responsibility. Finally, it is argued that there is no modern precedent for the crime of aggression, as none of the ad hoc tribunals exercised jurisdiction over the crime.

The debate over the inclusion of the crime of aggression has also touched on the potential intersection between the crime and the prohibitions against war crimes. Opponents of including the crime of aggression in the ICC Statute argue that the harms experienced by victims of war are captured by the prohibitions against war crimes (and even potentially those provisions governing crimes against humanity and genocide). They note that the crime of aggression adds little to the subject matter jurisdiction of the Court given the Rome Statute's comprehensive *jus in bello* provisions. Conversely, it is argued that aggression remains the supreme international crime that often gives rise to all other international crimes, as was noted by the Nuremberg Tribunal. Proponents of fully implementing Article 5(2) contend that a "clean" but nonetheless criminal war — that is, an act of aggression in which no war crimes are committed — still harms victims in a way that should be cognizable by the Court. In the words of Ben Ferencz, a former prosecutor in the post–World War II trials and a staunch advocate for the inclusion of the crime of aggression in the ICC Statute:

> Ever since the judgment at Nuremberg, it has been undeniable that aggressive war is not a national right but an international crime. War is the soil from which the worst human rights violations invariably grow. The U.N. Charter prescribes that only the Security Council can determine when aggression by a state has occurred but it makes no provision for criminal trials. No criminal statute can expand or diminish the Council's vested power. Only an independent court can decide justly whether any individual is innocent or guilty. Excluding aggression from international judicial scrutiny is to grant immunity to those responsible for "the supreme international crime" — omission [of the crime of aggression] encourages war rather than peace.[14]

In this way, it is argued that including the crime of aggression in the ICC Statute will deter political and military leaders from resorting to armed force in their relations with each other, because they will be on notice that the resort to armed conflict without Security Council approval, or without credible claims to be acting in self-defense, might give rise to individual criminal liability. This debate continues. As you cover this material in your course of study, you might refer to the Web page of the Working Group, which keeps relatively up-to-date records of ongoing deliberations.

JUS IN BELLO

Whereas the *jus ad bellum* governs the decision to utilize armed force, the *jus in bello* takes hold once an armed conflict exists. Historically, the codification of the *jus in bello* proceeded along two tracks: one, referred to as *Geneva law*, is based on the four Geneva Conventions of 1949 and their two 1977 Protocols and originated under the auspices of the Geneva-based ICRC; the other, referred to as *Hague law*, derives from a series of conventions concluded in The Hague in 1899 and 1907. Together, these sets of treaties regulate many aspects of the conduct of hostilities, at times in great detail. Geneva law creates interlocking legal regimes to protect classes of persons, such as prisoners of war (POWs) and noncombatants, who are particularly vulnerable in armed conflicts. By contrast, Hague law governs the means and methods of warfare.

Until the promulgation of the 1949 Geneva Conventions, which now bear the distinction of being the first multilateral conventions to receive universal ratification, a notion that there were crimes of war that would give rise to individual criminal responsibility existed only in customary international law and domestic law, primarily within national military codes. The Geneva Conventions for the first time considered certain "grave breaches" of the *jus in bello* to be war crimes, giving rise to individual criminal responsibility. The law of war crimes thus constitutes just one element of the *jus in bello*, as many applicable rules give rise only to state responsibility. The remainder of this chapter focuses on the penal provisions of the *jus in bello*, because only these aspects of international humanitarian law (IHL) fall under the rubric of ICL.

Given their long-standing pedigree, there was never any question that the ICC would exercise jurisdiction over violations of the *jus in bello* that give rise to individual criminal responsibility. The devil, as always, is in the details. This section sketches out the framework for understanding the current law of war crimes under ICL. It starts with the antecedent question of the applicability of IHL altogether, because the prohibitions against war crimes apply only where IHL applies. This section next touches on the choice of law question occasioned by the requirement of conflict classification. This is followed by a discussion of how ICL distinguishes between ordinary criminal acts committed in war and war crimes — the nexus problem. We then discuss the distinguishing features of Geneva and Hague law: protected persons and the principles of necessity, proportionality, and distinction, respectively. The section concludes with a brief tour of the ICC Statute's war crimes provision, because it encompasses many — but not all — of the war crimes contained within IHL treaties and adjudicated by the ad hoc tribunals as crimes under customary international law. The next chapter continues this discussion by concluding with a discussion of the intersections between the international criminal prohibitions against war crimes and terrorism.

Triggering International Humanitarian Law

Not all disturbances, acts of violence, or even uses of military force trigger the applicability of IHL and thus the prohibitions against war crimes. The Geneva Conventions themselves provide little insight into the question of their field of application, declaring at Article 2 only that the bulk of their provisions apply to "all cases of declared war or of any other armed conflict which may arise between two or more of the High Contracting Parties, even if the state of war is not recognized by one of them." Common Article 3 of those Conventions creates a mini-regime governing armed conflicts "not of an international character occurring in the territory of one of the High Contracting Parties" without further definition. It is not until Protocol II, which elaborates on and expands common Article 3, that we find a clear statement that its provisions do not apply to "situations of internal disturbances and tensions, such as riots, isolated and sporadic acts of violence and other acts of a similar nature, as not being armed conflicts."

Determining when and where IHL applies in the absence of more express treaty guidance was a central conundrum of the work of the two ad hoc international tribunals. In both the former Yugoslavia and Rwanda, the prosecutor charged individuals with war crimes for acts of violence committed well beyond the vicinity of active hostilities. For example, as part of a general challenge to the jurisdiction of the tribunal, defendant Tadić asserted that the war crimes counts in his indictment had to be dismissed, because his actions were not committed in the context of an armed conflict. In upholding the charges, the ICTY announced a broad test for determining when IHL is triggered within a particular situation, touching both on the question of when an armed conflict exists and the territorial scope of the prohibitions that then apply. It ruled:

> [A]n armed conflict exists whenever there is a resort to armed force between States or protracted armed violence between governmental authorities and organized armed groups or between such groups within a State. International humanitarian law applies from the initiation of such armed conflicts and extends beyond the cessation of hostilities until a general conclusion of peace is reached; or, in the case of internal conflicts, a peaceful settlement is achieved. Until that moment, international humanitarian law continues to apply

> in the whole territory of the warring States or, in the case of
> internal conflicts, the whole territory under the control of a
> party, whether or not actual combat takes place there.[15]

The tribunal reached this conclusion by noting that although
the Geneva Conventions are silent as to the geographical scope
of international "armed conflicts," they do imply that at least
some of the provisions of the Conventions apply to the entire
territory of the parties to the conflict, not just to the place of
actual hostilities. In particular, provisions addressing the treatment of POWs and other individuals captured by opposing
forces are not dependent on any proximity to actual hostilities.
Likewise, the beneficiaries of common Article 3 and Protocol
II governing noninternational armed conflicts are those taking
no active part (or no longer taking active part) in the hostilities.
Further, Article 6(2) of Geneva Convention IV indicates that
"[i]n the territory of Parties to the conflict, the application of
the present Convention shall cease on the general close of
military operations." The Tribunal ruled that all these provisions make clear that IHL applies broadly within the territory
of the conflict, such that the charges against Tadić should
stand.

Where IHL does not apply, other bodies of law may still
penalize the conduct in question. For example, Tadić was concurrently charged with crimes against humanity, the prohibition of which applies independently of any armed conflict
(although that had not been definitively established until the
Tribunal so ruled in *Tadić*). Acts of violence may also constitute acts of genocide (where protected groups are targeted with
the intent to destroy the group) or acts of terrorism under
international law. Where international law does not criminalize
particular acts of violence, recourse can always be had to extant
domestic penal law. Many of the war crimes prohibitions find
domestic analogs in the crimes of assault, kidnapping, murder,
and mayhem.

Conflict Classification

Determining that IHL applies to a particular situation (because it has reached the level of an armed conflict) immediately triggers a second inquiry: whether the conflict in question is an international or noninternational conflict. The 1949 Geneva Conventions primarily apply to international armed conflicts, defined at common Article 2 as "all cases of declared war or of any other armed conflict which may arise between two or more of the High Contracting Parties, even if the state of war is not recognized by one of them." This definition thus requires the presence of two embattled High Contracting Parties. There is a difference, however, between an international conflict and a conflict that is internationalized or that involves multiple state parties. Thus, the conflict in Afghanistan initiated after the events of September 11, 2001, began as an international armed conflict when the United States and its coalition parties fought the Taliban and its supporters. This was a conflict between two or more nation states and was thus "international" within the meaning of Article 2. Once the government of Hamid Karzai was installed, the conflict no longer pitted two sovereigns against each other. At that point, the conflict ceased to be an international armed conflict within the meaning of the Geneva Conventions, even though it remained internationalized by the presence of troops from multiple nations. Most of the articles of the Geneva Conventions thus no longer apply to this conflict as a technical matter.

Although the majority of the Geneva Conventions' provisions govern international armed conflicts (including situations of foreign occupation), the one exception is Article 3, common to all four Conventions, which applies in cases "of armed conflict not of an international character occurring in the territory of one of the High Contracting Parties." This article — called a "convention in miniature" — sets forth minimum protections that must be afforded to all individuals involved in noninternational armed conflicts. The latter terminology is employed in lieu of "civil war" or "internal war" to encompass the entire range of conflicts that do not meet the somewhat technical and unintuitive definition of international armed conflict contained in Article 2. The only textual requirement for the applicability of common Article 3 is the occurrence of an "armed conflict" within "the territory" of a High Contracting Party.

The international community adopted two protocols to the Geneva Conventions in 1977 in response to the changing nature of armed conflict, which involved the shift to predominantly noninternational armed conflicts, the movement of the battlefield to population centers, increased civilian involvement in armed conflicts, and the expansion of guerilla warfare. Most important, Protocol I expands the definition of international armed conflict to include "armed conflicts in which people are fighting against colonial domination and alien occupation and against racist regimes in the exercise of their right of self-determination." By elevating these conflicts to the status of international armed conflicts, and granting a political advantage to certain liberation movements, the protocol to a certain degree invokes the "just war" tradition of the *jus ad bellum*. Protocol I also provides a more detailed set of rules concerning the obligation to discriminate between military and civilian targets and to utilize proportionate force, and further defines and clarifies the rules with respect to mercenaries. It also expands the category of privileged combatants to include members of guerrilla movements or informal militias that adhere to certain rules to distinguish themselves from the civilian population. These rules are more relaxed than those contained within the Third Geneva Convention addressed to POWs, which has led to criticism that the protocol puts civilians at greater risk and provides greater protections to combatants and guerillas. With these provisions, Protocol I reflects elements of both Geneva and Hague law.

Protocol II elaborates on the minimum rules in common Article 3. Historically, states were reluctant to create legal rules governing the conduct of noninternational armed conflicts, primarily out of fear of legitimizing dissident or insurrectionary groups and of submitting what had been viewed as internal matters to international rules and scrutiny. During the drafting of the four Geneva Conventions, the ICRC and some state delegates proposed more detailed rules for noninternational armed conflicts. In the face of steep resistance, all that was achieved was the laconic common Article 3. The passage of Protocol II reflects a trend toward a greater acceptance of the need to regulate conflicts that do not fall within the bailiwick of the Geneva Conventions.

Protocol II also established a more precise test for determining its field of application than exists in common Article 3. Article 1 states:

1. This Protocol, which develops and supplements Article 3 common to the Geneva Conventions of 12 August 1949 without modifying its existing conditions or application, shall apply to all armed conflicts which are not covered by [Protocol I] and which take place in the territory of a High Contracting Party between its armed forces and dissident armed forces or other organized armed groups which, under responsible command, exercise such control over a part of its territory as to enable them to carry out sustained and concerted military operations and to implement this Protocol.

2. This Protocol shall not apply to situations of internal disturbances and tensions, such as riots, isolated and sporadic acts of violence and other acts of a similar nature, as not being armed conflicts.

Thus, Protocol II does not apply until the armed conflict involves armed groups under responsible command, who have sufficient control over territory to launch "sustained and concerted" military operations and also to conduct their operations in accordance with the rules of war contained in the protocol. Moreover, Protocol II applies only to a conflict between a State's armed forces and rebel or dissident movements on the State's territory. Common Article 3 is broader, and covers armed conflicts between such groups competing for power within a state when the central government is not involved or has ceased to exist. Common Article 3 also applies to those civil wars in which guerilla forces lack any fixed location from which to exercise territorial control or are not led by responsible command.

A further wrinkle in the exercise of conflict classification involves conflicts that appear to be noninternational armed conflicts, because they pit a state's military against rebel or insurrectionary forces, but involve the significant intervention of another nation state. The situation in the former Yugoslavia is an example of such a conflict. The armed conflict there began as a classic civil war when ethnic groups within Yugoslavia took up arms against each other. Eventually, however, various republics declared independence, including Bosnia-Herzegovina. Within Bosnia, the Bosnian Serbs (who favored continued union with Yugoslavia) and the Bosnian Croats (who favored union with the nascent Republic of Croatia) came to blows with the Bosnian authorities. The two groups enjoyed significant financial, logistical, and strategic support from Belgrade and Zagreb, respectively. In situations in which this level of support rose to the level of "overall control" over the Bosnian Serb and Croat paramilitaries, the ICTY has determined that the war became an international armed conflict, essentially pitting two nation states against each other, thus triggering the whole panoply of Geneva Convention rules.[16]

Viewed collectively, the Geneva treaty regime establishes a taxonomy of conflict classification that includes the following:

(a) situations that do not trigger IHL at all (e.g., riots, sporadic acts of violence);

(b) noninternational armed conflicts that trigger common Article 3's protections;

(c) noninternational armed conflicts that meet the heightened requirements of Protocol II;

(d) international armed conflicts within the meaning of Protocol I (e.g., situations in which an indigenous population is resisting colonial domination);

(e) sufficiently internationalized armed conflicts that satisfy the effective control test and thus trigger the 1949 Geneva Conventions; and

(f) traditional international armed conflicts pitting two High Contracting Parties against each other that also trigger the 1949 Geneva Conventions.

Choice of Law Implications of Conflict Classification

The question of conflict classification is more than academic in ICL. From the perspective of positive law, only the Geneva Conventions governing international (or sufficiently internationalized armed conflicts) create a penal regime of war crimes. Within those treaties, it is only certain "grave breaches" of the treaties that give rise to individual criminal responsibility. By their own terms, violations of other treaty provisions (including much of the four Geneva Conventions and common Article 3) and whole treaties (Protocol II and the Hague Conventions) only give rise to the civil liability of states and do not set forth any individual penal sanctions.

Nonetheless, the ad hoc tribunals have made quick work of dismantling distinctions between the norms applicable in international and noninternational armed conflicts that were so carefully crafted by states during the IHL treaty-drafting process. As a result, much conduct prohibited or criminalized in international armed conflicts now constitutes war crimes

even if committed in internal or other noninternational conflicts. With respect to the ICTY, this process was enabled by
the formulation of the war crimes provisions of the ICTY Statute. Article 2 of the ICTY Statute reproduced the grave
breaches regime of the Geneva Conventions. Article 3 of the
ICTY Statute extended the jurisdiction of the Tribunal to cover
"violations of the laws and customs of war," including a nonexhaustive list of violations of the Fourth Hague Convention.
The Tribunal interpreted this latter provision expansively to
penalize violations of common Article 3 as well as other prohibitions within the Geneva Conventions and their Protocols,
finding authority for this assertion in customary international
law rather than treaty law.

In penalizing violations of common Article 3 and Protocol
II, the ICTY has essentially merged the law governing
international and noninternational armed conflicts, rendering
conflict classification a virtually irrelevant exercise in its proceedings. The Appeals Chamber in *Tadić* was quite self-
conscious about this, having found that national practice
and the inroads made by the international human rights regime
into areas traditionally shrouded by state sovereignty have
"blur[red] the traditional dichotomy between international
wars and civil strife."[17] In addition, as most global conflicts
are internal in character, the distinction between the two bodies of law seemed increasingly arbitrary and outmoded to
modern tribunals.[18] This merger now finds positive expression
in Article 8 of the ICC Statute, indicating that this expansive
approach has been largely — although not entirely — ratified
by the community of states. As a result, the ICC can prosecute
almost all war crimes committed in any type of conflict as can
states that have harmonized their domestic penal codes with
the ICC Statute.

Despite the modern trend toward conflating the rules governing international and internal armed conflicts, the question
of conflict classification remains relevant to determine the

particular rules that apply in any armed conflict. Indeed, the question of conflict classification has been central to the jurisprudence arising out of the global "war on terror" and in particular for legal efforts to challenge the policy of the United States to detain individuals captured in Afghanistan and elsewhere at Guantánamo Bay and prosecute them before military commissions. In a case contesting the legality of the military commission scheme as originally established by the Bush administration, the U.S. Supreme Court dodged the question of whether the full Geneva Conventions applied to the hostilities.[19] It did rule, however, that at a minimum the protections of common Article 3 were applicable, and in particular found applicable the requirement that persons "taking no active part in the hostilities, including members of armed forces who have laid down their arms and those placed *'hors de combat'* by . . . detention" can only be tried by a "regularly constituted court, affording all the judicial guarantees which are recognized as indispensable by civilized peoples." The Court struck down the original military commission scheme in part because of its failure to adhere to the provisions of common Article 3. Expanding a penal regime to noninternational armed conflicts has also destabilized the conventional thinking about the intersection between war crimes and the crimes of terrorism, as will be discussed more fully in the next chapter.

Nexus to Armed Conflict

Establishing the applicability of IHL and of war crimes prohibitions does not end the inquiry of whether and how an individual can be prosecuted for the commission of a violent act in the context of an armed conflict. In particular, it must still be determined whether the act in question — such as an act of murder or the theft of property — constitutes a war crime as opposed to a simple domestic crime or some other international crime. Only offenses that have some sort of a nexus to an armed conflict fall within the category of war crimes under IHL. If there is no link between the offense and the armed conflict, then the act must be charged under some other head of ICL or under domestic criminal law.

The ad hoc tribunals have struggled with how to define this link. The ICTY Trial Chamber in *Prosecutor v. Delalić* stated that "there must be an obvious link between the criminal act and the armed conflict."[20] In *Tadić*, another Trial Chamber noted that "the offences [must be] closely related to the armed conflict as a whole."[21] Defining this link became particularly acute in the Rwandan context, because although the genocide occurred nationwide, the actual theater of war — which pitted the government armed forces against the Tutsi-led Rwandan Patriotic Front — only engulfed part of the country. This led to a number of acquittals on war crimes counts, although most defendants were convicted of genocide and crimes against humanity, which require no link to armed conflict.

In the *Akayesu* case, for example, the Trial Chamber acquitted the defendant of war crimes charges on the ground that "it has not been proved beyond reasonable doubt that the acts perpetrated by Akayesu . . . were committed in conjunction with the armed conflict."[22] Likewise, in *Kayishema*, the Trial Chamber ruled that it was insufficient to show a simple temporal concurrence between the crimes charged and the internal armed conflict ensuing elsewhere in the country. Rather, the Trial Chamber required a showing that "there was a direct link between crimes committed against these victims and the hostilities"[23] and that the defendants were connected to one of the two embattled parties.[24] The Trial Chamber also noted that the armed conflict had been used as a pretext to unleash an official policy of genocide, but that these two phenomena were distinct within the region in question.

The ICTY *sub silentio* disagreed with this approach. In the *Kunarac* case, it ruled that although the armed conflict must have "played a substantial part in the perpetrator's ability to commit [the charged crime], his decision to commit it, the manner in which it was committed or the purpose for which it was committed," it was enough if, as in the present case, "the perpetrator acted in furtherance of or under the guise of the armed conflict."[25] The Tribunal identified a nonexclusive series of factors that would help to guide this inquiry:

- the perpetrator is a combatant;
- the victim is a noncombatant;
- the victim is a member of the opposing party;
- the act may be said to serve the ultimate goal of a military campaign; and
- the crime is committed as part of or in the context of the perpetrator's official duties.[26]

In the ICC's Elements of Crimes, drafters settled on the following formulation: It must be shown that the charged conduct "took place in the context of and was associated with" an international or noninternational armed conflict. This formulation eases up on the strict requirements established in *Kayishema* and seems to imply the necessity of only a loose geographical and temporal nexus.

Protected Persons

The goal of the Geneva treaty regime is to mitigate the effects of war by primarily protecting four classes of persons who do not, or who can no longer, participate in hostilities. Thus, the four Geneva Conventions apply to (1) the sick and wounded on land (Geneva Convention I); (2) the sick and wounded at sea (Geneva Convention II); (3) POWs (Geneva Convention III); and (4) civilians, or more accurately, anyone who does not fall into one of the other treaties' protective regimes (Geneva Convention IV). Each treaty contains a provision defining the class of protected persons. The Fourth Geneva Convention acts as a catch-all for individuals who fall outside of the prior three regimes. For example, Article 4 of the Fourth Geneva Convention defines its protected persons as follows:

> Persons protected by the Convention are those who, at a given moment and in any manner whatsoever, find themselves, in case of a conflict or occupation, in the hands of a Party to the conflict or Occupying Power of which they are not nationals. Nationals of a State which is not bound by the Convention are not protected by it. Nationals of a neutral State who find themselves in the territory of a belligerent State, and nationals of a co-belligerent State, shall not be regarded as protected persons while the State of which they are nationals has normal diplomatic representation in the State in whose hands they are. . . . Persons protected by [one of the other three Conventions] shall not be considered as protected persons within the meaning of the present Convention.

Key elements of this definition are the fact that the individual is "in the hands of" a party "of which they are not nationals"— that is, a different nation state—and not protected by one of the other Conventions. This definition does, however, exclude from protection individuals who are nationals of a state that is aligned with their captors' state or that is neutral. Accordingly, although Geneva Convention IV's title indicates its aim is to protect "civilian persons in time of war," it also provides protection to combatants who do not meet the definition of POWs in Article 4 of Geneva Convention III. This includes so-called "unprivileged belligerents"—irregular combatants who are not part of a High Contracting Party's military force or who are nationals of states not formally at war—although this point remains contentious.

In connection with the global "war on terror," for example, the U.S. government has argued that none of the detainees held in Guantánamo or elsewhere is entitled to claim protection under the Geneva Conventions because, under the U.S. government's reading, these individuals meet neither the definition of "prisoner of war" under Geneva Convention III nor the definition of "civilian" pursuant to Geneva Convention IV. Instead, the Bush administration has employed an alternative terminology, calling these individuals "enemy combatants" or "unlawful enemy combatants" — terms that are not employed within IHL or any of its treaties. Furthermore, the Fourth Geneva Convention's definition of protected person set forth earlier does not turn on combatant or civilian status. That said, many of the individuals detained by the United States were captured within the context of a noninternational armed conflict, the regulation of which by international law does not contain a POW regime. In addition, many of these individuals are not nationals of a High Contracting Party with which the United States is at war. The U.S. courts have yet to rule definitively on how these individuals should be characterized under the well-established classificatory system of the Geneva Conventions and thus which protections should be accorded to them.[27]

Under the conventional regime, only protected persons can be the victims of war crimes. This requirement has been relaxed in the recent jurisprudence. For example, in the former Yugoslavia, Bosnian Muslims often found themselves "in the hands of" Bosnian Serb paramilitary troops with whom they shared a nationality, but not an ethnicity or ultimate allegiance. The ICTY rejected arguments that no war crimes were committed because the victim and the perpetrator shared a bond of citizenship when it held:

> While previously wars were primarily between well-established States, in modern inter-ethnic armed conflicts such as that in the former Yugoslavia, new States are often created during the conflict and ethnicity rather than nationality may become the grounds for allegiance. Or, put another

way, ethnicity may become determinative of national allegiance. Under these conditions, the requirement of nationality is even less adequate to define protected persons. In such conflicts, not only the text and the drafting history of the Convention but also, and more importantly, the Convention's object and purpose suggest that allegiance to a Party to the conflict and, correspondingly, control by this Party over persons in a given territory, may be regarded as the crucial test.[28]

By adopting a functional and teleological approach to the treaties and to the concept of "protected persons," the ICTY significantly diminished the significance of nationality in determining protected person status. This ruling has implications for the "war on terror," suggesting that nationality alone should not be the basis for excluding individuals from the protections of the Geneva Conventions.

Means and Methods of Warfare

Hague law is not organized by protected group; rather, it sets forth rules concerning the methods and means of warfare that seek to regulate what kinds of weapons are allowed, what constitutes a legitimate military target, and what type and degree of force is permissible. Hague law traditionally, and by its terms, only applied to international conflicts. Modern developments before the international criminal tribunals and within the ICC Statute, however, have extended many of these principles to noninternational armed conflicts.

The Hague Conventions originally established both basic principles and more specific rules governing the means and methods of warfare and the use of force in pursuit of a military objective. Protocol I to the 1949 Geneva Conventions recodified many of these principles and rules, thus signaling the convergence of the Hague and Geneva traditions. This body of law most importantly subjects the use of force within an armed conflict to the interlocking principles of necessity, distinction, and proportionality. Necessity requires that armed attacks be designed and intended to defeat the opponent militarily. Thus, Article 52(2) of Protocol I states:

> Attacks shall be limited strictly to military objectives. In so far as objects are concerned, military objectives are limited to those objects which by their nature, location, purpose or use make an effective contribution to military action and whose total or partial destruction, capture or neutralization, in the circumstances ruling at the time, offers a definite military of advantage.

The principle of distinction requires that parties to an armed conflict distinguish between legitimate military targets and illegitimate targets, such as civilians or civilian infrastructure. Article 48 of Protocol I provides that "[p]arties to the conflict shall at all times distinguish between the civilian population and combatants." Not surprisingly, interpretive problems arise with respect to so-called dual-use facilities, such as bridges, power plants, or communication facilities.

Indiscriminate attacks are also prohibited. Article 51 of Protocol I defines indiscriminate attacks to include "[t]hose [attacks] which employ a method or means of combat the effects of which cannot be limited as required by this Protocol; and consequently, in each such case, are of a nature to strike military objectives and civilians or civilian objects without distinction." This principle has also been interpreted to prohibit certain types of weapons (such as cluster bombs and land mines) that, by their very nature, do not discriminate among lawful and unlawful targets. The international community has promulgated multilateral treaties to this effect, although many of the major suppliers and consumers of these weapons have yet to sign or ratify these treaties.

The principle of proportionality states that when military force is used for a proper military objective, only that force that is proportional to the military objective to be gained may be used. If a choice of weaponry or tactics is available, the commander should choose those that will cause the least incidental harm. Civilian casualties in and of themselves are not necessarily unlawful. Rather, only those attacks that cause damage to civilian objects that is excessive in relation to the anticipated military advantage of the attack are prohibited. The greater the degree of military advantage anticipated, the more so-called "collateral damage" is allowed. Thus, civilian casualties do not indicate a violation of the laws of war where they are the result of an attack that is proportional to the military objective sought.

Hague law thus approaches the question of legality from the point of view of lawful military objectives and related activity. Geneva law takes a more rights-based approach, defining categories of people and the protections to which they are entitled. Although the focus of Hague and Geneva law is somewhat different, the rules serve to reinforce each other. Indeed, Geneva law's protection of vulnerable classes of individuals from the effects of armed conflict and the Hague rules governing the principle of distinction and the legitimate use of force during an armed conflict are in essence two sides of the same coin.

War Crimes Before the International Criminal Court

The ICC's list of war crimes contains a partial synthesis of Geneva and Hague law, the two major strands of *jus in bello*. Rather than adopt an open-ended provision along the lines of the ICTY Statute's Article 3, the drafters chose to specifically list chargeable crimes (51 in total) to better adhere to the principle of legality. The entire section is preceded by a threshold provision at Article 8(1) that emphasizes that the ICC has jurisdiction over war crimes "in particular when committed as part of a plan or policy or as part of a large-scale commission of such crimes."

The remainder of the article itself is quite unwieldy by virtue of the fact that it separately enumerates the crimes applicable in international armed conflicts (Article 8(2)(a) and (b)) and noninternational armed conflicts (Article 8(2)(c)–(f)). The latter provisions are subject to two different triggering prerequisites. Common Article 3 crimes can be charged with respect to noninternational armed conflicts that are distinct from "internal disturbances and tensions, such as riots, isolated and sporadic acts of violence, or other acts of a similar nature" (Article 8(2)(d)). In this way, the drafters essentially applied some of the provisions contained in Protocol II's material field of application (Article 1(2)) to common Article 3. The other crimes can be charged with respect to "armed conflicts that take place in the territory of a State when there is protracted armed conflict between governmental authorities and organized armed groups or between such groups" (Article 8(2)(f)). This limitation mirrors the *Tadić* test, as discussed previously.

Article 8 also contains separate subsections reproducing the grave breaches of the Geneva Conventions (Article 8(2)(a)) and the violations of common Article 3 (Article 8(2)(c)). The remainder of the article enumerates crimes according to the laws and customs of war, as drawn from the Hague Conventions, Protocol II, other IHL treaties (such as those protecting cultural property or prohibiting particular weapons of war), and other sources. In identifying these lists of customary crimes, the drafters were guided by two main considerations: the gravity of the acts in question and whether they merited international prosecution, and whether the particular acts gave rise to individual criminal responsibility under either customary or treaty law. Although the drafters often claimed that they were merely codifying existing law, it is impossible not to conclude that some progressive development in the law occurred, especially with respect to the crimes that may be committed within noninternational armed conflicts.

~ 7 ~

The Crimes
of Terrorism

Terrorism is a concept with a colloquial meaning that lacks a consensus definition under international law. An omnibus definition of the crime of terrorism has eluded the international community to date largely because of the now trite adage: "One man's terrorist is another man's freedom fighter." Indeed, many international instruments condemning terrorism seem to carve out exceptions for national liberation movements and groups struggling for self-determination in the context of a history of colonialism and oppression. For example, a 1991 UN General Assembly Resolution denounced terrorism but, in virtually the same breath, reaffirmed "the inalienable right to self-determination and independence of people under colonial and racist and other forms of alien domination and foreign occupation."[1] As a result of this normative ambivalence, codification efforts have yielded a number of treaties that require states to criminalize only specific terrorist acts (such as aircraft hijacking or attacks against internationally protected persons).

Owing in part to these definitional challenges, the architects of the International Criminal Court (ICC) excluded the crime of terrorism from the ICC Statute altogether. Nonetheless, vocal support for the crime's eventual inclusion in the Court's subject matter jurisdiction remains. A number of terrorism prosecutions are proceeding in domestic courts around the world, and a hybrid court in Lebanon will be devoted to adjudicating terrorism crimes. As a result of the catastrophic attacks of September 11, 2001 and subsequent events, countering the threat of terrorism remains high on the agendas of individual states and the international community. For these reasons, we include this category of crimes within the "canon" of international criminal law (ICL).

This chapter endeavors to identify the elements of terrorism that distinguish it from other international crimes. It also considers the way in which the phenomenon of terrorism at times implicates and intersects with international humanitarian law (IHL) and the prohibitions against war crimes. Finally, it explores the extent to which terrorism crimes might be prosecutable before the ICC, notwithstanding that these crimes were purposefully excluded from the Court's subject matter jurisdiction.

TERRORISM UNDER INTERNATIONAL LAW

Although there have been efforts to codify a global prohibition against terrorism under international law for decades, there is no universal treaty or international instrument that defines the crime of terrorism writ large. The League of Nations embarked on the first major attempt in the modern era to prohibit the crime of terrorism after the 1934 assassination by Croatian separatists of King Alexander of Yugoslavia and others. The treaty—the Convention for the Prevention and Punishment of Terrorism (1937)—defined terrorism as follows: "All criminal acts directed against a State and intended or calculated to create a state of terror in the minds of particular persons or a group of persons or the general public."[2] The treaty attracted 24 state signatories; only India ultimately ratified the Convention. The onset of World War II scuttled any further efforts to bring the treaty into effect. After the dissolution of the League of Nations, the treaty was never revived.

From this abortive start, the international community has proceeded in a piecemeal fashion by criminalizing various manifestations of terrorism (such as offenses committed on board aircraft, crimes against internationally protected persons, hostage-taking, crimes involving maritime navigation, crimes involving nuclear material, and the financing of terrorism), often in response to particular terrorist incidents. In addition to providing penal definitions, many of these treaties obligate state parties to incorporate the relevant prohibitions into their domestic criminal codes, to treat enumerated acts of terrorism as extraditable offenses, to grant mutual legal assistance in the investigation and prosecution of the proscribed acts, and to either extradite or prosecute offenders pursuant to broad principles of extraterritorial jurisdiction. In this regard, the crimes of terrorism have been largely responsible for the greater acceptance of passive personality jurisdiction in international law, as states increasingly assert jurisdiction over extraterritorial acts of terrorism committed against their nationals.

This proliferation of definitions has led courts and commentators to conclude that there is no established definition of terrorism under customary international law. Nonetheless, many definitions of terrorism share certain basic structural elements:

1. The perpetration of violence by enumerated or unenumerated means;
2. The targeting of innocent civilians or elements of the civilian infrastructure;
3. Conduct that is undertaken:
   a. With the intent to cause violence or with wanton disregard for the act's consequences;

187

b. For the purpose of causing fear or terror, coercing a government, or intimidating an enemy;

c. To achieve some political, military, ideological, or religious goal.

As you review the various definitions of terrorism provided in your primary text or in the literature, try to identify common and divergent elements. You will see that although many instruments and penal codes addressing terrorism do not list prohibited acts with specificity, most contain one or more specific intent or motive element requiring proof of the existence of some mental state over and above the general intent to commit acts of violence.* In some cases, this mental element is aimed at the civilian population (the intent to cause terror) or a government (the intent to influence a government). This emphasis on the perpetrator's motive markedly distinguishes crimes of terrorism from other domestic and international crimes.

Many multilateral instruments limit their application to terrorism committed by non-state actors, implicitly or explicitly failing to recognize any notion of state terrorism. Thus, some

---

*In these formulations, it is often unclear if this mental element is the equivalent of a specific intent requirement (along the lines of the definition of genocide) or simply a required motive. Specific intent is generally defined as the purpose that the perpetrator intends to accomplish by committing a specific criminal act. It is usually a special mental element that is required above and beyond any mental state associated with the underlying *actus reus* of the crime. (For example, burglary — the breaking and entering into of a dwelling of another — requires a showing of the specific intent to commit a felony therein.) The concept of specific intent often elides with that of motive, which is the guiding purpose or goal behind an individual's criminal action. Normally, proof of motive is not required for a criminal conviction, although proving the defendant's motive is often an integral part of any prosecution and is often relevant at the time of sentencing. By contrast, the prosecution must prove the existence of specific intent if it is an element of a crime. One exception to this general rule involves hate crimes, which require proof that the defendant was motivated by animosity toward a protected group.

definitions — such as the one contained in the 1997 Terrorist Bombing Convention — prohibit acts committed, *inter alia*, against governmental facilities or public installations.[3] Other treaties limit their application to acts of "international terrorism," thus implicitly excluding jurisdiction over acts of terrorism committed by substate actors operating solely within a state. The Nuclear Terrorism Convention, for example, provides at Article 3 that

> This Convention shall not apply where the offence is committed within a single State, the alleged offender and the victims are nationals of that State, the alleged offender is found in the territory of that State and no other State has [grounds to assert territorial, nationality, or passive personality jurisdiction].

By contrast, others treaties include no specific place or manner restrictions.

The 1999 International Convention for the Suppression of the Financing of Terrorism in certain respects unifies these various terrorism treaties. Article 2(1) of that treaty incorporates a number of extant treaties in its annex by providing that

> Any person commits an offence within the meaning of this Convention if that person by any means, directly or indirectly, unlawfully and wilfully, provides or collects funds with the intention that they should be used or in the knowledge that they are to be used, in full or in part, in order to carry out [any violation of an annexed treaty].

In addition, the treaty prohibits

> [a]ny other act intended to cause death or serious bodily injury to a civilian, or to any other person not taking an active part in the hostilities in a situation of armed conflict, when the purpose of such act, by its nature or context, is to intimidate a population, or to compel a government or an international organization to do or to abstain from doing any act.[4]

This latter provision comes close to an omnibus definition of the phenomenon. The Financing Convention is bolstered by a Chapter VII Security Council Resolution passed in the weeks following the attacks of September 11, 2001, requiring all states to, *inter alia*, suppress the financing of acts of terrorism and freeze financial assets of persons or entities involved in terrorism.[5]

Since the 1990s, members of the United Nations have been pushing for a truly Comprehensive Convention on International Terrorism with a definition of terrorism that would reconcile and harmonize the disparate definitions in prior treaties. Such a convention, however, has yet to come to fruition. More recently, the UN Security Council adopted a resolution condemning the incitement of terrorist acts as well as the justification or glorification thereof.[6] It called on

> all States to adopt such measures as may be necessary and appropriate and in accordance with their obligations under international law to:
>
> (a) Prohibit by law incitement to commit a terrorist act or acts;
>
> (b) Prevent such conduct;
>
> (c) Deny safe haven to any persons with respect to whom there is credible and relevant information giving serious reasons for considering that they have been guilty of such conduct.

Additionally, the resolution called on all states to strengthen security at international borders and passenger screening facilities, promote tolerance, and "prevent the subversion of educational, cultural, and religious institutions by terrorists and their supporters."

None of the functioning international criminal tribunals includes terrorism in its subject matter jurisdiction. The Special Tribunal for Lebanon (STL), which is still under construction, will be the first.[7] The STL is a hybrid tribunal established by the United Nations and Lebanon to investigate and prosecute those "responsible for the terrorist crime which killed the former Lebanese Prime Minister Rafiq Hariri and others."[8] The Tribunal has a mandate to apply only the domestic laws of Lebanon "relating to the prosecution and punishment of acts of terrorism, crimes and offences against life and personal integrity, illicit associations and failure to report crimes and offences, including the rules regarding the material elements of a crime, criminal participation and conspiracy." Article 314 of the Lebanese Penal Code, one of several terrorism-related provisions that may be litigated before the STL, "defines 'terrorist acts' as all 'acts designed to create a state of alarm which are committed by means such as explosive devices, inflammable materials, poisonous or incendiary products or infectious or microbial agents likely to create a public hazard.'"[9] The *mens rea* element requires knowledge and a will to commit the terrorist act along with a specific intent to create a state of alarm or fear. The STL is thus a quasi-international tribunal effectively specializing in the law of terrorism. As such, although it will be interpreting Lebanese domestic law, the STL's jurisprudence will no doubt be persuasive as other tribunals consider terrorism crimes in the future.

TERRORISM WITHIN THE ICC STATUTE

As originally envisioned, the ICC's constitutive statute was to be primarily procedural in nature, incorporating the "core" international crimes of genocide, crimes against humanity, and war crimes by reference and as defined by customary international law along with certain "treaty crimes" set forth in discrete multilateral treaties already in existence, such as treaties addressing terrorism, drug trafficking, money laundering, and the like. To that end, nine of the terrorism treaties referenced earlier (for example, those addressing terrorism against aircraft, ships, hostages, and diplomats) were included in an annex to a draft of the ICC Statute.

Early on, delegates expressed concern that customary international law alone would not define the relevant crimes as clearly as would be necessary to provide adequate notice to an accused pursuant to the principle of *nullum crimen sine lege*. In addition, with respect to treaty crimes, delegates anticipated that it would be necessary to confirm that the treaty was in force with respect to the relevant states (e.g., the territorial and nationality state) for a treaty crime prosecution to proceed. These concerns led states to agree to set out the operative definitions of all the crimes in the Statute (and later adopt Elements of Crimes) rather than to incorporate such crimes by reference to preexisting treaties or customary international law.

As the negotiations proceeded at the 1998 Rome Conference, the treaty crimes eventually either fell out of the Statute, as was the case with terrorism *stricto sensu* and drug trafficking, or were incorporated into the core crimes, as was the case with respect to crimes against internationally protected persons (which are enumerated as war crimes at Article 8(2)(b)(iii)) and apartheid (which is listed as a crime against humanity at Article 7(1)(j)). With respect to terrorism crimes, drafters articulated several reasons for eventually excluding these crimes from the Statute altogether: (1) terrorism has no universally accepted definition; (2) terrorism was not considered to be one of "the most serious crimes of international concern" as contemplated by Article 1; (3) at the time, terrorism was not clearly recognized as a crime under customary international law; (4) including crimes of terrorism would unnecessarily politicize the ICC; and (5) there are alternative domestic venues for terrorism prosecutions such that establishing international jurisdiction would be unnecessary or duplicative.

In addition, delegates at the Rome Conference were committed to concluding the treaty in five weeks, and the inclusion of terrorism was proving to be a sticking point in the negotiations.

With respect to the politicization argument, states contended that the inclusion of terrorism would impede ratification of the Rome Statute for fear of politicized prosecutions and proceedings, especially in cases in which states were battling subversive groups or internal rebellions. As one scholar has noted, terrorism "is not only a phenomenon, it is also an invective, and there are many examples of States using this invective in a most subjective manner to de-legitimize and demonize political opponents, associations or other States."[10] This argument overlooks the fact that many of the crimes within the jurisdiction of the Court have significant political ramifications, not the least of which is the crime of aggression.

Terrorism was also excluded under the rationale that effective systems of national and international cooperation are already in place for the prosecution of terrorism crimes. Because governments are usually the direct or indirect target of terrorist acts, states are highly motivated to prosecute criminally acts of terrorism, to cooperate with each other toward this end, and to encourage the pursuit of civil actions by victims. Indeed, as compared to the "atrocity crimes," terrorism crimes are more often incorporated into domestic penal codes and are more frequently prosecuted by states. Given this observation, it was argued that the principle of complementarity would likely prevent the prosecution of acts of terrorism before the ICC in many cases.* Moreover, it was argued that effective

---

*The principle of complementarity is fundamental to the ICC framework and provides that the Court will exercise jurisdiction only where the relevant domestic authorities (for example, the territorial and nationality states) are either unwilling or unable to prosecute offenders. Notably, complementarity is not triggered, at least according to the plain text of Article 17, where the domestic courts are overly zealous toward prosecutions or where the defendant's due

counterterrorism requires "long-term planning, infiltration into the organizations involved, the necessity of giving immunity to some individuals involved, and so forth"[11] — all functions more effectively exercised by national jurisdictions than an international court far from the events in question and the relevant political milieu.

In the end, the final ICC Statute supports jurisdiction over only the four core crimes, namely genocide, crimes against humanity, war crimes, and the undefined crime of aggression. Some drafters remained uneasy with this result and managed to secure the adoption of Resolution E at the Rome Conference, which recommended that a review conference assemble in 2009 or 2010 to consider the inclusion of the crime of terrorism in the ICC Statute. As this Conference approaches, many states and scholars continue to argue that terrorism should eventually be included within the Court's jurisdiction. In particular, these advocates question the assumption made during the Rome Conference — which occurred in 1998, prior to the attacks of September 11, 2001 — that terrorism is not a serious crime of international concern. They argue that terrorism represents a substantial and growing threat, especially given the possibility of attacks with nuclear, chemical, or biological weapons of mass destruction.

Although there is no question that the threat of terrorism enjoys a greater level of international recognition and concern since the Rome Conference, the question of how best to address terrorist crimes as a legal matter is still very much an open one. One of the fundamental issues is whether the more established international crimes currently within the jurisdiction of the ICC adequately provide redress for terrorist acts, or whether there is a jurisdictional lacunae that needs to be filled.

---

process rights are potentially in jeopardy — two risks for terrorism prosecutions where the state is the target of the acts in question.

THE INTERFACE BETWEEN TERRORISM AND WAR

One of the challenges to creating a penal regime for acts of terrorism stems from the fact that the crimes encompassed within the concept of terrorism sit at the intersection of the *jus ad bellum* (governing the legality of the resort to armed force *ab inicio*) and the *jus in bello* (governing the legality of the use of armed force and the conduct of hostilities once an armed conflict has been initiated). As was discussed in Chapter 6 on the legal regulation of war, contemporary international law treats these two bodies of law as conceptually distinct. Yet acts of terrorism are often justified by the justness of the cause on behalf of which they are committed. Indeed, there remains a deep-seated unwillingness within segments of the international community to fully relinquish the idea that certain forms of otherwise prohibited violence are legitimate if they are employed in opposition to a colonial, racist, alien, occupying, or oppressive regime by a group seeking independence or self-determination. In such situations of asymmetrical power, an armed conflict fought "according to the rules" would undoubtedly result in a military victory for the dominant power; thus, the apparent inevitability of terrorism. This also explains the rhetorical persistence of the bromide "One man's terrorist is another man's freedom fighter."

Likewise, a certain degree of uncertainty surrounds the interface between the law governing the crimes of terrorism and IHL. This is especially true where terrorists' organizational capabilities and destructive potential rival that of conventional militaries. Acts that would be criminal under domestic law, or would constitute acts of terrorism under the various treaty prohibitions against terrorism, may be lawful acts of war under IHL when committed within the context of an armed conflict. This section attempts to untangle these bodies of law based on a series of scenarios.

Violent Acts Committed Within International Armed Conflicts

Imagine two signatories to the 1949 Geneva Conventions and their Protocols, Alpha and Beta, at war with each other. Alpha's troops launch two attacks against Beta's troops: one on a traditional battlefield along the border between the two states and one against a military barracks within Beta's territory in the dead of night while Beta's troops are asleep. Both attacks by Alpha's combatants against Beta's combatants are legitimate acts of warfare. Combatants representing nation states at war with each other are deemed "privileged belligerents," which is to say that under IHL they are entitled to use force against each other. Combatants and military installations are lawful objects of attack. Assuming the only individuals deliberately targeted are combatants, and that appropriate levels of force and types of weaponry are utilized, this attack generates no prosecutable event by Beta, Alpha, or the international community. Presumably, if Beta attempted to prosecute either of these acts as war crimes or as violations of domestic law, the defendants would have a strong defense of combat immunity that would find support in IHL and trump domestic law as the *lex specialis*. Thus, although we often think of the laws of armed conflict as limiting the use of force, the same laws provide legal justification for certain acts of violence that would otherwise be illegal outside of an armed conflict.

By contrast, imagine an attack by Alpha's troops against a civilian hospital that contained no Beta military personnel and served no military purpose. A deliberate attack by Alpha's combatants on Beta's civilians (that is, noncombatants) and on a civilian object in the context of an international armed conflict is the quintessential war crime. The perpetrators of this act remain privileged belligerents, but they become war criminals when they deliberately misuse their military might against a protected class of persons or target. Alpha's combatants may be prosecuted for the war crimes of willfully killing protected persons or the "extensive destruction and appropriation of property, not justified by military necessity and carried out unlawfully and wantonly," within the lexicon of the 1949 Geneva Conventions.[12]

Violent Acts Committed Outside of Armed Conflict

Now, remove the state of war between Alpha and Beta, but imagine there exists a nonviolent political conflict between the two states over contested territory in Beta that is inhabited by individuals who practice the same religion as the inhabitants of Alpha. A deliberate armed attack on civilians hailing from Beta by a radical group hailing from Alpha whose members are motivated by some political or ideological purpose is the quintessential terrorist act. Under current international treaties governing terrorism, only the Terrorist Bombing Convention is implicated by this scenario, and even then only if a "place of public use," "state or government facility," "transportation system," or "infrastructure facility" is intentionally targeted using an "explosive or other legal device" as those terms are defined by the treaty. An attack on a civilian neighborhood would likely not qualify.

Either Alpha or Beta would be entitled to prosecute this act as the crime of murder, or attempted murder, under their domestic penal codes pursuant to the nationality or territorial principles of jurisdiction, respectively. If the penal codes of Alpha and Beta codify any crimes of terrorism or crimes against humanity, the attack may also be prosecutable as such under domestic law if the elements of those crimes are met. Without the existence of an armed conflict between the two states, IHL is not implicated and no war crimes have been committed. Likewise, the perpetrators from Alpha are not entitled to prisoner of war status when captured or any form of combatant immunity if prosecuted.

The distinction between war crimes and acts of terrorism seems relatively comprehensible under these scenarios. Once we start altering the operative variables, however, this categorization gets murkier.

The Initiation of an International Armed Conflict

Going back to our situation involving the radicalized group from Alpha, depending on how catastrophic the initial attack by Alpha was, how organized the perpetrators were, and whether the group was under the overall control of the government of Alpha, this violence may constitute the initiation of an international armed conflict between the two states, thus triggering the application of the IHL governing international armed conflicts and a right of Beta to engage in self-defense within the meaning of Article 51 of the UN Charter. (An attack by an organized militia not under the overall control of Alpha might constitute the initiation of a noninternational armed conflict within Beta, as discussed more fully later.)

Determining when IHL is initiated, and whether the rules governing international or noninternational armed conflicts apply, returns us to a topic in Chapter 6. Recall that the International Criminal Tribunal for the Former Yugoslavia (ICTY) in *Tadić* concluded that "an armed conflict exists whenever there is a resort to armed force between States or protracted armed violence between governmental authorities and organized armed groups or between such groups within a State."[13] The ICTY also noted that IHL applies "from the initiation of such armed conflicts and extends beyond the cessation of hostilities until a general conclusion of peace is reached."[14] In terms of conflict classification, an armed attack by the

formal armed forces of Alpha would constitute the initiation of an international armed conflict within the meaning of Article 2 of the Geneva Conventions. Likewise, an attack by an informal militia under the "overall control" of Alpha — the test devised by the ICTY to establish the existence of an *international* armed conflict — would also trigger the Geneva Conventions.*
This brings us full circle to our original IHL scenarios discussed earlier. Once the IHL governing international armed conflicts applies, acts that would otherwise be criminal under international or domestic law may become legitimate acts of war. A deliberate attack on civilians, however, is never a lawful act of war and could be prosecuted as a war crime.

Violent Acts Committed Within Noninternational Armed Conflicts

Another obvious amendment to our scenario involves entirely internalizing the conflict. Imagine a civil war within Beta in which citizens of Beta who practice the same religion as inhabitants of Alpha seek secession from Beta to achieve irredentist aspirations to join Alpha. In the dark of night, the secessionists attack Beta's military barracks and a civilian hospital.

The Geneva Conventions (by common Article 3) and Protocol II regulate military conduct in civil wars and other noninternational armed conflicts. The attack on the civilian hospital

---

*These militia might not qualify for prisoner of war treatment, however, if captured. Article 4 of Geneva III contemplates the involvement of "militias . . . belonging to a [High Contracting] Party to the conflict and operating in or outside their own territory" in addition to formal forces. To qualify as privileged belligerents, and to be entitled to prisoner of war treatment, these militia must (a) be commanded by a person responsible for his or her subordinates; (b) have a fixed distinctive sign recognizable at a distance; (c) carry arms openly; and (d) conduct their operations in accordance with the laws and customs of war.

is prohibited by common Article 3* and Articles 4 and 13 of Protocol II, which protect persons who do not take direct part in hostilities, including the civilian population. By contrast, neither instrument prohibits the attack on the military barracks. (The penal consequences of these acts are discussed later). Under IHL, Beta's combatants remain legitimate objects of attack even when they are not actively engaged in combat. In other words, once the fact of an armed conflict is established, members of the armed forces of a state are combatants, always considered to be taking a direct part in hostilities and thus targetable. It is only once they are officially *hors de combat* as a result of illness, injury, capture, or surrender that combatants may not be targeted. In our scenario, Beta's combatants have certainly "laid down their arms" for the night, but that terminology is not meant to cover combatants who have simply retired for the night. Indeed, the billeting of these combatants in the barracks is not dispositive; these individuals could conceivably be attacked in their homes as well, although IHL would condemn the deaths of any civilians deliberately targeted or the unintentional deaths of civilians if the force

---

*Common Article 3 reads in relevant part:

(1) Persons taking no active part in the hostilities, including members of armed forces who have laid down their arms and those placed "hors de combat" by sickness, wounds, detention, or any other cause, shall in all circumstances be treated humanely, without any adverse distinction founded on race, colour, religion or faith, sex, birth or wealth, or any other similar criteria. To this end, the following acts are and shall remain prohibited at any time and in any place whatsoever with respect to the above-mentioned persons:

(a) violence to life and person, in particular murder of all kinds, mutilation, cruel treatment and torture;

(b) taking of hostages;

(c) outrages upon personal dignity, in particular humiliating and degrading treatment;

(d) the passing of sentences and the carrying out of executions without previous judgment pronounced by a regularly constituted court, affording all the judicial guarantees which are recognized as indispensable by civilized peoples.

used was disproportional to any military advantage to be gained by attacking off-duty troops.

A rather unintuitive asymmetry in IHL reveals itself if we alter our facts a bit. Imagine that as our secessionists attack government troops, the government troops advance around the perimeter and attack the secessionists from behind, causing them to disband and scatter. Under IHL, this is a lawful act of war. The secessionists are taking direct part in hostilities and, as such, are lawful objects of attack. Further imagine that during this confrontation, government troops identified particular individuals during the attack who subsequently escaped capture. Can government troops later track these individuals down and kill them in their homes? The answer according to Protocol II is no. Unlike the government troops mentioned earlier, who are always considered to be taking direct part in hostilities and are thus always targetable, our secessionists are not technically combatants. As noncombatants, they may be targeted only when they are taking direct part in hostilities pursuant to Article 13(3) of Protocol II, which states "[c]ivilians shall enjoy the protection afforded by this part [not to be targeted], unless and for such time as they take a direct part in hostilities." This answer might change, however, if the secessionists were billeted in a rebel camp somewhere in the territory of the state, because this might still qualify as participation in hostilities. The thorny question of when precisely noncombatants "take a direct part in hostilities" is the subject of ongoing discussions within the International Committee of the Red Cross pursuant to a joint initiative with the T.M.C. Asser Institute in the Netherlands.

The Initiation of a Noninternational Armed Conflict

To alter our scenario somewhat again, imagine the same situation as given previously in which a group of individuals in Beta who practice the same religion as inhabitants of Alpha desire secession from Beta to join Alpha. Assume that, for the moment, this is merely a political and not an armed conflict. Imagine that the group in Beta radicalizes and eventually decides to utilize violence within Beta to draw attention to their cause. Eventually, the group becomes more and more organized and the violence escalates in terms of the frequency and severity of attacks. At a certain point, the IHL governing a noninternational armed conflict will begin to apply.

Recall from Chapter 6 that common Article 3 and Protocol II have different thresholds of applicability.* The former requires simply an armed conflict "occurring in the territory of one of the High Contracting Parties," with the ICTY defining "armed conflict" as "protracted armed violence between governmental authorities and organized armed groups." The latter (at Article 1(1)) requires an armed conflict within the territory of a party to the Conventions in which the non-state actors are under responsible command and exercise a degree of control over the state's territory that enables them "to carry out sustained and concerted military operations and to implement [the] Protocol." The Protocol at Article 1(2) makes clear that it does not apply to "situations of internal disturbances and tensions, such as riots, isolated and sporadic acts of violence and other acts of a similar nature." If our secessionists do not meet this standard — for example, if they possess no territory or are not under responsible command — their acts of violence will be governed only by common Article 3.

---

*In *Hamdan v. Rumsfeld* (548 U.S. 557 (2006)), for example, the U.S. Supreme Court determined that common Article 3 applied to the armed conflict between the United States and al Qaeda.

The Penal Consequences of Violent Acts Committed Within Noninternational Armed Conflicts

Classic IHL, as derived from the four Geneva Conventions of 1949 and their Protocols, would treat all these events quite differently than would modern IHL in terms of their penal consequences. Most important, although the Geneva Conventions identify a list of "grave breaches" that constitute war crimes under IHL, neither common Article 3 nor Protocol II creates, or mandates the domestic creation of, a penal regime for noninternational armed conflicts. As a result, if we consider only the Geneva Conventions and their Protocols, any penal liability for acts of violence committed within a noninternational armed conflict would be governed by domestic law.

So, assuming that Beta has domestically incorporated the Geneva Conventions and their Protocols, but gone no further, the killing by the secessionists of civilian patients in the hospital and members of Beta's military quartered in their barracks would be treated as acts of ordinary murder by Beta's authorities. The crimes against both targets may thus be treated exactly the same; it is of no moment that the military barracks would be a lawful object of attack within the context of an international armed conflict. The classic treaty law governing noninternational armed conflicts entitles states to treat our secessionists as common criminals rather than privileged belligerents. Individuals who are not considered privileged belligerents under IHL are not entitled to combatant immunity for what would otherwise be lawful acts of war. Nor, for that matter, need they be treated as prisoners of war when they are captured, but the state's standard constitutional and human rights protections would still apply.

Some states have gone beyond their treaty obligations and domestically penalized certain violations of the Geneva treaty provisions governing noninternational armed conflicts. The

United States did so with the passage of the 1996 War Crimes Act.* The original version of that statute defined war crimes to include acts that constitute "a violation of common Article 3 of the international conventions signed at Geneva, 12 August 1949, or any protocol to such convention to which the United States is a party and which deals with non-international armed conflict." Common Article 3(1)(a) prohibits "violence to life and person, in particular murder of all kinds" when committed against a person "taking no active part in the hostilities, including members of armed forces who have laid down their arms." As codified as a war crime in U.S. law, this provision would render the secessionists' attack against the civilian hospital the war crime of violence to life and murder. (The attack could also be prosecuted as ordinary murder under U.S. law.) Because common Article 3 does not prohibit the attack on the government barracks, it would generate no criminal liability under the U.S. war crimes statute. It, too, however, could be prosecuted under the domestic penal code.

Modern developments in IHL have significantly expanded the concept of war crimes. In particular, the statutes of the two ad hoc criminal tribunals, and the jurisprudence thereunder, significantly collapsed the distinction between international and noninternational armed conflicts in terms of the penal consequences of acts of violence within the latter. In so doing, the tribunals now regularly prosecute violations of treaty provisions that are not identified as crimes by the treaties themselves. For example, the general prohibition against inflicting

---

*The original version of the War Crimes Act of 1996 criminalized all violations of common Article 3 of the Geneva Conventions so long as they were committed by or against a member of the Armed Forces of the United States or a national of the United States. 18 U.S.C. § 2441(3). A subsequent amendment to this statute by the Military Commissions Act of 2006 decriminalized certain violations of common Article 3, namely "(c) outrages upon personal dignity, in particular humiliating and degrading treatment" and "(d) the passing of sentences and the carrying out of executions without previous judgment pronounced by a regularly constituted court, affording all the judicial guarantees which are recognized as indispensable by civilized peoples."

terror on a population appears in the Additional Protocols to the 1949 Geneva Conventions at Article 51(2) in Additional Protocol I and Article 13(2) in Additional Protocol II.* In *Prosecutor v. Galić*, the ICTY had occasion to interpret these provisions when the prosecution charged the defendant with "inflicting terror on the civilian population" as a war crime under Article 3 of the ICTY Statute (providing for jurisdiction over an exemplary list of "violations of the laws and customs of war"). Even though neither of these provisions contemplates individual criminal liability or defines "spreading terror" as a criminal offense, the ICTY nonetheless convicted the defendants of the charged crime. In particular, the ICTY identified the following elements of the crime of inflicting terror on the civilian population:

(i) Acts of violence directed against the civilian population or individual civilians not taking direct part in hostilities causing death or serious injury to body or health within the civilian population.

(ii) The offender willfully made the civilian population or individual civilians not taking direct part in hostilities the object of those acts of violence.

(iii) The above offence was committed with the primary purpose of spreading terror among the civilian population.[15]

The tribunals' approach to war crimes in noninternational armed conflicts was largely adopted and codified by the ICC Statute at Article 8.** This suggests an emergent customary international law governing the commission of war crimes in noninternational armed conflicts. Most states, however, could

---

*These provisions identically provide that "[t]he civilian population as such, as well as individual civilians, shall not be the object of attack. Acts or threats of violence the primary purpose of which is to spread terror among the civilian population are prohibited." Article 4(2) of Protocol II also prohibits "acts of terrorism" against civilians or others *hors de combat* as a Fundamental Guarantee.

**Domestic war crimes statutes are increasingly following suit as states adjust their penal codes after ratification of the ICC Statute. This suggests that customary international law now recognizes the possibility of war crimes being committed within noninternational armed conflicts.

not prosecute such acts without first incorporating these prohibitions into their domestic penal codes.

PROSECUTING ACTS OF TERRORISM BEFORE THE ICC

Despite the clear omission of terrorism from the ICC Statute, some argue that the Court could adjudicate certain acts of terrorism within its existing subject matter jurisdiction. This is because in certain situations, acts of terrorism may satisfy the elements of other international crimes. As exemplified earlier, the high degree of intersection between acts of terrorism and war crimes suggests that the former may be prosecutable before the ICC and other international tribunals with jurisdiction over war crimes.

Considering our scenarios involving states Alpha and Beta, the ICC could consider Alpha's attack on the hospital, if committed during an international armed conflict, to qualify as the following war crimes, *inter alia*, within the Rome Statute:

- Willful killing (Article 8(2)(a)(i));
- Violence to life and persons (Article 8(2)(a)(iii);
- Extensive destruction of property . . . not justified by military necessity (Article 8(2)(a)(iv));
- Intentionally attacking civilians (Article 8(2)(b)(i));
- Intentionally directing attacks against civilian objects (Article 8(2)(b)(ii)); or
- Intentionally directing attacks against hospitals (Article 8(2)(e)(iv)).

Likewise, if the attack on the hospital occurred within the context of a noninternational armed conflict, the following provisions may be applicable:

- Violence to life and person, in particular murder (Article 8(2)(c)(i));

- Intentionally directing attacks against civilians (Article 8(2)(e)(i)); or
- Intentionally attacking hospitals (Article 8(2)(e)(iv)).

Note that neither Article 51(2) of Additional Protocol I nor Article 13(2) of Additional Protocol II was included in these lists.

None of the provisions of Article 8 penalizes the attack on the military barracks, whether committed in an international or noninternational armed conflict. The targeting of a military objective is generally a lawful act of war; however, it becomes a war crime where disproportionate force is used such that there is an incidental loss of life, long-term or severe environmental damage, or superfluous injury.* Absent this, any prosecution of the barracks attack would have to occur before domestic courts under domestic law.

In addition to these war crimes, where violent acts (such as murder, torture, or kidnapping) are committed within the context of a widespread or systematic attack against a civilian population, they may constitute crimes against humanity under Article 7. The definition of crimes against humanity in the ICC Statute requires proof that the attack was "pursuant to or in furtherance of a State or organizational policy to commit such attack" (Article 7(2)(a)). Presumably, many terrorist groups could be shown to possess such a policy to attack civilians. Terrorist attacks may also implicate the prohibition against genocide, where the acts target a protected group with the intent to destroy that group. Although there are many instances of acts of terrorism being directed against a protected group (such as those committed during "the troubles" in Northern Ireland or even the attacks of September 11, 2001), it may be

---

*Article 8 prohibits the use of weapons that cause unnecessary or superfluous suffering, such as poison or poisoned weapons, asphyxiating gases, or so-called dum dum bullets (bullets that expand on impact). *See* ICC Statute, Articles 8(2)(b)(xvii)–(xx).

difficult to prove the specific intent to commit genocide as opposed to the intent to intimidate or coerce a government— the hallmark of terrorism.

Isolated or exceptional violent acts, committed in times of peace (or without any nexus to an armed conflict) and absent more systemic repression, might not be considered a war crime or a crime against humanity. Prosecuting such acts at the international level may require the existence of a stand-alone crime of terrorism. As you review the terrorism materials in your course, and the degree of normative redundancy in ICL, reflect on whether terrorism crimes should be expressly included within the ICC Statute or whether such acts are better prosecuted before domestic courts. In addition, given the clear intent of the majority of drafters to exclude crimes of terrorism from the ICC, consider to what extent the ICC should apply its existing crimes to acts that would otherwise be considered acts of terrorism under the terrorism treaties or pursuant to an emerging customary international law prohibition.

~ 8 ~

Genocide and Crimes Against Humanity

G enocide and crimes against humanity are the criminal counterparts of many human rights prohibitions. Called "atrocity crimes" by some, these two great crimes sit at the pinnacle of international criminal law (ICL). This chapter presents the history and scope of genocide and crimes against humanity, and the relationship between them, with an eye toward exploring their division of labor in ICL and whether a conceptual distinction between them should be maintained.

Although an ancient scourge, the concept of genocide as a distinct international crime arose out of the Nazi Holocaust and World War II. We think of Nazi crimes as the paradigmatic case of genocide, but treaty codification of the crime came too late to prosecute anyone for what has sometimes been called "the crime of crimes." The perpetrators of the Nazi Holocaust were instead prosecuted for crimes against humanity, another international crime that traces its formal origins to the World War II period. Although genocide became the subject of a dedicated multilateral treaty in 1948, additional codification of crimes against humanity beyond the charters for the two post–World War II tribunals did not happen until the UN

Security Council created the International Criminal Tribunal for the Former Yugoslavia (ICTY) in 1993.

In addition to a shared history, the two crimes are also conceptually similar. Crimes against humanity are a constellation of acts made criminal under international law when they are committed within the context of a widespread and systematic attack against a civilian population with knowledge of that attack. This crime's very name captures two important facets of the crime: Crimes against humanity are considered to be committed against all of humanity, not just the individual victims or their immediate communities, and crimes against humanity "violat[e] the core humanity that we all share and that distinguishes us from other natural beings."[1] Genocide involves the commission of one of a set of enumerated acts against members of a protected group with the intent to destroy the group, in whole or in part. The goal of genocide is thus to eradicate a very segment of humanity, defined by race, ethnicity, religion, or nationality.

Notwithstanding this similarity, there are clear doctrinal distinctions between crimes against humanity and genocide. First, only acts committed against groups identified by a common race, ethnicity, religion, or nationality may qualify as genocide; criminal acts committed against any "civilian population," not necessarily defined by any common group identity, can qualify as crimes against humanity. Second, genocide requires that the perpetrator have the specific intent to "destroy" a group because its members share a common racial, ethnic, religious, or national identity, whereas crimes against humanity do not require any form of specific intent. Third, crimes rise to the level of crimes against humanity when they are committed within the context of a "widespread or systematic" attack against a civilian population; there is no similar threshold qualification for genocide. As a result, a single isolated act (such as the killing of a member of a protected group) could qualify as genocide if the perpetrator acted with the requisite specific intent,[2] whereas a single isolated act against a civilian is unlikely to qualify as a crime against humanity on its own.

Given the parallels between these two crimes, this chapter expressly raises the question of whether there is a legal justification for continuing to distinguish between these two types of crimes, or whether the acts of crimes against humanity encompass all those that would also qualify as genocide in all circumstances. Most pressing is the question of whether the unique characteristics of the crime of genocide warrant preserving the two separate crimes. To guide our inquiry, this chapter provides the basic history of the two crimes followed by a discussion of their elemental similarities and differences.

CRIMES AGAINST HUMANITY

Crimes against humanity were first codified in response to the atrocities of World War II. There were, however, some earlier references to crimes against the laws of humanity during the post–World War I period, when international prosecutions were first contemplated. In particular, the deportation and massacre of the Armenian population of the Ottoman Empire prompted the Allied governments of France, Great Britain, and Russia to issue in 1915 a joint Declaration to the Ottoman Empire denouncing these acts as "crimes against humanity and civilization for which all the members of the Turkish Government will be held responsible together with its agents implicated in the massacres."[3] The majority of the Allies originally envisioned international trials against "[a]ll persons belonging to enemy countries, however high their position may have been, without distinction of rank, including Chiefs of States, who have been guilty of offences against the laws and customs of war or the laws of humanity."[4] The U.S. delegation dissented from the reference to crimes against humanity, arguing that the notion of crimes committed against all of humanity was too inchoate and contextual to support criminal justice. The U.S. position ultimately prevailed, and the 1919 Treaty of Versailles ending World War I excluded reference to "crimes against humanity" in the provisions addressing criminal responsibility (Articles 228–229).[5] In the end, the whole project of international justice was scrapped, and only a few trials before domestic tribunals were held.

When the prospect of international criminal justice was revived at the end of World War II, it was clear that existing ICL would be insufficient to condemn the full horror of the recent war. As philosopher Hannah Arendt wrote, the Holocaust was "a new crime, [a] crime against humanity — in the sense of a crime 'against the human status,' or against the very nature of mankind."[6] More precisely, the well-established prohibitions against war crimes did not reach the acts of international aggression committed against peaceful states or acts of violence committed against a state's own civilians or against civilians from allied countries. The framers of the Nuremberg Charter thus dusted off the previously discarded concept of crimes against humanity to address the latter phenomenon, in many ways the defining brutality of the Nazi enterprise.* Although the crime of aggression — deemed "the greatest menace of our times" — was the centerpiece of the Charter and the Nuremberg Trial, the notion of crimes against humanity has proven to be the real legacy of Nuremberg, albeit with chronic definitional confusion.

---

*The charge of crimes against the peace, now termed the crime of aggression, was devised to address the crimes committed against the society of sovereign states, the traditional subject of public international law. Crimes against humanity addressed crimes against all of humankind, cutting across particular state affiliations. The notion that humanity itself could be the victim of an international crime is at the core of the human rights movement, which also traces its broadest roots to the post–World War II period.

Unlike the crimes of genocide, torture, and crimes against humanity never became the subje prehensive penal treaty in the postwar period. considerable definitional confusion has plagued the crime over its life span. During the negotiations surrounding the International Law Commission's (ILC) Draft Code of Crimes Against the Peace and Security of Mankind, drafters experimented with various elements of the crime in an effort to arrive at a consensus definition. The hodgepodge of definitions produced by the ILC and national legislatures did little to satisfy the principle of legality. It was not until the promulgation of the statutes of the two ad hoc international criminal tribunals that an official modern definition emerged. Yet, in spite of the proximity in time and subject matter of the statutes of the two ad hoc tribunals — essentially Irish twins of the Security Council — their definitions of the crime contain significant variations.

The International Criminal Tribunal for Rwanda (ICTR) definition of crimes against humanity includes a requirement that the attack against a civilian population be "on national, political, ethnic, racial, or religious grounds." This addition of a discriminatory motive to the definition is an anomaly; no legal definition before or since has included such a requirement. The ICTY definition was also not without its unique aspects, reintroducing the nexus to armed conflict requirement that was present at Nuremberg but that all had assumed was no longer a necessary condition for an act to constitute a crime against humanity. These definitions, including their noted idiosyncrasies, were further refined in the case law of the two tribunals. All these doctrinal developments were codified, with some additional modifications, in a consensus definition in Article 7 of the Statute of the International Criminal Court (ICC). Through this iterative process of codification and interpretation, many definitional issues left open in the postwar period have been finally resolved, as discussed in greater detail later.

The prohibition against crimes against humanity is increasingly important in ICL. It applies where the prohibition against genocide does not, such as where the group targeted is not a protected group (i.e., it is not a national, religious, ethnic, or national group) or where the defendant did not act with the specific intent to destroy the group. It also applies where the technical requirements of the war crimes prohibitions are not satisfied, such as where there is no armed conflict or where the victims do not constitute "protected persons." Finally, the crime against humanity of "persecution" is potentially far reaching, as it may "criminalize" violations of certain economic, social, and cultural rights.

GENOCIDE

Unlike crimes against humanity, the term *genocide* occupies a singular position in our lexicon. Yet a variance exists between the legal or technical definition of genocide, as embodied within the Convention on the Prevention and Punishment of the Crime of Genocide (the Genocide Convention) and its progeny, and lay conceptions of the crime.[7] The exclusion of certain instances of mass killing from the legal definition of genocide (although such killings often qualify as crimes against humanity) generates extreme dissatisfaction among victim groups who define their own experience in terms of genocide, which they view as the supreme international crime.[8] This disjuncture is in many respects the result of a series of political compromises that occurred during the drafting of the Genocide Convention. Modern adjudications of the crime of genocide have to a certain degree begun to unravel these compromises, although the technical requirements in the definition of the crime continue to challenge international criminal lawyers.

Genocide is a modern word for an old crime. The term was originally coined by Polish jurist Raphael Lemkin, who, after learning of the Armenian massacre of World War I, campaigned tirelessly for the drafting of a multilateral treaty prohibiting the crime. Despite his efforts, it took the events of World War II to compel the international community to finally bring Lemkin's project to fruition. The charters of the Nuremberg and Tokyo Tribunals did not include genocide as an enumerated crime; instead, they provided for the prosecution of war crimes, crimes against humanity, and crimes against the peace. However, the Nuremberg indictment did charge the Nazi defendants with committing genocide, which it defined as "the extermination of racial and national groups . . . in certain occupied territories in order to destroy particular races and classes of people, and national, racial or religious groups, particularly Jews, Poles, and Gypsies."[9] Further, the Judgment clearly addressed acts that would amount to genocide under the contemporary definition of the crime.

Following the Nuremberg Judgment in 1946, the UN General Assembly took up the matter of genocide and passed a resolution confirming that genocide constituted a crime under international law, the punishment of which was a matter of international concern.[10] The unanimous resolution also recommended that the United Nations draw up a draft convention on genocide to be submitted to the full General Assembly for signature and ratification. Throughout this drafting process, the provisions concerning the element of intent (*mens rea*), the enumerated protected groups, the inclusion of cultural genocide, and application of universal jurisdiction received the most intense debate. The Convention entered into force in January 1951 and, to date, it has been ratified by 133 states.

THE ELEMENTS OF THE TWO CRIMES

Like many international crimes, crimes against humanity and genocide are characterized by two sets of elements.* The first set of elements is referred to as the *chapeau* ("hat") of the definition of the crime.[11] The *chapeau* elements apply to any subsequent enumeration of prohibited acts. Thus, for an act to qualify as either a crime against humanity or genocide, it must meet the requirements of these *chapeau* elements. For genocide, the *chapeau* requires that the perpetrator acted with "the intent to destroy, in whole or in part, a national, ethnical, racial, or religious group, as such." For crimes against humanity, the key *chapeau* elements are twofold: The perpetrator's act must be "part of a widespread or systematic attack directed against any civilian population" and the perpetrator must have acted "with knowledge of the attack."

The second set of elements identifies the specific acts (such as killings) that, if committed in the context of the elements set forth in the *chapeau*, qualify as either a crime against humanity or an act of genocide. As with the *chapeau* elements, the definitions of genocide and crimes against humanity include very different constituent acts.

The *Chapeau* Elements

The *chapeau* elements of the definition of crimes against humanity and genocide contain the core difference between these two crimes. We compare four significant issues raised by the *chapeau* elements of each of these crimes. First, and most significant, is the *mens rea* requirement of each. Second is the

---

*We focus here on the definitions of crimes against humanity and genocide as set forth in the Rome Treaty. As noted earlier, the definition of crimes against humanity varies among the Rome Treaty and the statutes of the ad hoc tribunals. All definitions of genocide mirror that found in the Genocide Convention.

definition of the victim group for each crime. Related to this second issue is a third issue of whether an armed conflict is necessary to prove a crime against humanity, an issue that does not arise with respect to the crime of genocide. Fourth is the question of whether either crime requires the showing of a formal policy or plan as an element of the offense.

Mens Rea and the Challenge of Specific Intent

The concept of *mens rea* — the mental component of criminal liability — is a fundamental precept of the criminal law, as the definitions of most crimes contain such a subjective element (with the exception of a limited quantity of strict liability regulatory crimes). To be found guilty, a defendant must have committed a criminal act (*actus reus*) with the required mental state (*mens rea*). With respect to most crimes, a prosecutor must show that the defendant acted either intentionally or with reckless disregard to the potential consequences of his or her action. It may also be sufficient if the perpetrator acts with knowledge of particular facts or circumstances.

The most significant difference between crimes against humanity and genocide is the *mens rea* element of specific intent (*dolus specialis*) required for genocide. The notion of specific intent indicates that the perpetrator acted with the intent to bring about a certain consequence. In the case of genocide, this consequence is the complete or partial destruction of a protected group. Accordingly, to make out a charge of genocide, the prosecutor must demonstrate that the accused acted with the specific intent to destroy a protected group in whole or in part. This mental state transforms what would otherwise be a municipal law crime (such as murder) or a crime against humanity (such as extermination) into genocide — the "crime of crimes."[12] This distinguishing feature of genocide makes it a particularly difficult crime to prove. Prosecutors may thus choose to charge someone with a crime against humanity rather than genocide if the evidence of specific intent is weak.

By contrast, the ICTY and ICTR Statutes contain no express *mens rea* element for crimes against humanity. Nonetheless, the tribunals have through their jurisprudence constructed a two-tier *mens rea* for the crime: One *mens rea* requirement relates to the particular charged constitutive act and the other is essentially a *chapeau* element that applies to all crimes against humanity. With respect to the latter, it must be shown that the defendant knew that his or her actions were part of the widespread or systematic attack against the civilian population. This overarching *mens rea* is in addition to the primary *mens rea* that is required for the underlying constitutive offense, such as murder (the intent to kill) or deportation (the intent to transport someone across an international boundary). The drafters of the ICC Statute adopted this approach in Article 7. The ICC's Elements of Crimes make clear that the defendant need not have knowledge of all details of the attack or any underlying plan or policy.[13] Indeed, knowledge of the attack can be actual or constructive.[14]

Although proving the *mens rea* required for crimes against humanity may be challenging, it is far less onerous on its face than the specific intent required to prove genocide. Absent a guilty plea or incriminating manifesto (something that most *génocidaires* have today learned to avoid), it is difficult to ascertain whether an accused in fact acted with the necessary specific intent. The two ad hoc tribunals, however, have developed a jurisprudence with respect to the specific intent requirement that allows an inference to be drawn with respect to the mental state of the accused from the surrounding nature of the crimes alleged and other contextual factors. For evidence of specific intent, the tribunals have looked at, *inter alia*, the relative proportionate scale and systematicity of the actual or attempted destruction, the status of the victims, the existence of discriminatory propaganda, the nature of the acts committed, attendant acts of violence, and statements or speeches made at the time the acts were committed. For example, the Trial Chamber of the ICTR noted that:

> in the absence of a confession from the accused, his intent can be inferred from a certain number of presumptions of fact. . . . [I]t is possible to deduce the genocidal intent inherent in a particular act charged from the general context of the perpetration of other culpable acts systematically directed against that same group, whether these acts were committed by the same offender or by others. Other factors, such as the scale of atrocities committed, their general nature, in a region or a country, or furthermore, the fact of deliberately and systematically targeting victims on account of their membership of a particular group, while excluding the members of other groups, can enable the Chamber to infer the genocidal intent of a particular act. [It is also] possible to infer the genocidal intention that presided over the commission of a particular act, *inter alia*, from all acts or utterances of the accused.[15]

Can one look to the commission of acts that would not themselves qualify for genocide as evidence of genocidal intent? A Trial Chamber of the ICTY has so ruled. In the Rule 61 proceedings confirming the indictment against Radovan Karadžić and Ratko Mladić, a Trial Chamber of the ICTY noted that genocidal intent may also be inferred from "the perpetration of acts which violate, or which the perpetrators themselves consider to violate, the very foundation of the group — acts which are not in themselves covered by the list in Article 4(2) [corresponding to Article II of the Genocide Convention] but which are committed as part of the same pattern of conduct."[16] In other words, even acts that would not satisfy the *actus reus* element of genocide, such as acts of economic discrimination or "cultural genocide" (the destruction of the cultural manifestations of a protected group), may support a finding that an accused acted with genocidal intent.* The existence of acts of cultural genocide — such as the destruction of centers of learning, cultural artifacts, houses of worship, or other institutions associated with a particular group — also neutralize arguments that casualties within the protected group were incidental to a traditional armed conflict. The ICTY Trial Chamber in the case against Krstić noted that "the deliberate destruction of mosques and houses belonging to members of the group" was evidence of an intent to destroy the Bosnian Muslims.[17]

This circumstantial and inferential approach to genocidal intent does not mean that international tribunals are quick to conclude that an accused is guilty of genocide. In the case against Goran Jelisić, a Trial Chamber of the ICTY acquitted the defendant on a single count of genocide, finding no genocidal intent despite some direct evidence pointing to such an intent.[18] Jelisić had, among other things, called himself the "Serb Adolf," stated that his mission was to "kill Muslims," and admitted that he had killed a number of Muslim individuals because they were Muslims. The Trial Chamber concluded that although the defendant acted with "discriminatory intent," he did not act with the requisite specific intent to destroy the Muslim group. In particular, the Trial Chamber ruled that the evidence did not establish that there was a plan or policy in place to kill Muslim individuals. (We discuss the plan or policy issue with respect to genocide and crimes against

---

*Lemkin's conception of the crime of genocide encompassed all forms of destruction of a group as a distinct social entity. Accordingly, early formulations of the legal prohibition against genocide defined the crime broadly to involve coordinated actions against a protected collectivity's culture, religion, language, and social institutions as well as physical acts of violence. The drafters of the Genocide Convention, however, ultimately excluded reference to acts of "cultural genocide" on the grounds that such an offense was too vague and too far removed from physical destruction to merit inclusion in the treaty. The crime of forcibly transferring children from the protected group is a vestige of this notion of cultural genocide.

humanity later.) The Trial Chamber implied that although it may be theoretically possible for a single person to commit genocide acting alone, it would be difficult to do so. In this case, the Chamber found that the defendant "killed arbitrarily rather than with a clear intention to destroy a group."[19]

On appeal, the Appeals Chamber reversed. It reviewed the evidence and determined that the defendant believed himself to be following a plan established by superiors to eradicate the Muslim population of Brčko and that, regardless of the existence of such a plan, Jelisić was on "a one-man genocide mission, intent upon personally wiping out the protected group."[20] Accordingly, the Appeals Chamber ruled that a reasonable finder of fact could have convicted the defendant of genocide and so the motion for acquittal should not have been granted.

The ad hoc tribunals have also lessened the difficulties associated with proving specific intent by removing it as a requirement in cases involving accomplice liability to genocide. The Genocide Convention at Article III prohibits "complicity in genocide" along with genocide, conspiracy to commit genocide, and direct and public incitement to commit genocide. The same types of liability are recognized by the ad hoc tribunals and the ICC. With respect to cases against individuals accused of being accomplices to genocide, the ad hoc tribunals have held that the accomplice need only act "knowingly" with respect to the primary perpetrator, thus paving the way for genocide convictions without genocidal intent. In other words, under this approach, if a defendant charged with complicity knew that the principal actor was acting with the specific intent to commit genocide, the accomplice could be liable for genocide as well, even though the accomplice did not himself or herself possess genocidal intent. If the defendant accomplice did not know the principal offender was acting with genocidal intent, however, the accomplice could only be charged as an accessory to the predicate act (for example, murder or cruel treatment).[21] This result is not without its detractors. It has been argued that genocide is — by definition — a specific-intent crime such that anyone convicted of genocide must possess the special *mens rea* that sets genocide apart from other international or domestic crimes.

What about a subordinate who acts pursuant to the orders or direction of a superior? Can a subordinate who committed an enumerated act, such as the killing of members of a protected group, escape a charge of genocide by arguing that he or she acted under superior orders and thus did not himself or herself possess the requisite genocidal intent? The ICTY confirmed that under international law generally, the fact that a defendant acted under superior orders does not absolve him or her of liability for the acts committed, although such a defense may mitigate punishment. However, it has yet to be determined whether the fact that a subordinate acted under superior orders could negate the intent requirement to transform a municipal crime or a crime against humanity into genocide. Notably, Article 33 of the Rome Statute states that "orders to commit genocide . . . are manifestly unlawful," thereby signaling that acting under superior orders may not mitigate punishment or negate the intent requirement before the ICC.

Protected Groups

The second major element distinguishing genocide from crimes against humanity is the definition of the victim group. The definition of the protected group within the prohibition against crimes against humanity is broad, merely requiring that crimes take place within the context of an attack "directed against a civilian population." This element is satisfied where the civilian population is the primary object of attack and may be proven with reference to "the means and method used in the course of the attack, the status of the victims, their number, the discriminatory nature of the attack, the nature of the crimes committed in its course, the resistance to the assailants at the time, and the extent to which the attacking force may be said to have complied or attempted to comply with the precautionary requirements of the laws of war."[22]

In developing a jurisprudence around crimes against humanity, the ad hoc tribunals have given content to the notion of a *civilian population*. Although the interpretive issues with respect to civilian population are not as prominent or perhaps as consequential as those raised with respect to the definition of protected groups under genocide, as discussed later, the ad hoc tribunals have also clarified some of the open issues and have generally interpreted the term in a way that expands, rather than contracts, the definition of crimes against humanity.

One issue with respect to the definition of civilian population concerns the presence of combatants as victims. In other words, if an attack is directed against civilians and combatants (for example, members of a guerrilla movement), is this attack more correctly characterized as a war crime rather than a crime against humanity? The jurisprudence of the ad hoc tribunals has established that so long as the population is "predominantly civilian,"[23] even if it is actively involved in a resistance movement,[24] this element is satisfied. Crimes against humanity may also be committed against combatants who are *hors de combat*, thus giving rise to a potential overlap between the prohibitions against war crimes and crimes against humanity during situations of armed conflict.[25] This overlap has been cited as justification for the elimination of the distinction between war crimes and crimes against humanity (and even perhaps genocide). As one former ICTY prosecutor reasoned, "[i]ssues relating to classification of a conflict, the significance of the law of war to that conflict, or the jurisdiction of a tribunal over an alleged act of genocide would all fade into insignificance if they were brought within the rubric of crimes against humanity."[26] Under the current law, however, where an act is lawful under humanitarian law (for example, the killing of a combatant in an armed conflict), it would not constitute the crime against humanity of murder by operation of the principle of *lex specialis derogat legi generali*, which states that when two rules are in conflict, the more specific law takes precedent.

By contrast to the broad notion of "civilian population" developed by the tribunals, the prohibition against genocide applies only to acts intended to destroy groups based on four characteristics: nationality, ethnicity, religion, or race. The drafters of the Genocide Convention intentionally excluded political, social, linguistic, economic, and other groups from the list of protected groups. All subsequent definitions of genocide have mirrored this approach. As a result, many twentieth-century episodes of mass killings — such as the Stalinist pogroms against the kulaks (petty bourgeoisie opposed to state ownership) in the former Soviet Union in 1929–1930, the targeting of communists in Indonesia in the 1960s, the majority of the repression in Cambodia during the Khmer Rouge era of 1975–1979, and the dirty wars in Latin America in the 1970s and 1980s — do not cleanly satisfy the elements of the crime of genocide as they are defined by the Convention (although crimes committed in these eras would constitute crimes against humanity and perhaps war crimes).

The limitation on the groups to which the crime of genocide applies raises the question of whether genocide has been defined too narrowly to be useful in today's world. Proponents of maintaining a distinct crime of genocide and of resisting its expansion argue that the crime of genocide captures something distinct from more generic crimes against humanity. Unlike the latter, genocide is a crime committed with the ultimate goal of eliminating a people from the face of the earth because they share some largely immutable and innate characteristic. It is argued that such a crime not only harms the targeted group, but also harms the rest of humanity by threatening to diminish the racial, religious, ethnic, or national diversity of the world's population in a way that is irreversible.

On the other hand, it can be argued that the genocide definition is artificially restrictive as it excludes the wholesale slaughter of human groups that do not happen to share one of the four characteristics listed in the genocide definition. This gives rise to two broad critiques. First is the critique that the definition excludes attacks against groups that share characteristics other than the four listed — such as political affiliation, sexual orientation, sex, language, economic class, and so on — and are targeted because of that characteristic. If these crimes are committed with the intent to destroy in whole or in part all communists, gays and lesbians, women, Basque speakers, or bourgeois, why should they not also fall under the moniker of genocide, the ultimate crime? A common response to the argument to expand the list of protected groups is that the four listed characteristics are immutable ones with which a person is born. This explanation is problematic, as some of the characteristics may clearly be adopted out of choice (e.g., religion or nationality), and our postmodern sensibility recognizes that attributes like "ethnicity" and "race" are as much socially constructed as they are based on any firm, objective biological reality. In addition, sex and sexual orientation are arguably as immutable as any of the four listed groups.

The second critique is that any instance of the mass slaughter of civilians should be considered genocide, in keeping with the lay understanding of the crime. This argument is weaker than the first, as it argues for eliminating any notion of discriminatory animus from the genocide definition, thus treating the killing of 1 million people because of their ethnicity the same as the killing of 1 million civilians (although proof of discrimination could operate as an aggravating factor at sentencing much as domestic hate crimes statutes operate). We think there is value in the law recognizing the discriminatory motive and intent of some mass killings, and that such acts committed with a genocidal intent are different from, and perhaps worse than, the same acts committed without that intent.

The two ad hoc international tribunals, and the ICTR in particular, have to a certain extent relaxed the protected group requirement for genocide. For example, the ICTR has adopted a subjective approach to defining the four protected groups. In the case against Kayishema and Ruzindana, a Trial Chamber noted that an ethnic group could be "a group identified as such by others, including the perpetrators of the crimes."[27] In other words, the victim group can be identified by using the "criteria of stigmatization" employed by the perpetrators of the crime on the basis of perceived national, ethnical, racial, or religious characteristics, even if the victim group has no objective indicia of a protected group.[28] According to this interpretive approach, protected groups can be identified within the sociohistoric context in which they operate or exist, and it is of no moment that the group in question has no "objective" existence. Indeed, the ICTY has noted that this approach is warranted by the difficulty of objectively defining and identifying the four protected groups. In particular, it noted:

> Although the objective determination of a religious group still remains possible, to attempt to define a national, ethnical or racial group today using objective and scientifically irreproachable criteria would be a perilous exercise whose result would not necessarily correspond to the perception of the persons concerned by such categorisation. Therefore, it is more appropriate to evaluate the status of a national, ethnical or racial group from the point of view of those persons who wish to single that group out from the rest of the community. The Trial Chamber consequently elects to evaluate membership in a national, ethnical or racial group using a subjective criterion.[29]

At the same time, another ICTR Trial Chamber in the case against Musema muddied the waters by noting that subjective definitions of groups alone are insufficient, because the drafters of the Genocide Convention specifically intended to exclude political and economic groups from the genocide prohibition.[30] This suggests that a group that was erroneously considered to be an ethnic group by an attacker, but was in fact more properly considered to be an economic group, could not claim to be the victim of genocide.

The case against Jean-Paul Akayesu — the inaugural international genocide prosecution — first established this subjective approach. In adjudicating the genocide counts, the ICTR had to determine whether Hutu and Tutsi groups within Rwanda constitute different "ethnic groups" within the meaning of the statute's definition of genocide. The Tribunal noted at the outset that "the Tutsi population does not have its own language or a distinct culture from the rest of the Rwandan population."[31] The Tribunal conceded that the term "ethnic group is, in general, used to refer to a group whose members speak the same language and/or have the same culture. Therefore, one can hardly talk of ethnic groups as regards Hutu and Tutsi, given that they share the same language and culture."[32] The Tribunal concluded nevertheless that within the Rwandan context, the two groups should be considered separate ethnic groups: "in the context of the period in question, they were, in consonance with a distinction made by the colonizers, considered both by the authorities and themselves as belonging to two distinct ethnic groups; as such, their identity cards mentioned each holder's ethnic group."[33]

To come to this conclusion, the ICTR identified "a number of objective indicators of the group as a group with a distinct identity."[34] The majority of these "objective indicators" stem from the colonial experience within Rwanda and not from any innate linguistic, cultural, or biological characteristic. For example, the Tribunal noted that "[e]very Rwandan citizen was required before 1994 to carry an identity card which included an entry for ethnic group."[35] Further, the Civil

Code of 1988 provided that all persons are to be identified by sex and ethnic group. The ICTR also noted that the Rwandan witnesses who testified before the Chamber identified themselves by ethnic group, and generally knew the ethnic group to which their friends and neighbors belonged. Finally, the Tribunal found dispositive that "the Tutsi were conceived of as an ethnic group by those who targeted them for killing."[36] The Trial Chamber thus concluded that the identification of persons as belonging to the group of Hutu or Tutsi had become embedded in Rwandan culture. In this way, the Tribunal was willing to accept the social construction of ethnicity in Rwanda and treat acts taken with the intent to destroy the Tutsi group as acts of genocide.

The Khmer Rouge period in Cambodia offers a fundamental test of the definition of genocide. The roughly 2 million deaths are largely considered by the general public — within Cambodia and abroad — to be genocide. Indeed, Cambodia often bears the dubious distinction of being described as the first post-Holocaust genocide. Yet a close read of the Genocide Convention reveals that much of the violence committed by the Khmer Rouge in Cambodia may not technically constitute genocide, primarily because the perpetrator group and the victim group shared the same nationality, ethnicity, race, and religion. Instead, the majority of the victims were targeted on the basis of what an objective assessment would describe as their membership in an undesirable political, social, or economic group. By the time a Vietnamese invasion in 1979 revealed the killing fields for the world to see, "a greater proportion of the population [had] perished than in any other revolution during the twentieth century."[37] As the Extraordinary Chambers in the Courts of Cambodia (ECCC) began their work in 2008, it remains to be seen how any indictments for genocide will fare. So far, prosecutors before the ECCC have not pushed the legal envelope; none of the current defendants has been indicted for genocide.

Crimes Against Humanity and Armed Conflict

The other major definitional issue with respect to crimes against humanity, now resolved, was the question of whether an armed conflict is a necessary condition for the crime. This is an issue that does not arise with respect to genocide, as there was never any requirement that acts of genocide be linked to armed conflict. Under general ICL today, the attack against the civilian population need not rise to the level of an armed conflict. At Nuremberg, however, crimes against humanity were intimately tied to the crimes involving the war. Specifically, the Nuremberg Tribunal required the prosecution to demonstrate a "nexus" between the charged crime against humanity and the war of aggression launched by Nazi Germany or Imperialist Japan.

This nexus element was in part a function of the definition of the crime employed in the Nuremberg and Tokyo Charters. The Nuremberg Charter defined crimes against humanity at Article 6(c) as follows (emphasis added):

> [M]urder, extermination, enslavement, deportation, and other inhumane acts committed against any civilian population, before or during the war, or persecutions on political, racial, or religious grounds in execution of or *in connection with any crime within the jurisdiction of the Tribunal*, whether or not in violation of the domestic law of the country where perpetrated.

The Nuremberg Tribunal interpreted the italicized passage to preclude the prosecution of events preceding the commencement of World War II, which it pegged to Germany's invasion of Poland in 1939. This rendered crimes against humanity a by-product of war rather than an autonomous offense. This ruling was only partially supported by the text, as this interpretation required the Tribunal to ignore the preceding phrase "before or during the war." Notwithstanding the war nexus requirement, the Nuremberg Tribunal was satisfied by evidence of a relatively fragile connection between the crimes against humanity charged and other war crimes or acts of aggression. For example, the Nuremberg Tribunal found a war nexus with respect to charges against defendant Schirach (who was convicted of crimes against humanity only) where he committed crimes against Austrian nationals while Austria was annexed by Germany, an act that constituted a crime against the peace under the Charter.

The war nexus served two important purposes in the post–World War II proceedings. First, it helped to satisfy the principle of legality by tying the new charge of crimes against humanity to the relatively well-established prohibition against war crimes. Second, it justified the intrusion of international law into the domestic affairs of a sovereign state. Crimes against humanity effectively trumped domestic authority by criminalizing acts "whether or not in violation of the domestic law of the country where perpetrated." The war nexus ensured that only after a state had already breached international peace by committing acts of aggression would crimes committed internally be susceptible to international scrutiny and prosecution. This concern has become less acute over time with the rise of the human rights movement, which is premised on the idea that a state's treatment of individuals within its territory and under its control is now beyond doubt a matter of international concern.

Although the purposes served by the war nexus at the founding of crimes against humanity have become largely obsolete, the UN Security Council nonetheless included reference to armed conflict in its definition of crimes against humanity in the ICTY Statute (but not the ICTR Statute). Specifically, Article 5 of the ICTY Statute requires that crimes against humanity be committed "in armed conflict, whether international or internal in character," and directed against any civilian population. In the first modern prosecution for crimes against humanity, defendant Dusko Tadić argued that the ICTY Statute's formulation offended the *nullum crimen sine lege* (NCSL) principle because it allowed a link to a non-international armed conflict, and thus was inapplicable. He reasoned that the Nuremberg definition required a nexus to an international armed conflict, which — in his estimation — was not occurring in the former Yugoslavia (a position that was ultimately rejected by the ICTY). The Tribunal confirmed that NCSL was not offended by the statute's definition when it ruled that:

> the definition of Article 5 is in fact more restrictive than the general definition of crimes against humanity recognised by customary international law. The inclusion of the nexus with armed conflict in the article imposes a limitation on the jurisdiction of the International Tribunal and certainly can in no way offend the *nullum crimen* principle so as to bar the International Tribunal from trying the crimes enumerated therein. Because the language of Article 5 is clear, the crimes against humanity tried in the International Tribunal must have a nexus with an armed conflict, be it international or internal.[38]

The Trial Chamber had held that the formulation of the war nexus in the ICTY Statute "necessitates the existence of an armed conflict and a nexus between the act and that conflict." The Appeals Chamber overruled this aspect of the judgment, finding that "a nexus between the accused's acts and the armed conflict is *not* required" and that the "armed conflict requirement is satisfied by proof that *there was* an armed conflict."[39]

Policy or Plan

Is it necessary to prove a formal policy or plan to establish a genocide or crime against humanity? Neither crime contains this requirement in its definition. As we noted earlier in the case of Goran Jelisić, the ICTY noted that there was no evidence of a plan or policy to destroy the Muslim population, although the ICTY suggested in *dicta* that such a policy or plan was not required as a formal matter. The existence of a policy or plan may contribute to the effectiveness of a genocidal attack or a crime against humanity, but this is separate from the question of whether such a plan or policy is legally required to constitute the offense.

Although the jurisprudence, admittedly sparse, suggests that a policy or plan is not required in the case of genocide, there is conflicting authority with respect to such a requirement for crimes against humanity. When crimes against humanity are adjudicated, defendants generally argue that there is such a requirement, whereas prosecutors (and plaintiffs) argue that proof of a policy or plan is not an element of the offense *sensu stricto*, although it is useful as an evidentiary matter. Arguably, where the attack against a civilian population is systematic (as opposed to widespread), a policy is likely at work. In fact, it is hard to imagine a systematic attack that is not the result of some entity's nefarious policy.

The Appeals Chamber of the ad hoc tribunals has held that a policy or plan is not required as an element of the offense.[40] In contrast, however, the ICC Statute seems to define the term *attack* with reference to a policy in Article 7(2)(a). The Statute's Elements of Crimes clarifies that the policy language "requires [evidence] that the State or organization actively promote or encourage such an attack." At the same time, such a policy "may, in exceptional circumstances, be implemented by a deliberate failure to take action, which is consciously aimed at encouraging such attack." The failure to intervene in an attack, combined with the intention of allowing the attack to continue, may thus satisfy any policy element in the ICC Statute.

Although there is no requirement that an act be part of a policy or plan to qualify as a crime against humanity, a nexus is required between the attack against the civilian population and the act of the accused. This does not mean, however, that the accused must have the purpose of furthering the overall attack. The ad hoc tribunals have held that a defendant need not have a formal connection with the group or entity carrying out the attack[41] or to be acting with nonpersonal motives.[42] So long as the accused has knowledge of the overall attack, and of the fact that his or her act is contributing to the attack, it does not matter if the accused intended to further the overall attack.

In addition, because the descriptors "widespread" and "systematic" modify the term "attack," a single act may constitute a crime against humanity so long as it manifests the necessary nexus to a larger attack against a civilian population, regardless of motive.[43] For example, a U.S. district court found that the assassination of Salvadoran Archbishop Oscar Romero constituted a crime against humanity. The court reasoned that this nexus was demonstrated where the single act was shown to be "part of an overall policy or a consistent pattern of inhumanity."[44] Thus, as a general rule, an isolated criminal act cannot be prosecuted as a crime against humanity unless the act is itself a "widespread or systematic" attack, such as the attack of September 11, 2001.*

Enumerated Acts

In addition to different *chapeau* elements, the crime of genocide and crimes against humanity differ with respect to their *actus rea*, or the enumerated acts that trigger individual liability. In part because of its early codification, the list of acts that

---

*Note, however, that the United States led the charge to prevent terrorism from being listed as a crime against humanity in the Rome Statute. If future adjudicators want to remain faithful to this original intent, they may deny jurisdiction over acts that are primarily acts of terrorism, notwithstanding that such acts may also be characterized as the crimes against humanity of murder, extermination, and so on.

constitute genocide is much shorter than the list found in codified versions of crimes against humanity. In addition to killing members of a protected group, the Genocide Convention provides that genocide can be committed through the causing of bodily harm, inflicting adverse conditions of life on the group, interfering with the ability to procreate, and transferring children from the group. The theory is that these acts, although not directly amounting to the full or partial destruction of a group, have the potential to bring about this destruction through a process of "slow death."[45]

The Nuremberg and Tokyo definition of crimes against humanity distinguishes between two broad categories of offenses: inhumane acts ("murder, extermination, enslavement, deportation, and other inhumane acts") and acts of persecution ("on political, racial, or religious grounds").* Gradually, this bifurcation has almost entirely collapsed, and modern definitions include persecution in the general list of constitutive offenses. Reflecting humankind's seemingly inexorable ability to devise new ways to brutalize its members, the list of predicate crimes has lengthened over time with the addition in the ICC Statute of new crimes against humanity, such as forms of arbitrary detention or imprisonment, gender violence, disappearances, and apartheid. These additions are clearly in reaction to past atrocities and the failure of the international community adequately to condemn them, most notably the crime of apartheid and the use of systematic violence against women to terrorize a civilian population. In total, the ICC Statute lists 11 enumerated acts under its definition of crimes against humanity.

Although the listed enumerated acts differ between the two crimes, can one argue that the same acts could qualify as either

---

*The Tokyo Charter recognized only political and racial persecutions, probably because religious persecution was less present in the Pacific theater.

genocide or crimes against humanity, depending on the existence of the *chapeau* elements? Certainly one could interpret the phrases "causing serious bodily or mental harm" or "deliberately inflicting" adverse conditions of life under genocide as including all of the more specific acts listed under crimes against humanity. The ICTR, for example, has held that "serious bodily and mental harm" includes acts of physical or mental torture, disfigurement, cruel treatment, rape and other sexual violence, and persecution.[46] The two ad hoc tribunals have interpreted "inflicting adverse conditions of life" to include a lack of adequate housing, hygiene, medical care, or subjecting individuals to a subsistence diet, starvation, or excessive physical exercise. Likewise, the expulsion of people from their homes with the requisite intent can also satisfy this element of genocide.[47]

One could also interpret the phrase "other inhumane acts" in the definition of crimes against humanity to encompass most of the enumerated acts under genocide. The ICTY, for example, has interpreted "other humane acts," at times in *dicta*, to include forced displacement, mutilation, beatings, degrading treatment, and forced prostitution.[48] Although the jurisprudence testing the outer contours of this residual clause is still in its infancy, an ICTY Trial Chamber defined "inhumane acts" as "intentional acts or omissions which infringe fundamental human rights causing serious mental or physical suffering or injury of a gravity comparable to that of other crimes covered by Article 5 [the article defining crimes against humanity]."[49] Looking to international human rights standards for guidance, the Chamber identified "inhumane acts" to include the infringement of basic human rights, including "serious forms of cruel or degrading treatment of persons belonging to a particular ethnic, religious, political or racial group, or serious widespread or systematic manifestations of cruel or humiliating or degrading treatment with a discriminatory or persecutory intent."[50] Upholding a conviction for "other inhumane acts," the Appeals Chamber affirmed the Trial Chambers' judgment that the forcible removal of a family from its home and the destruction of the family house constituted inhumane acts that were properly charged alongside the crime against humanity of murder based on the killing of a family member.[51]

International tribunals prove themselves to be quite nimble when interpreting the listed acts under both genocide and crimes against humanity to encompass the same *actus reus*. At the same time, the particular crimes against humanity of persecution and extermination appear to incorporate the *chapeau* elements of genocide within crimes against humanity. In other words, it would appear that every act that constitutes genocide would also constitute a crime against humanity.

Persecution

Definitions of persecution generally contain a discriminatory intent element, thus approximating the specific intent required under genocide. Article 7 of the ICC Statute, for example, requires proof that the defendant acted "on political, racial, national, ethnic, cultural, religious, gender . . . or other grounds that are universally recognized as impermissible under international law." This latter reference would presumably cover persecutions on grounds of sexual orientation, age, profession, mental disability, health status, and so forth, although the statute leaves the cognizability of these other "suspect classes" open to litigation. The ICTY has interpreted the requirement of discriminatory animus broadly. For one, it is enough that the perpetrator subjectively believed that the victim was a member of a protected group.[52] As discussed earlier, this is similar to the decisions of tribunals adjudicating genocide claims, which have found that it is the subjective perceptions of the perpetrator, rather than any "objective" identity of the victim groups, that matters. In addition, the ICTY has ruled that groups may be defined negatively, as for example, non-Croats.[53] In this way, the crime against humanity of persecution contains three *mens rea* elements: the mental state necessary for the underlying act, knowledge that the act is committed within the context of a widespread or systematic attack against a civilian population, and a discriminatory intent.

A Trial Chamber of the ICTY has set forth a four-part test for determining what constitutes persecution: (1) a gross or blatant denial (2) on discriminatory grounds (3) of a fundamental right found in customary or treaty law (4) reaching the same level of gravity as other enumerated crimes against humanity.[54] Applying this test, one Trial Chamber found that denying people the right to employment, freedom of movement, judicial process, and medical care all constituted criminal persecution when committed on invidious grounds.[55] As noted earlier, these types of acts may also be found to constitute "deliberately inflicting adverse conditions of life" under the crime of genocide. In this way, the tribunals have looked to the pantheon of human rights treaties to add content to these open-ended ICL provisions.

Extermination

Through adjudicating the concept of "extermination" as an enumerated crime against humanity, the ICTY has identified another category of crimes that closely parallels genocide. Indeed, extermination encompasses the crime of mass killing, which most lay persons equate with genocide. In *Krstić*, the Trial Chamber noted the two crimes' normative overlap and entered only a conviction for genocide on the grounds that extermination was, in essence, a lesser included offense of genocide.[56] Yet, even extermination differs from genocide in that it is a result crime, requiring proof of multiple deaths, rather than a crime of intent.[57] The ICC Elements of Crimes emphasize that it must be shown that the perpetrator killed one or more persons "as part of a mass killing of members of a civilian population." In addition, the ICTY established the following *mens rea* for extermination:

> inten[t] to kill, to inflict grievous bodily harm, or to inflict serious injury, in the reasonable knowledge that such act or omission is likely to cause death, or otherwise [the] inten[t] to participate in the elimination of a number of individuals, in the knowledge that his action is part of a vast murderous enterprise in which a large number of individuals are systematically marked for killing or killed.[58]

The requirement that there be a large number of deaths is a significant difference between extermination as a crime against humanity and genocide (which as noted earlier might be found with only one or a handful of deaths). Despite this difference, however, there is a large overlap between extermination and genocide. Unlike the crime of genocide, the crime of extermination is not limited to groups with a common characteristic. Given the limited number of protected groups within the definition of genocide and the difficulties of proving a defendant's specific intent to destroy the group, the crime against humanity of extermination may over time take on greater prominence in the prosecutor's arsenal as it does much of the work of genocide, and more.

CONCLUSION: CONVERGENCE OR DISTINCTION?

As noted earlier, there are significant differences between the crimes of genocide and crimes against humanity. First, the prohibition of genocide requires a showing of specific intent, whereas the prohibition against crimes against humanity requires only that the defendant acted with knowledge of a widespread or systematic attack against a civilian population. Second, the prohibition against crimes against humanity requires the existence of a widespread or systematic attack as a circumstantial element, whereas genocide in theory could consist of a single isolated act. Third, crimes against humanity may be committed against any civilian population, whereas genocide is limited to populations with a common race, religion, nationality, or ethnicity.

Despite these significant differences, the emerging jurisprudence tends to downplay them. The ad hoc tribunals have interpreted the four protected categories in the prohibition against genocide in an expansive way, incorporating subjective perceptions of difference into the definition of each category. Although the *actus reus* of crimes against humanity contains a more numerous list of acts than does the prohibition against genocide, the list of crimes against humanity includes the act of extermination, which has been interpreted by the ad hoc tribunals to effectively capture all discrimination-based killings and persecutions that are not covered by genocide. Given these similarities between the two crimes, and given the fact that they both describe some of the worst atrocities known to humankind, is it necessary to preserve these two crimes as distinct, or should we instead combine them in a way that ensures that all such atrocities are equally punished and deterred?

~ 9 ~

Immunities, Amnesties, and Excuses

lthough opportunities to hold individuals accountable for violations of international crimes have increased tremendously in the last century, potential defendants are not without their own arsenal of defenses. Most of the defenses found in domestic legal systems — such as mistake of law, mistake of fact, incapacity, consent, and self-defense — are also found in the jurisprudence of international criminal law (ICL). We focus here on those defenses that have been most commonly raised in ICL proceedings, or those that raise special issues at the international level.

In particular, individuals accused of the commission of international crimes may benefit from the application of immunities, amnesties, and a variety of excuses that predate the development of modern ICL. The first two — immunities and amnesties — have been weakened with the creation of an increasingly robust ICL regime (with the significant exception of combatant immunity, which remains a hallmark of international humanitarian law). Most forms of immunity and many amnesty laws are viewed with skepticism by the human rights and international justice advocacy communities, although amnesties are still used frequently by states to facilitate the demise of regimes of atrocity. Excuses, a third form of defense, play a similar role at the international level as they do in a domestic system — they lessen, and sometimes negate, liability for an otherwise illegal act.

All three of these exceptions to criminal accountability are justified as furthering important social values. Immunities are justified as protecting the necessary and legitimate functions of government officials by, for example, protecting such officials from politically motivated or otherwise distracting and disruptive legal claims. Combatant immunity is justified to further the regulation of permissible and impermissible warfare. Amnesties are justified as means to achieve peace and social stability by providing a "carrot" to members of the government or military (and even to rebel forces) responsible for atrocities so they will lay down their arms. Excuses (such as self-defense) are justified as furthering fundamental moral values and ensuring that criminal liability follows true fault on the part of the defendant.

IMMUNITIES

The historic immunities from legal process afforded to diplomats, other state officials, and heads of state have eroded in the last few decades. Defenses that once provided absolute protection to official actors under both domestic and international law now appear to provide little, if any, protection for violations of ICL, especially before international tribunals. The Statute of the International Criminal Court (ICC) with its categorical rejection of most immunities, the transnational prosecutions of Augusto Pinochet (Chile) and Hissène Habré (Chad), the international prosecutions of Charles Taylor (Liberia) and

Omar Al-Bashir (Sudan), and recent decisions of the International Court of Justice (ICJ) all reflect the demise of official state immunity for certain international crimes. As noted later, the one exception to this general trend weakening legal immunities is the doctrine of combatant immunity under international humanitarian law (IHL), although its application to the global "war on terror" remains contested.

Functional and Personal Immunities

Under international law, there are two general types of immunity enjoyed by state officials: functional and personal. Functional immunity is also referred to as immunity *ratione materiae*, or subject matter immunity. *Functional immunity* protects an individual from liability for conduct performed on behalf of the state, or "official acts." Thus, a state official who engages in an ordinary criminal act for his or her own benefit (for example, theft or murder) will not be protected from liability by functional immunity. Personal immunity is also referred to as immunity *ratione personae*. *Personal immunity* attaches to the person and provides protection from legal process regardless of the nature of the act in question. The enjoyment of personal immunity has historically been limited to diplomats, foreign ministers, and heads of state, and up until recently it provided absolute protection from legal process while the individual held office. As illustrated by the recent indictments of sitting heads of state (such as Milošević, Taylor, and Al-Bashir), personal immunities are no longer absolute guarantees of protection.

Immunities are strongest when deployed within domestic legal systems and weakest before international courts. Thus, state officials still enjoy the benefit of strong immunity claims (both functional and personal) before national courts. Before international courts, however, state officials increasingly have little access to immunity claims. In addition, a similar erosion is taking place with respect to functional immunities before national courts, especially where serious violations of ICL are at issue.

Since the start of the modern development of ICL at Nuremberg and Tokyo, officials accused of the worst international crimes have been unable to claim functional immunity as a defense. Although it is clear that a state official may not be held criminally liable for his or her official acts, it is also clear that, since Nuremberg, certain acts have become, per se, unofficial. These include acts of torture, genocide, crimes against humanity, war crimes, and aggression.* Thus, although such acts are often committed by individuals in their official capacities — and, in fact, official action is required to trigger international liability for some crimes — as a matter of law such acts are not considered official for purposes of immunity doctrines. As Lord Brown-Wilkinson succinctly stated in the *Pinochet* case before the English House of Lords, "How can it be for international law purposes an official act to do something which international law itself prohibits and criminalises?"[1] Functional immunity thus does not apply to acts that violate ICL.

At first glance, this gives rise to a contradiction. A prosecution for torture, for example, requires proof of official action, as the Convention Against Torture defines torture with reference to state action. For purposes of immunity, however, torture is never an official act. This seeming contradiction is explained by the different contexts in which the notion of "official action" is used. For purposes of criminal liability, ICL borrows the definition of torture from international human rights law to

---

*Note, however, that although there is a general consensus that an act of aggression is a violation of international law that may lead to criminal liability, there is as yet no consensus concerning the definition of this offence.

criminalize those acts undertaken by government officials or otherwise pursuant to state action.*

Diplomats enjoy a strong form of personal immunity, as codified internationally in the Vienna Convention on Diplomatic Relations (1961). As a result, diplomats are entitled to absolute personal immunity from any civil or criminal process while in a host country and even while transiting through a third country. This immunity applies to any criminal act they may commit, either before or after they assumed office, regardless of whether the act was committed as part of their official duties. Notwithstanding this seemingly impenetrable barrier to prosecution, diplomats may still be subject to legal process for their activities under certain circumstances. First, personal immunity may be waived by the diplomat's state, as the immunity is a right of the state and not of the individual. If a state waives a diplomat's immunity, he or she may be prosecuted while still in office even for acts committed in his or her official capacity. Second, diplomats may be prosecuted after they no longer hold a diplomatic position for unofficial acts committed while they held their diplomatic posts — in other words, they enjoy functional immunity after they leave office, but not personal immunity.

Heads of state enjoy the same form of personal immunity as diplomats, although head of state immunity is not as clearly codified in international law. Heads of government and certain ministers (such as ministers of foreign affairs) enjoy such personal immunity. Dapo Akande noted in 2004 that he could find no case "in which it was held that a state official possessing immunity *ratione personae* is subject to the criminal jurisdiction of a foreign state when it is alleged that he or she has committed an international crime."[2] Some claim that the

---

*This is true only when torture is prosecuted as a stand-alone crime. Where torture rises to the level of a crime against humanity or constitutes a war crime, a showing of state action is not required.

one exception to this assertion is the prosecution and conviction of the former President of Panama, Manuel Noriega, by the United States.[3] In that prosecution, however, the U.S. government took the position that Noriega was not in fact the legitimate head of state, because he had been replaced by Guillermo Endara in an election that Noriega annulled to stay in power. The Noriega precedent, relying as it does on a claim that Noriega was not in fact a current head of state, does not provide a clear exception to Akande's observation.

Although functional and personal immunities may provide protection to a state official from a criminal prosecution by another state, the weight of authority suggests that such immunities do not apply before international tribunals. The lack of such immunity is primarily based on the powers accorded to the particular international tribunal by their constitutive instruments (that is, the statutes of the various international criminal tribunals). The post–World War II criminal tribunals — the International Criminal Tribunal for the Former Yugoslavia (ICTY), the International Criminal Tribunal for Rwanda (ICTR), the Special Court for Sierra Leone (SCSL), and the ICC — all include provisions asserting jurisdiction over state officials regardless of any conflicting immunity doctrines.[4] Some argue, however, that it is premature to conclude that personal immunity does not apply before an international criminal tribunal as a matter of customary international law.

Combatant Immunity

A specialized form of immunity is available under IHL for combatants. Although the IHL embodied in the Geneva Conventions primarily provides protection to innocent or vulnerable individuals (such as civilians, prisoners of war [POWs], the wounded, and the shipwrecked) in international armed conflicts, it also tacitly provides immunity to combatants for acts of violence committed in furtherance of a military campaign. This immunity applies to privileged combatants for acts of war they commit that are not in violation of IHL. By contrast, no immunity is granted for war crimes — acts that violate IHL and give rise to individual criminal responsibility. Although an attack against a military base or other military facilities might be illegal as a matter of municipal law, an individual involved in such an attack within the context of an international armed conflict is immune from such liability so long as he or she meets the requirements of a privileged combatant.

None of the treaties expressly sets forth a definition of "privileged combatant." The Third Geneva Convention at Article 4, however, provides that members of the armed forces of a party to the conflict qualify as POWs in the event of capture or surrender. In addition, members of a militia, volunteer corps, and organized resistance movements that "belong" to a party may also qualify as POWs if they satisfy the following four requirements:[5]

i. the organization must be commanded by a person responsible for his subordinates;

ii. the organization's members must have a fixed distinctive emblem or uniform recognizable at a distance;

iii. the organization's members must carry arms openly; and

iv. the organization's members must conduct their operations in accordance with the laws and customs of war.

That article also identifies other individuals who may also qualify as POWs when they accompany combatants, such as war correspondents and civilian crews.

Individuals entitled to POW treatment can only be prosecuted for acts that violate IHL. The definition of POW thus largely governs when combatant immunity attaches. Note that the IHL governing noninternational armed conflicts does not contain a POW regime or recognize the notion of combatant immunity. As a result, rebel combatants may always be prosecuted for their acts of violence, even when committed within the context of a noninternational armed conflict. In most circumstances, such combatants will be prosecuted under municipal penal law, unless the state has adopted a special penal regime to govern noninternational armed conflicts.

The question of combatant immunity has recently been raised in the context of the global "war on terror." The question is when an act of violence qualifies as a lawful incident of an armed conflict, and is thus subject to the permissions and prohibitions of IHL, versus when the act is one of terrorism, in which case international terrorism conventions and the municipal law of interested states applies. The consequences of such a determination are significant. For example, both regular armed forces and al Qaeda operatives were the object of attack in the international armed conflict initiated by the United States against the Taliban regime in Afghanistan in the immediate aftermath of the September 11, 2001 attacks. The U.S. government has taken the position that neither members of the Afghan armed forces nor al Qaeda members qualified as privileged combatants. As a result, it has argued that they are not entitled to POW status when captured or combatant immunity for acts of violence they may commit. The President also stated, however, that the United States would treat captured individuals humanely and consistent with the spirit, if not the letter, of the Geneva Conventions.

Although we agree with the U.S. government and most international lawyers that al Qaeda members are not privileged combatants, some members of the armed forces of the Taliban when it was the lawful government of Afghanistan may qualify as such. If so, acts of war committed by Taliban troops should give rise to combatant immunity so long as no war crimes were committed. As unprivileged combatants, al Qaeda operatives are not entitled to combatant immunity. As a result, if they participate in hostilities without the privilege of doing so, they can be prosecuted for acts of terrorism, murder, mayhem, and the like to the extent that there are applicable penal statutes.

The question still arises with respect to how a determination of combatant status should be made. The Third Geneva Convention (concerning POWs) states that if there is any doubt with respect to the lawful combatant status of a captured person (and thus whether that person is entitled to POW status), then such person must be treated as a POW until a "competent tribunal" determines his or her status.[6] In response to a challenge by individuals detained at the U.S. naval base in Guantánamo Bay, Cuba, the U.S. Supreme Court held that the United States was obligated to provide some legal process to establish the combatant status of those being detained.[7] As a result, the U.S. government established Combatant Status Review Tribunals, although the focus of these tribunals has been to determine whether the individual detainee qualifies as an "enemy combatant," and thus whether he may still be detained, and not whether he is entitled to POW status.

The defense of combatant immunity has been raised in other litigation in U.S. courts. John Walker Lindh, the so-called American Taliban, was prosecuted for his involvement with the Taliban forces in Afghanistan and in particular for remaining with the Taliban after the attacks of September 11, 2001. Lindh raised combatant immunity as a defense, arguing that he was part of an organized military force that was resisting an incursion by forces of the Northern Alliance. The federal court in which Lindh's case was heard concluded that Lindh had not met his burden of showing that the Taliban met the requirements of privileged combatants under the Geneva Conventions, and thus the defense of lawful combatant immunity was denied.

Immunity Before the ICC

The Rome Treaty establishing the ICC has uncompromising provisions with respect to immunities, some of which go further than those of any other international court in making clear that traditional immunities do not apply to those officials suspected of committing acts prohibited by the treaty. These provisions are somewhat complicated, however, by other provisions that appear to recognize, and even defer to, those same immunities. So, Article 27(1) makes clear that functional immunity is inapplicable to any individual before the ICC, specifically identifying heads of state and government. In addition, Article 27(2) rejects the traditional doctrine of personal immunity for sitting state officials. This latter provision is not found in the statutes of any of the earlier international criminal tribunals, and thus is unique to the ICC. Article 98(1), by contrast, provides that a state is not obligated to hand an individual over to the ICC if doing so would be "inconsistent[] with its obligations under international law with respect to the State or diplomatic immunity of a person . . . of a third State, unless the Court can first obtain the cooperation of that third State for the waiver of the immunity."

These two provisions (Articles 27 and 98(1)) may, and should, be interpreted to complement each other in keeping with standard rules of treaty interpretation. In particular, Article 27 should be construed as a waiver by a state party of any immunity (both personal and functional) that might otherwise apply to their officials before the ICC, and Article 98(1) should be interpreted to apply only in the case of officials from a state that is not a party to the Rome Treaty. Article 98(1) would thus apply with respect to officials whose state has not waived their immunity through Article 27, thus requiring the ICC to seek a waiver with respect to such an official. This is not the only interpretation of these two articles, of course. Article 98 could be interpreted to mean that a state party to the ICC is not obligated to hand over an official from another state, regardless of whether that state has ratified the Rome Treaty. This interpretation, however, would seem to be contrary to the general purpose of the ICC as it would require the consent of an official's government before that official could be subject to the jurisdiction of the ICC. A number of states have passed domestic legislation incorporating the ICC statute that is consistent with the interpretation just proposed.[8]

There is thus created a two-tier immunity structure for state officials before the ICC: one for officials from states that are parties to the Rome Treaty, and one for officials from states that are not parties. For officials from state parties, neither functional nor personal immunity applies with respect to any proceeding connected to the ICC, as the state has waived any rights such officials may have to such immunities through acceptance of Article 27. With respect to officials from non-state parties, those states that have not ratified the Rome Treaty have not, as a matter of treaty law, waived any otherwise applicable immunities enjoyed by their officials. Article 98(1) thus applies to these officials. In such a case, the Court would have to secure from a non-state party the waiver of its official's immunity before a third state would be obligated to hand that individual over to the ICC.

Article 98(2) provides a challenge similar to Article 98(1) with respect to the anti-immunity provisions of Article 27. Article 98(2) provides that a State is not required to hand over a suspect to the Court if to do so would conflict "with . . . obligations under international agreements" that would require it to obtain the consent of the State of which the suspect is a national, "unless the Court can first obtain the cooperation of the sending State for the giving of consent for the surrender." It is generally accepted that this subsection is meant to apply to Status of Forces Agreements. The United States, however, has entered into a number of bilateral agreements by which the treaty parties agree not to surrender a national of the other party to the ICC. Although there is debate about the effect of such agreements entered into with state parties to the Rome Treaty, which have obligations to approach the ICC in good faith and not hinder its functions, such agreements may be effective with respect to non-state parties. In other words a state that is not party to the Rome Treaty (such as the United States) could refuse to surrender to the ICC a national of Zimbabwe (which is also not a party to the Rome Treaty) if an Article 98(2) agreement had been entered into by those two states. With respect to states that are parties to the Rome Treaty, however, the better approach is that such agreements should not protect their citizens from being surrendered to the Court.

Immunity and Customary International Law

As a matter of treaty law, personal and functional immunities will not shield an official from accountability for violations of ICL before the ICC. Can one, however, say that official immunities do not apply to such crimes as a matter of customary international law?

This is less clear, and at the moment the answer is probably no. Evidence in support of the existence of a rule of customary international law voiding such immunities includes the ICC Statute (and the fact that it has attracted more than 100 state parties), the statutes of the ICTY and ICTR created by the UN Security Council, and the prosecution of Charles Taylor before the SCSL.* On the other hand, as a matter of domestic law, most states continue to provide some form of immunity to their own government officials, as well as to officials of other states. In addition, in a significant and somewhat controversial opinion, the ICJ found that customary international law provides personal immunity to certain government officials with respect to transnational prosecutions. (The case in question involved a Belgian attempt to prosecute the sitting Foreign Minister of the

---

*The SCSL declined to accord immunity to Charles Taylor, then a sitting head of state, despite the fact that Liberia was not a party to the agreement creating the SCSL and thus could not be said to have waived any official immunity.

Democratic Republic of the Congo.) In *dicta*, the ICJ stated that such immunity would not apply in the case of a prosecution before "certain international criminal courts" such as the ICTY, ICTR, or ICC.[9] Finally, as noted previously, the ICC Statute acknowledges the residual existence of such immunities through Article 98. Recall, however, that Article 98 of the Rome Statute appears to preserve such immunity before the ICC only for officials from states that have not ratified the Rome Statute.

The so-called *Belgian Arrest Warrant* case is significant because it extends personal immunity beyond the category of individuals to whom it traditionally applied, namely heads of state, heads of government, and diplomats. In extending personal immunity to foreign ministers, the ICJ reasoned that without such immunity, foreign ministers would be hindered in performing a crucial function of their position (that is, international travel and diplomacy). It would thus appear that before domestic courts, a wide variety of government officials may benefit from personal immunity.

The most significant recent development with respect to official immunities is probably the erosion of immunities traditionally afforded a sitting head of state under customary international law when such individuals are prosecuted before an international tribunal. Until recently, it was generally accepted that sitting heads of state were absolutely immune while in office from any legal process. This is no longer the case. The first indictment against a sitting head of state by an international tribunal was issued by the ICTY against the president of Yugoslavia, Slobodan Milošević. Milošević challenged the indictment on a number of grounds, including the absolute immunity traditionally enjoyed by sitting heads of state. The ICTY dismissed Milošević's claims of immunity and upheld the indictment.[10] In Africa, the first international indictment of a sitting head of state was that of Charles Taylor of Liberia in June 2003 by the SCSL.[11] This was followed by the ICC's indictment of President Omar Al-Bashir of Sudan. That the

SCSL is a hybrid tribunal (that is, a court with a mix of domestic and international law attributes) complicates the ICJ's dichotomous result in the *Belgian Arrest Warrant* case (the assertion that personal immunities are inapplicable before international tribunals and the holding that such immunities continue to apply as a matter of international law before domestic courts). In the end, the SCSL held that Taylor could not claim personal immunity, concluding that the Special Court qualifies as an international tribunal and thus, per the *Belgian Arrest Warrant* case, such immunities are inapplicable before it.[12]

AMNESTIES

Throughout recorded history, officials have enacted amnesties to prevent the prosecution of state officials for crimes they may have committed while in office. This practice continues today, especially in light of the limitations of functional immunity. Until very recently, state practice has been uncritical of the use of such amnesties. In fact, with a few notable exceptions, every state court to consider the question has upheld the legality of a challenged amnesty.[13] In addition to limiting the applicability of traditional immunities to state officials responsible for international crimes, international law is also eroding the strength of amnesties. Indeed, whenever international courts and other similar institutions (such as human rights courts) have confronted domestic amnesties, they have always declared such enactments to be illegal.

Amnesties Before the Special Court for Sierra Leone

The first non-domestic criminal tribunal to address directly the legality of an amnesty was the SCSL. In *Prosecutor v. Kallon & Kamara*, the SCSL held that the amnesty provision in the

Lomé Accord does not apply to those prosecuted before the Special Court.[14] The Court reasoned that the Lomé Accord was in fact a creature of domestic law, and thus was subordinate to international law. Being subordinate to international law, the Accord must give way to the jurisdiction and powers of the Special Court.

The Court took up the issue more directly a short two months later in *Prosecutor v. Gbao*, asserting, first, that "there is a *crystallized* international norm to the effect that a government cannot grant amnesty for serious crimes under international law,"[15] and second, that "[u]nder international law, states are under a duty to prosecute crimes whose [sic] prohibition has the status of *jus cogens*."[16] Robert Cryer has correctly noted that both of these statements are controversial, and that the latter — concerning the duty to prosecute — "cries out for greater discussion."[17] Specifically, although there has been a good deal of attention in the academic literature concerning a duty to prosecute violations of ICL, it is far from clear both whether such a duty exists and what, if any, are its limits. Treaties concerning torture and many acts of terrorism establish a general obligation to either prosecute or extradite a suspect to a state that will prosecute, but it is not clear if such an obligation extends to other crimes as a matter of customary international law, and thus applies regardless of whether a state is a party to a particular treaty.

As some of the following discussion with respect to amnesties will suggest, there is a stronger argument that international law requires some form of justice with respect to violations of ICL, but it is less clear that such justice must take the form of traditional retributive-based criminal prosecutions.

Amnesties and the ICC Statute

The ICC Statute does not address amnesties expressly. This was a deliberate decision made by the delegates at the Rome

Conference, who clearly rejected the arguments of the South African delegation, among others, that some amnesties should be given effect before the ICC. The ICC Statute's silence with respect to amnesties means that we will have to wait for the development of the Court's jurisprudence on this issue before we can say with any certainty which, if any, amnesties may provide protection from prosecution before the ICC. There is no question, however, that the ICC Statute provides ample room for the Court and prosecutor to defer to a specific amnesty in deciding not to prosecute an individual suspect.

Indeed, there are four ways in which an amnesty may be given effect before the ICC. First, the office of the prosecutor may suspend an investigation "in the interests of justice" (Article 53(c)(2)). Second, the Court may find that an amnesty satisfies the requirements of domestic prosecution under the Statute's complementarity provisions (Article 17). Third, the UN Security Council may suspend an investigation or prosecution under its Chapter VII powers (Article 16). Fourth, the Court may conclude that the amnesty is the equivalent of a conviction or acquittal and thus triggers its *ne bis in idem* (double jeopardy) provision (Article 20).

Interests of Justice

First, Article 53 of the ICC Statute provides that the prosecutor may decline to initiate an investigation if it would "serve the interests of justice." Such a decision is, however, reviewable by the Pre-Trial Chamber on its own initiative, and the Chamber may reverse the prosecutor's decision per Article 53(3)(b).*

---

*This is in contrast to a decision by the prosecutor not to proceed on other grounds (for example, lack of legal or factual basis), which is only reviewable if a state party so requests, or if the Security Council requests a review in a case initiated by its referral. *See* Article 53(3)(a). In these other cases, however, the Chamber may only *request* that the prosecutor reconsider the question, rather than reversing the prosecutor's decision as can be done in the case of the prosecutor not proceeding in the interest of justice.

The question then is what would qualify as a basis for declining to initiate an investigation "in the interest of justice." Certainly one could accept as reasonable an interpretation that would allow the prosecutor to reach such a decision if the individual suspect is participating in a justice or reconciliation process other than a traditional criminal prosecution. In other words, one could imagine a prosecutor declining to prosecute (and a pre-Trial Chamber upholding that decision) if the suspect was subject to alternative accountability mechanisms, whether it be something like the South African amnesty process (which provided some level of accountability) or an alternative dispute resolution mechanism like the *gacaca* process in Rwanda.

Although such an interpretation is plausible, the ICC has not been operating long enough, and thus has not created enough of a jurisprudential track record, for us to predict with any accuracy whether such an interpretation would be adopted by the prosecutor and approved by the Court. Central to this determination would be whether the alternative mechanism implemented in the country provides some notion of justice. We argue that justice requires some form of individual accountability, although others have argued that achieving "peace" alone (meaning the immediate end of an armed conflict) qualifies as a form of justice. The latter argument may be summarized as follows: The ending of hostilities protects future victims from harm, and this achievement outweighs the lack of retrospective justice with respect to past victims.

The ICC prosecutor appears to have adopted a definition of justice that requires some individual accountability, as he made a distinction in a recent policy document between "justice" and "peace,"[18] and noted that although "interests of justice" incorporates a broader notion of justice than criminal justice, it "should not be conceived of so broadly as to embrace all issues related to peace and security."[19] Human Rights Watch has argued in a very sophisticated policy paper that the phrase "interests of justice" should be interpreted narrowly, and should not be used to decline an investigation or prosecution in the face of a national amnesty, truth commission, or other alternative justice system or process of reconciliation.[20]

A related question is whether the inquiry concerning interest of justice is focused on the justice of an individual case, or whether it encompasses the more generalized justice policies of a society. In other words, does the inquiry concerning the interest of justice focus on the specific facts and circumstances of an individual suspect, or is it a more general inquiry concerning a particular society's approach to justice in the post-conflict or postrepression situation? Carsten Stahn argues that the proper inquiry is on the individual case, and not on the general approach of the state from which that individual comes.[21] There is a good deal of textual support for this position in the language of the treaty, referring for example to "the crime" and "the victims."

Complementarity

Article 17 of the Rome Statute concerning complementarity also provides a possible textual basis for the ICC to defer to a local amnesty. There are two possible avenues for this interpretation: Article 17(1)(a) and Article 17(1)(b). Under Article 17(1)(a), the ICC will defer to a national mechanism if "[t]he case is being investigated or prosecuted by a State which has jurisdiction over it, unless the State is unwilling or unable genuinely to carry out the investigation or prosecution." Under Article 17(1)(b), the ICC will defer to a national mechanism if "[t]he case has been investigated by a State which has jurisdiction over it and the State has decided not to prosecute the person concerned, unless the decision resulted from the unwillingness or inability of the State genuinely to prosecute." The one other provision in this article, subsection (c), only applies if there has been a "trial" by a "court." Even the South African amnesty, which is the most "court-like" amnesty ever adopted, would not qualify under any reasonable interpretation of "trial" or "court."

In considering the way in which complementarity might lead to the application of a domestic amnesty before the ICC, there are three issues worth highlighting: (1) the interpretation of the term "investigation," (2) the proper focus of an investigation, and (3) the presumptions created by the provisions. The first issue concerns the scope of an investigation. Is a general investigation into the causes, effects, and contours of a history of violations sufficient, or is a more focused and individualized investigation required? As with the idea of taking into account the "interest of justice" under Article 53, it appears clear that investigation refers to an individual investigation — an investigation focused on the facts of a specific atrocity or perpetrator — and not the type of general investigation of the causes and contours of violations that one often finds conducted by a truth commission.

The second question concerns the *type* of individualized investigation. Some have interpreted the concept of an investigation to mean a criminal investigation that could result in a prosecution and conviction, and then concluded that an amnesty could never satisfy this requirement. A variation of this argument is that the granting of an amnesty after an investigation is *prima facie* evidence of an "unwillingness" to investigate or "to bring the person concerned to justice," and thus fails under Article 17. Indeed, a definition of investigation anchored in a process of criminal prosecution precludes any form of amnesty. By contrast, a definition of investigation that focuses on gathering and publicizing evidence with respect to the crimes in question but that may not result in a prosecution would describe some amnesties, such as the one adopted by South Africa in 1995.

This distinction between criminal investigation and amnesty is misplaced in this context. A conditional amnesty like that adopted in South Africa is consistent with a definition of "criminal investigation," as the investigations undertaken in that amnesty process could have led (and in many cases did lead) to a denial of amnesty and thus the possibility of criminal prosecution. The fact that such prosecutions have not been forthcoming in post-amnesty South Africa is an argument that South Africa's amnesty process might not qualify under this interpretation of "investigation," not that a similar amnesty could never qualify. Support for the position that some amnesties might qualify as an investigation can be found in statements by some of the negotiators at Rome, although such statements are of course not authoritative interpretations of the treaty.

The third issue under Article 17 concerns the way in which its presumption operates. Stahn rightly argues that the exceptions to Article 17 should be interpreted narrowly, "since it is drafted in a negative fashion."[22] In other words, the general presumption of the complementarity regime is admissibility unless one or more of the exceptions clearly applies. Stahn thus argues that an amnesty *must* be accompanied by some form of investigation to qualify as a proceeding that would render a case inadmissible. In other words, an amnesty without more would be insufficient, for it would not provide strong evidence of a state's commitment to providing some form of individual justice. All three of these interpretive points underscore the fact that an amnesty could conceivably qualify as an investigation under Article 17, but that such an amnesty must meet a minimum threshold of accountability.

Security Council Deferral

Article 16, under which the UN Security Council can invoke its Chapter VII power to stop an investigation or prosecution for a year at a time, may also provide a mechanism for giving *de facto* effect to a domestic amnesty before the ICC. The legal question is whether deferral to an amnesty could ever be justified as triggering the Security Council's Chapter VII powers—in other words, whether not deferring to the amnesty could be characterized as a threat to the peace or a breach of the peace. There are clearly some circumstances in which the question of whether to defer to a domestic amnesty might affect international peace. An amnesty included as part of a peace deal to end a serious armed conflict could be easily characterized as part of an effort to address a breach of the peace or threat to the peace. The Security Council might distinguish such a negotiated amnesty from a self-amnesty. A negotiated amnesty is more likely to garner the long-term support of the parties to a conflict, and its invalidity is more likely to endanger the related negotiated settlement. A self-amnesty, on the other hand, is likely to lack legitimacy or acceptance by other parties to a conflict, and thus its lack of enforcement before the ICC may be less likely to threaten international peace (either because such peace remains elusive, or because conditioning peace upon the impunity of one side to a conflict is less likely to create a stable peace). Likewise, the differential timing of an amnesty—that is, one enacted in the midst of a conflict or peace process versus one enacted while a repressive regime is in office or during peacetime—might be relevant. Amnesties passed in peacetime, after the end of a conflict, are less likely to affect international peace than amnesties passed in the midst of a conflict as part of a peace process.

Security Council deferral might provide a means of implementing a temporary amnesty—in other words, a temporary suspension from prosecution. Such a temporary amnesty could be conditional on a number of things, including a requirement that the beneficiaries not take up arms again and actively support peace and reconciliation efforts (for example, through revealing information and testifying before a truth commission, and by providing some form of reparation to their victims, whether monetary or through good works). One could thus imagine a state working with the Security Council to craft a period of deferral based on conditions that further peace, justice, and reconciliation. Such a scenario would only arise if the prosecutor initiated an investigation or prosecution under Article 53 or Article 17, as discussed earlier. In other words, a deferral on the basis of an amnesty would only come into play if there was a strong difference of opinion between the prosecutor and a suspect's state and the Security Council.

Ne Bis In Idem

Article 20 codifies the generally recognized principle of criminal law forbidding double jeopardy, referred to as *ne bis in idem* in ICL. That provision provides that a suspect will not be prosecuted before the ICC if he or she has already been convicted or acquitted by a court, unless the proceedings were: (1) designed to shield the suspect from responsibility for crimes within the jurisdiction of the court, or (2) were not conducted independently or impartially, but rather, in a manner inconsistent with bringing the person concerned to justice.

For this provision to apply to an amnesty, two interpretive hurdles must be overcome. First, the granting of an amnesty would have to qualify as a conviction or acquittal. Second, such conviction or acquittal would have to be achieved by a court. On the first point, an amnesty cannot be characterized as an acquittal. An individual is acquitted when it is determined that he or she is not responsible for an alleged crime for either factual or legal reasons. An amnesty, by definition, assumes that the individual is guilty, but withholds punishment. An amnesty might more easily be characterized as a conviction if one could establish that the individual was found to be responsible or guilty and subject to some form of punishment. The first element — a determination of guilt or responsibility — is an easier requirement, as most amnesties implicitly, and some explicitly, establish individual responsibility. The second element — the imposition of some form of punishment — is less common with respect to an amnesty. For instance, the East Timorese amnesty law did require some form of reparation from its beneficiaries, whereas the South African amnesty law did not.

On the second point, an amnesty administered by a court may more clearly qualify as a prior adjudication. The question arises when the amnesty is administered by a quasi-judicial body like a truth commission. Some argue that such quasi-judicial bodies cannot qualify as a court. We do not think the issue is so clear, and one could argue that a body like the South African Amnesty Committee — consisting solely of judges or attorneys and operating independently of the executive branch — could sufficiently qualify as a court to trigger the attachment of double jeopardy.

EXCUSES AND JUSTIFICATIONS

Most of the defenses found in domestic criminal law are also found in ICL, such as the defenses of mistake, duress, incapacity, self-defense, superior orders, and necessity. The source and elements of many of these defenses within ICL is found in customary international law and general principles of law. Rather than discuss each of these defenses in turn, we focus here on one as an illustrative example — the debate concerning necessity as an excuse for torture.

The prohibition against torture is one of the most codified prohibitions in international human rights law. It can be found in the Universal Declaration of Human Rights, the International Covenant on Civil and Political Rights (ICCPR), all regional human rights treaties, the Geneva Conventions, the Cairo Declaration on Human Rights in Islam, the statutes of all hybrid and ad hoc international criminal tribunals, and the Rome Treaty establishing the ICC. In addition, the prohibition against torture has its own dedicated treaty, the Convention Against Torture, which also prohibits acts that fall short of torture but constitute cruel, inhuman, or degrading treatment or punishment. None of these manifestations of the prohibition of torture contains any codified exception. The ICCPR, for example, does not list the prohibition against torture as one of the rights from which a state may derogate in times of emergency. It is also generally accepted that torture has risen to the level of a *jus cogens* prohibition, binding on all states regardless of treaty commitments or persistent objection.

Despite the universal formal acceptance by states of the absolute prohibition against torture, since the launching of the so-called "global war on terror", some, including government officials in the United States, have argued that there may be circumstances in which torture and other forms of harsh treatment would be morally permissible, and thus should be legally permissible. This debate about justifications for torture has proceeded alongside a second debate about what constitutes torture. The United States, for example, has argued that "waterboarding," or the controlled drowning of an individual, does not constitute torture. By contrast, the Committee Against Torture—the body of experts appointed to interpret the Convention Against Torture—and other experts conclude that such a procedure does constitute torture.

Those who argue that there are some circumstances in which torture may be permissible most often use the defense of necessity to support their position. The necessity defense has been invoked in two ways to justify torture. First, the necessity defense has been cited to support the use of torture in response to threats of terrorism. The argument is that the threat from terrorism is so great, and the consequences of terrorist acts are so immense, that the use of torture on suspected terrorists is justified to prevent a future attack. This defense is more properly characterized as a justification, rather than a legal defense. A legal defense is premised on the idea that the underlying act is in fact wrongful, but that the circumstances remove liability for this otherwise wrongful act.

This first use of the necessity defense attempts to provide an *ex ante* justification for torture, in effect arguing quite broadly that the act of torture is legal in all cases involving suspected terrorists.

The two states where this issue has been raised at the highest levels of government are the United States and Israel. The question has not been squarely faced by a court in the United States, but it has been the subject of a Supreme Court decision in Israel.[23] In the Israeli case, the Israeli security forces argued that the necessity defense justified the adoption of an interrogation policy that includes severe physical and mental techniques (such as prolonged sleep deprivation and a form of shaking that, in some cases, has resulted in death) given the ongoing threat of terrorism. The Israeli Supreme Court rejected this argument, noting that the necessity defense could not be used as "a general authority to establish directives respecting the use of physical means during the course of a[n] . . . interrogation."[24] In other words, the necessity defense cannot be used as the basis of forward-looking authority for, in this case, interrogation policy.

Whereas this first use of the necessity defense is forward looking, the second use is backward looking. The second use of the necessity defense would be employed by the torturer as an individualized defense in a criminal prosecution or other form of accountability mechanism. The Rome Treaty allows a form of necessity defense before the ICC in Article 31(1)(d), which provides for the exclusion of criminal liability if the act is (1) caused by duress (2) that results from a threat of imminent death or continuing or imminent serious bodily harm (3) against the actor or another person, where (4) the act is reasonable and necessary to avoid the threat, and (5) where the actor does not intend to cause a harm greater than the one sought to be avoided. Note in particular that the act must be in response to an imminent threat, and that there are requirements of both reasonableness and proportionality.

The paradigmatic example cited to illustrate this use of the necessity defense is the "ticking time bomb" scenario. This scenario contains several elements: A state has in custody an individual who knows the location of a bomb that is set to detonate imminently, the detonation will result in the death of a number of people, the individual will reveal the location of the bomb under torture, and the authorities will be able to defuse it in time to save innocent civilians. The necessity theory is that torturing the suspect to force him or her to reveal the location of the bomb is justified by the number of lives saved. This scenario of course is dependent on a number of factual premises that will be rarely — if ever — all present in the real world: (1) that the detonation of the bomb is imminent, (2) that the person in custody in fact knows the location of the bomb, (3) that the person will reveal that information if tortured, (4) that the authorities will be able to defuse the bomb, (5) that detonation is the only way to save lives, and (6) that no other techniques will get the individual to talk.

Consider the following, which sets forth the consequentialist justification for the necessity defense:

> Necessity as a justification derives from consequential moral theories, according to which wrongful actions may be morally deemed by the goodness of their consequences. It justifies the sacrifice of legitimate interests to protect other interests of substantially higher value. It does not grant the individual "a license to determine social utility." It is rather limited to emergency cases in which there is an imminent and concrete danger to an interest recognized by the legal system. In the context of this discussion, such an emergency exists in the "ticking bomb" situation, in which a bomb has been set to explode imminently and innocent people are likely to be killed. The only hope for saving their lives is to get information about the location of the bomb in order to defuse it. Should necessity justify the use of force in an attempt to coerce the person under interrogation to reveal such information?

The justification of necessity rests on the balance between interests of innocent persons. The sacrifice of an innocent person's interests is justified when necessary to save those of another, when that other person's interests have a higher value. Therefore, if necessity is to apply to ticking bomb situations it will justify the use of interrogational force against the *innocent*. Taken to extreme, necessity might prima facie justify the use of force against a terrorist's child in order to force the terrorist to reveal the information about the location of a bomb he has planted. Even to consequentialists the use of force against the child might seem morally repugnant. No one should torture innocent children — even when done to produce a sizeable gain in aggregate welfare.[25]

Although necessity may not be available in all cases involving the use of torture, might there be some situations when it would be justified under ICL? As you study defenses under ICL, consider when a necessity defense might be applicable to a charge of war crimes, crimes against humanity, or genocide.

CONCLUSION

Immunities, amnesties, and excuses all limit the ability to hold individuals accountable for violations of ICL. Immunities are historically well established under international law, although as we have seen they are weakening before institutions of international criminal accountability. The recent pronouncement of the ICJ on the issue would limit some immunities to situations involving transnational assertions of jurisdiction by coequal sovereigns and remove their use before international tribunals. Although ICJ decisions are not considered precedential or binding on parties not before the court, numerous treaties ratified by the vast majority of states (including the Genocide Convention and the Rome Treaty) make clear that such immunities are no longer available to those who commit the most serious international crimes.

Like immunities, the legality of amnesties has also been reduced by a variety of recent developments, including challenges before the Inter-American Court of Human Rights. Amnesties are still used by states negotiating the end of a period of violent conflict, but the general consensus is that such amnesties are illegal if they do not allow for some form of individualized accountability.

Finally, ICL, like its domestic counterpart, allows a number of defenses, excuses, and justifications to criminal liability. We highlighted one of the more controversial applications of an excuse in the context of torture. Whereas in the first two cases — immunities and amnesties — one sees a trend toward increasing accountability by limiting historically-used mechanisms, in the case of torture and the necessity defense, one sees a challenge by some states (most notably the United States) to the generally accepted absolute prohibition against torture. The struggle over defining the proper contours of immunities, amnesties, and excuses is a microcosm of the more general struggle between those who push for increased accountability for international crimes and those who resist such incursions on powers historically reserved to states.

～ 10 ～

Forms of Individual Responsibility

Crimes against international law are committed by men, not by abstract entities, and only by punishing individuals who commit such crimes can the provisions of international law be enforced.

So wrote the Nuremberg Tribunal in its historic judgment. Modern international criminal law (ICL) is premised on individual — as opposed to state or collective — responsibility. Shifting responsibility from the collective to the individual was a doctrinal revolution that has made possible the multitude of international criminal proceedings going forward today. In fact, at the moment, it is far easier to hold individuals responsible for international crimes than states or other collectives.

The shift from collective to individual responsibility required the development of *forms* of individual responsibility. Like domestic law, ICL recognizes different types of responsibility that trigger individual liability. Some forms of responsibility employed in ICL — like complicity, conspiracy, and incitement — trace their origins to familiar domestic law principles. Other forms of responsibility — such as superior responsibility — are more unique to international law.

Liability may be divided into two broad types: principal and accessory. Thus, a defendant can be found liable as a principal if he or she committed, planned, or ordered a crime. Likewise, the defendant may be found liable as an accessory if he or she instigated, incited, aided and abetted, or was complicit in a crime. Many of these forms of liability inevitably involve two or more participants in criminal behavior: the direct perpetrator (who personally commits the crime and is directly liable) and the accessory (who is responsible for making some knowing and substantial contribution to the crime). Domestic criminal law recognizes various forms of complicity liability during the life of a crime, including the roles of accessories before and after the fact. To a certain extent, these forms exist in ICL as well.

Because international crimes often involve the participation of multiple individuals over vast expanses of time and space, premising liability on the defendant's relationship, association, or joint action with others has become increasingly important in ICL. In addition, criminal law has long recognized the particular dangers posed by group criminality, where individuals may be influenced and encouraged by their peers and be less willing to abandon a criminal enterprise if others are involved. In the United States in particular, prosecutors use the doctrine of conspiracy to capture the web of activity associated with organized criminal activity. Internationally, the concept of conspiracy is somewhat disfavored, except with respect to the crime of genocide.* Instead, we find a related

---

*The Genocide Convention included the crime of conspiracy to commit genocide because the goal of the Convention was not only to punish perpetrators, but also to prevent acts of genocide. In the case against Musema, one Trial Chamber of the Rwandan Tribunal, drawing on the Convention's *travaux* (drafting history) and common law and civil law understandings of conspiracy, defined conspiracy to commit genocide as "an agreement between two or more persons to commit the crime of genocide." *Prosecutor v. Musema*, Case No. ICTR-96-13-A, Judgment & Sentence, at ¶ 191 (Jan. 27, 2000). That Trial Chamber held that an accused cannot be convicted of both genocide and conspiracy to commit

doctrine of liability in the joint criminal enterprise, although the two forms present some significant differences.

Forms of liability in ICL find expression in three primary sources of international law: treaty law, customary international law, and general principles of law. Many international treaties, as well as the statutes of the ad hoc international tribunals, expressly set forth applicable forms of liability. For example, the Genocide Convention at Article III makes punishable acts of conspiracy, incitement, attempt, and complicity to commit genocide, in addition to the direct commission of genocide. Likewise, the Torture Convention at Article 4(1) obliges states to punish attempts to commit torture and complicity in torture. Superior responsibility first found expression in Protocol I to the Geneva Conventions at Article 86(2). Superior responsibility was later codified in the statutes of the ad hoc war crimes tribunals (see Article 7(3) of the Yugoslav Tribunal Statute and Article 6(3) of the Rwanda Tribunal Statute) and the International Criminal Court (see Article 28 of the ICC Statute).

Although these treaties identify applicable forms of responsibility, they provide little in the way of concrete standards for determining when the participation of an individual in the principal crime rises to the level of complicity, conspiracy, or attempt. For this, the modern international criminal tribunals have had to rely on general principles of law, World War II precedent, and other indicia of customary international law to identify more precise elements of proof for establishing liability. Furthermore, as is the case in domestic law, the line between these various forms of participation is not a sharp

---

genocide, as the latter crime merges with the former if genocide is actually committed, *id.* at ¶ 198, and that it must be demonstrated that the defendant possessed the specific intent to commit genocide. *id.* at ¶ 192. Musema was ultimately acquitted of conspiracy to commit genocide, because there was insufficient evidence that he conspired with others to commit genocide or reached an agreement to that end. *id.* at ¶ 940.

one. As you read the materials in your primary text, consider whether the standards of liability being developed in ICL are consistent with domestic criminal law standards. Where ICL departs from domestic law concepts and standards, ask yourself whether this is attributable to something special about ICL and whether judges are adequately explaining the disparity.

In this chapter, we briefly discuss two forms of responsibility: superior responsibility and complicity (including joint criminal enterprise). This is not a complete discussion of the forms of liability used within ICL, or a thorough discussion of these two specific forms of accessory liability. Instead, we focus on these two forms of accessory liability to highlight some of the more interesting and controversial challenges facing the development and adjudication of ICL. In particular, these forms of responsibility have the potential to extend liability far beyond the direct perpetrator of international crimes. Consider to what extent these extensions are warranted in light of the nature of international crimes and whether ICL, by sanctioning expansive forms of indirect liability, has remained faithful to a foundational principle of the criminal law: individual fault.

SUPERIOR RESPONSIBILITY

The doctrine of superior (or command) responsibility originated in international humanitarian law (IHL), although it is often invoked in domestic military justice proceedings. The doctrine of superior responsibility in the military context is a direct consequence of the principle of responsible command, which grants military superiors the privilege of ordering their subordinates to engage in acts of violence that — outside of a state of war — would be unlawful. The assumption is that the most effective way to prevent abuses is by placing potential liability on a superior operating within the context of a disciplined military structure. The essence of the doctrine of superior responsibility is that a defendant can be held legally responsible, either criminally or civilly, for unlawful acts committed by his or her subordinates. Superior responsibility attaches if the defendant had actual or constructive knowledge that his or her subordinates were committing abuses and he or she did not take necessary and reasonable measures to prevent these abuses or to punish the perpetrators. The theory of liability is thus premised on the commander's failure to exercise powers of command and control over subordinates in the face of a duty to act. Although originally developed in the military context, the doctrine of superior responsibility applies to both military and civilian superiors, albeit with some distinctions.

History of the Doctrine

By way of background, although the concept of superior responsibility can be found in early IHL treaties, it was in the post–World War I period that individual criminal responsibility for command responsibility was first contemplated at the international level. The Commission on the Responsibility of the Authors of the War and on Enforcement of Penalties recommended that the German ex-Kaiser and other leaders be tried for war crimes because they "were cognizant of and could at least have mitigated the barbarities committed during the course of the war. A word from them would have brought about a different method in the action of their subordinates on land, at sea and in the air."[1]

The contemplated trials of responsible World War I leaders, however, never came to fruition. It was not until the post–World War II period that international courts and military commissions first adjudicated the doctrine of superior responsibility, although neither the Nuremberg nor the Tokyo Charters set forth the elements of the doctrine. With respect to the International Military Tribunal at Nuremberg (IMT), a U.S.

proposal to refer to the responsibility for the "omission of a superior officer to prevent war crimes when he knows of, or is on notice as to, their commission or contemplated commission and is in a position to prevent them" was not included in the IMT Charter. Nonetheless, the Nuremberg Tribunal invoked superior responsibility without enunciating the precise elements of the doctrine, no doubt because of the strong evidence of the direct involvement of the accused in the design and implementation of the atrocities that were the subject of the Indictment. In contrast, the International Military Tribunal for the Far East (the Tokyo Tribunal) was much more diligent in applying the theory of liability to each defendant pursuant to Count 55 of the Indictment, which read:

> The Defendants . . . being by virtue of their respective offices responsible for securing the observance of the said Conventions and assurances and the Laws and Customs of War in respect of the armed forces in the countries hereinafter named and in respect of many thousands of prisoners of war and civilians then in the power of Japan belonging to the [Allies] deliberately and recklessly disregarded their legal duty to take adequate steps to secure the observance and prevent breaches thereof, and thereby violated the laws of war.

Both military and civilian superiors, including high-level members of the Japanese Cabinet, were convicted by the Tokyo Tribunal solely on the basis of the activities of their subordinates.

The most famous, and indeed infamous, of the command responsibility trials held in the postwar period concerned General Tomoyuki Yamashita, who was charged with liability under a theory of command responsibility for war crimes committed by Japanese troops in the occupied Philippines. General Yamashita's conviction by a U.S. military commission was brought before the U.S. Supreme Court on a petition for the writ of *habeas corpus*. The Supreme Court denied the appeal, finding that the military commission had authority to try General Yamashita and that it was without jurisdiction to rule on the substantive issue of the defendant's guilt or innocence. The Court found no issue with the charge asserted, stating that military commanders have "an affirmative duty to take such measures as were within his power and appropriate in the circumstances to protect prisoners of war and the civilian population."[2]

Justices Rutledge and Murphy vigorously dissented from the judgment. In an opinion that has resonance today, Justice Murphy strongly criticized the military commissions that were used to prosecute General Yamashita and the way in which they framed the charge of superior responsibility:

> [General Yamashita] was rushed to trial under an improper charge, given insufficient time to prepare an adequate defense, deprived of the benefits of some of the most elementary rules of evidence and summarily sentenced to be hanged. In all this needless and unseemly haste there was no serious attempt to charge or to prove that he committed a recognized violation of the laws of war. He was not charged with personally participating in the acts of atrocity or with ordering or condoning their commission. Not even knowledge of these crimes was attributed to him. It was simply alleged that he unlawfully disregarded and failed to discharge his duty as commander to control the operations of the members of his command, permitting them to commit the acts of atrocity. The recorded annals of warfare and the established principles of international law afford not the slightest precedent for such a charge. . . . No one in a position of command in an army, from sergeant to general, can escape those implications. Indeed, the fate of some future President of the United States and his chiefs of staff and military advisers may well have been sealed by this decision. . . . To subject an enemy belligerent

> to an unfair trial, to charge him with an unrecognized crime, or to vent on him our retributive emotions only antagonizes the enemy nation and hinders the reconciliation necessary to a peaceful world.[3]

General Yamashita was thereafter hanged. The *Yamashita* precedent continues to "cast a long shadow" over subsequent superior responsibility jurisprudence because of lingering concerns about the unfairness of the proceedings against him.[4]

Subsequent World War II–related prosecutions built on this initial application of command responsibility. Most notably, the so-called High Command Case, brought under the authority of Control Council Law No. 10, involved the trial of senior German officers for the execution of civilians and prisoners of war. The tribunal rejected the notion — advanced by the prosecution — that the command responsibility doctrine provided for the *per se* liability of a commander within a chain of command. Rather, the tribunal established the principle that to be held liable, the commander must have had knowledge of abuses by subordinates and must have failed to act in the face of such knowledge.[5] In the Hostage Case, the tribunal convicted top German officers for war crimes, including the unlawful taking and killing of hostages. The tribunal elaborated on what constitutes negligence with respect to knowledge of the acts of subordinates:

> An army commander will not ordinarily be permitted to deny knowledge of reports received at his headquarters, they being sent there for his special benefit. Neither will he ordinarily be permitted to deny knowledge of happenings within the area of his command while he is present therein. It would strain the credulity of the Tribunal to believe that a high ranking military commander would permit himself to get out of touch with current happenings in the area of his command during wartime.[6]

Superior Responsibility in Treaty Law

Given these and other precedents, one would have expected the drafters of the Geneva Conventions of 1949 — still today the most authoritative source of IHL — to codify the doctrine of command responsibility. It was only with the drafting of the 1977 Protocols to the Geneva Conventions, however, that a command responsibility standard first entered positive law. Protocol I (which defined international armed conflicts to include those armed conflicts waged for self-determination against colonial domination, alien occupation, and racist regimes) set forth the test for command responsibility in Articles 86 and 87:

> Article 86: Failure to Act
>
> 2. The fact that a breach of the Conventions or of this Protocol was committed by a subordinate does not absolve his superiors from penal or disciplinary responsibility, as the case may be, if they knew, or had information which should have enabled them to conclude in the circumstances at the time, that he was committing or was going to commit such a breach and if they did not take all feasible measures within their power to prevent or repress the breach.
>
> Article 87: Duty of Commanders
>
> 1. The High Contracting Parties and the Parties to the conflict shall require military commanders, with respect to members of the armed forces under their command and other persons under their control, to prevent and, where necessary, to suppress and to report to competent authorities breaches of the Conventions and of this Protocol. . . .
>
> 3. The High Contracting Parties and Parties to the conflict shall require any commander who is aware that subordinates or other persons under his control are going to commit or have committed a breach of the Conventions or

of this Protocol, to initiate such steps as are necessary to prevent such violations of the Conventions or this Protocol, and, where appropriate, to initiate disciplinary or penal action against violators thereof.[7]

Although Protocol I applies only to international armed conflicts, the ad hoc tribunals have held that the doctrine of command responsibility exists in noninternational armed conflicts as a matter of customary international law, regardless of whether a relevant state party has ratified the 1977 Protocols to the Geneva Conventions.[8]

Subsequent codifications have subtly altered the formulation of the doctrine in important ways. This doctrinal evolution is most notable with respect to the *mens rea* requirement, resulting in some uncertainty about what level of knowledge is required for a commander to be held liable for the acts of his or her subordinates. Article 6(3) of the Statute of the Rwanda Tribunal (ICTR), for example, provides:

> The fact that any of the acts [criminalized in] the present Statute was committed by a subordinate does not relieve his or her superior of criminal responsibility if he or she knew or had reason to know that the subordinate was about to commit such acts or had done so and the superior failed to take the necessary and reasonable measures to prevent such acts or to punish the perpetrators thereof.

The ICTR thus replaces Protocol I's "had information which should have enabled them to conclude in the circumstances at the time" with the "had reason to know" standard, which sounds more like a traditional negligence test. The ICC has another, more elaborate, formulation that for the first time expressly distinguishes between military and civilian superiors:

Article 28
Responsibility of commanders and other superiors
In addition to other grounds of criminal responsibility under this Statute for crimes within the jurisdiction of the Court;

(a) A military commander or person effectively acting as a military commander shall be criminally responsible for crimes within the jurisdiction of the Court committed by forces under his or her effective command and control, or effective authority and control as the case may be, as a result of his or her failure to exercise control properly over such forces, where:

(i) That military commander or person either knew or, owing to the circumstances at the time, should have known that the forces were committing or about to commit such crimes; and

(ii) That military commander or person failed to take all necessary and reasonable measures within his or her power to prevent or repress their commission or to submit the matter to the competent authorities for investigation and prosecution.

(b) With respect to superior and subordinate relationships not described in paragraph (a), a superior shall be criminally responsible for crimes within the jurisdiction of the Court committed by subordinates under his or her effective authority and control, as a result of his or her failure to exercise control properly over such subordinates, where:

(i) The superior either knew, or consciously disregarded information which clearly indicated, that the subordinates were committing or about to commit such crimes;

(ii) The crimes concerned activities that were within the effective responsibility and control of the superior; and

(iii) The superior failed to take all necessary and reasonable measures within his or her power to prevent or repress their commission or to submit the matter to the competent authorities for investigation and prosecution.

Elements of the Contemporary Doctrine

According to most modern formulations as set forth earlier, the doctrine of superior responsibility comprises three primary elements:

1. A relationship of *subordination* between the direct perpetrators of the unlawful acts and the superior/ defendant.
2. The superior/defendant knew or should have known that his or her subordinates were committing, had committed, or were about to commit abuses (the *mens rea* element).
3. The superior/defendant failed to take adequate steps to prevent or punish such abuses (the *actus reus* element).

In adjudicating a case against a defendant superior, the finder of fact considers these elements in logical sequence. Thus, the finder of fact's first step is to determine whether the direct perpetrators of the acts that underlie the indictment were subordinates of the defendant. This prong of the doctrine ensures that any measures undertaken by the defendant to prevent or punish abuses would have reached the individuals accused of directly perpetrating the acts in question. If this prong is satisfied, it must be determined whether the defendant was on notice that his or her subordinates were committing abuses. It is this knowledge, which may be actual or constructive, that triggers the superior's duty to act. Finally, if the defendant possessed the requisite knowledge, then the finder of fact must determine whether the defendant fulfilled his or her duty to act in the face of this knowledge. In this regard, the finder of fact must determine whether the defendant did all that was necessary and reasonable under the circumstances to prevent and punish criminal conduct by his or her subordinates. A defendant is legally responsible for the acts complained of where there is sufficient evidence that he or she failed to implement appropriate preventative and punitive measures in light of his or her knowledge that subordinates were committing, or had committed, abuses.

Subordination

The requirement of subordination is an inquiry concerning the relationship between a superior and his or her subordinate, and more particularly determines the point at which we feel comfortable holding the former accountable for the actions of the latter. If the test is too lax, then we may hold individuals liable for actions over which they effectively had little control (as many argue was the case with Yamashita). If the test is too strict, we risk absolving individuals who had the power to stop ongoing atrocities, and thus send a weak signal of deterrence to current and future military and civilian leaders.

The International Criminal Tribunal for the Former Yugoslavia (ICTY) has ruled that the required relationship of subordination between the defendant and the direct perpetrator(s) is established if the defendant exercised "effective control" over the individual perpetrator(s).[9] This requires showing that the defendant had the "material ability to prevent and punish the commission of the offenses" at issue.[10] Under this formulation, a showing of de jure command over the direct perpetrators within a military hierarchy or formal chain of command is a relevant but not sufficient showing to satisfy this first prong of the doctrine. Thus, even where a commander had the legal authority to control the actions of his or her subordinates by virtue of his or her rank or position within a military hierarchy, a finding of liability under the doctrine of command responsibility requires proof that the commander could actually exercise that power as a factual matter. Thus, the Trial Chamber required a showing of de facto control in addition to de jure command. The theory behind the adoption of this standard is that the "doctrine of command responsibility is ultimately predicated upon the power of the superior to control the acts of his subordinates."[11]

The ICTY developed the effective control standard in the context of allegations that certain defendants' de jure positions did not accurately reflect their de facto powers to prevent or punish criminal conduct by subordinates. These allegations came from both the prosecution and the defense. For example, in *Delalić* the prosecution argued that Delalić exercised considerable control and authority within a prison camp, even though there was no official instrument or letter of appointment conferring to him any formal responsibility over the camp. In adopting the effective control standard, the *Delalić* Trial Chamber noted that such situations are often found in the context of civil wars, in which "previously existing formal structures have broken down and where, during an interim period, the new, possibly improvised, control and command structures may be ambiguous and ill-defined."[12] In other cases, defendants argued that they actually possessed less power than their de jure positions would suggest. The ICTY has accepted this defense, although it developed a rebuttable presumption that de facto control exists where there is de jure command. The ICTY thus confirmed that the effective control standard governs the determination of the subordination prong in all superior responsibility situations, including those involving de jure commanders whose formal rank or position is uncontested.[13]

Although the *Delalić* tribunal purported to adopt a uniform standard, the doctrine of effective control requires different inquiries and produces different legal strategies with respect to de facto and de jure command and control. With respect to de facto commanders, the effective control standard ensures that individuals lacking formal rank or title, or operating outside of any official or sanctioned chain of command, can still be held liable for abuses committed by individuals under their actual command or control. Conversely, with respect to de jure commanders, the effective control standard ensures that they can be held liable for abuses by individuals not formally under their command, but who are nonetheless under their control, such as death squad members or civilians within occupied territory. The effective control standard also ensures that commanders possessing formal command or authority are not held responsible for the criminal conduct of individuals who may be formal subordinates, but who are not under a commander's actual control by virtue of the prevailing circumstances (where, for example, lines of communication or the chain of command have been severed).

With respect to civilian superiors, the existence of a superior–subordinate relationship may be even more difficult to prove. As noted earlier, the ICC Statute defines subordination in the civilian context in terms of "effective authority and control" rather than "effective command" to reflect the fact that civilian subordinates are not generally considered under the "command" of their superiors. The prosecutor must also show that the direct perpetrator's actions "concerned activities that were within the effective responsibility and control of the superior." This reflects the fact that political and civilian leaders rarely possess formal powers of control that match those of military commanders. This does not mean that such individuals cannot exercise high degrees of de facto control over their subordinates, but this can be more difficult to prove.[14]

Mens Rea

The superior responsibility *mens rea* standard has been formulated in several different ways in the jurisprudence and in treaty law. These permutations span the gamut from those sounding of strict liability to those requiring a showing of negligence, recklessness, willful blindness, or even actual knowledge. A more liberal view of the evidence required to show knowledge (for example, an assumption that reports prepared by subordinates were in fact submitted to and read by a superior) has the effect of expanding the scope of superior liability. On the other hand, requiring a showing of actual knowledge might be impossible from the perspective of available proof in a wartime situation. Regardless of the standard employed, most tribunals agree that this prong may be satisfied by circumstantial evidence. As you read through cases involving superior or command responsibility, pay particular attention to the evidence presented to prove the knowledge requirement, and ask yourself if the tribunal's decision is fair to the accused or creates reasonable expectations and incentives for civilian and military leaders in the future.

The ICC Statute introduced a significant alteration with respect to the knowledge requirement for cases involving a civilian versus a military superior. For a military superior, the knowledge requirement is a form of the familiar "knew or should have known" test; for a civilian superior, the burden on the prosecutor is higher, requiring a showing of actual knowledge or "conscious disregard" of information that "clearly indicated" subordinate wrongdoing. The assumption behind this more rigorous standard is that military organizations have more formal and more efficient channels of communication than do civilian organizations, and thus it is reasonable to place the more onerous "should have known" test on a military commander. The easier test for liability places a greater incentive on military commanders to seek out information about the actions of their subordinates so as to ensure their adherence to the laws of armed conflict.

Actus Reus (Omission)

The doctrine of superior responsibility premises liability on an omission: The superior is found liable for failing to act when under a duty to do so. As noted by the ICTY in *Halilović*:

> Command responsibility is responsibility for an omission. The commander is responsible for the failure to perform an

act required by international law. This omission is culpable because international law imposes an affirmative duty on superiors to prevent and punish crimes committed by their subordinates.[15]

Under the doctrine of superior responsibility, the defendant superior is thus liable for his or her own omissions and not vicariously liable for the acts of his or her subordinates.

This third prong of the command responsibility doctrine is formulated in the disjunctive, providing that a superior is liable when he or she either fails to prevent abuses or fails to punish them after the fact. That said, the failure to prevent and the failure to punish criminal conduct are related inquiries. A failure to punish infractions may be viewed as a failure to prevent by essentially giving the "green light" to future abuses and contributing to a climate of impunity. Determining what concrete measures the defendant should have taken is intimately connected to the degree of actual power possessed by the superior, so this prong must be established on a case-by-case basis.

Superior responsibility should not be confused with liability for ordering an act, which is a form of direct, not accessorial, liability. The act of ordering usually occurs in the context of a superior–subordinate relationship as well, although proof of de jure subordination is not required.* A superior prosecuted for ordering a subordinate to commit a crime, however, is held

---

*The ICTY and ICTR have differed over the presence of a superior–subordinate relationship in the context of a charge of ordering a crime. The ICTR presumed such a relationship in the *Akayesu* case: "Ordering implies a superior–subordinate relationship between the person giving the order and the one executing it. In other words, the person in a position of authority uses it to convince another to commit an offense." *Prosecutor v. Akayesu,* Case No. ICTR-96-4-T, Judgment, ¶ 483 (Sept. 2, 1990). In contrast, the ICTY has stated that "no formal superior–subordinate relationship is required for a finding of 'ordering' so long as it is demonstrated that the accused possessed the authority to order." *Prosecutor v. Kordić & Čerkez,* Case No. IT-95-14/2, Judgment, ¶ 388 (Feb. 26, 2001).

liable for his or her own affirmative act — the issuing of an unlawful order — not an omission.*

This discussion of the elements of superior responsibility confirms that the doctrine is not predicated on a strict liability standard. If the prosecution fails to establish any of the three elements, a defendant should be exonerated. This should occur where there is insufficient evidence that the direct perpetrators were the defendant's subordinates or under the defendant's effective control, or where there is insufficient evidence that the defendant had knowledge, either actual or constructive, of subordinates' abuses. Likewise, acquittal is appropriate where the evidence indicates that the defendant undertook sufficient measures to prevent and punish criminal conduct given his or her level of command and other relevant circumstances. In any of these situations, a defendant should be exonerated notwithstanding that the crimes were committed.

As important as the doctrine of command responsibility is in ICL, the ad hoc tribunals have expressed a distinct preference for convicting defendants on the basis of some more direct form of liability (ordering offenses, complicity in offenses, and so on) if both have been proven. As the ICTY held in *Blaškić*:

> the Appeals Chamber considers that, in relation to a particular count, it is not appropriate to convict under both Article 7(1) [listing forms of direct and accessory responsibility] and

---

*The doctrine of superior orders works in tandem with direct liability for ordering abuses to ensure that criminal responsibility exists up the chain of command. As formulated by the Nuremberg Charter, the doctrine of superior orders provides that "the fact that a Defendant acted pursuant to order of his Government or of a superior shall not free him from responsibility, but may be considered in mitigation of punishment if the Tribunal determines that justice so requires." Charter of the International Military Tribunal of Aug. 8, 1945, art. 8, *annexed to* Agreement for the Prosecution and Punishment of the Major War Criminals of the European Axis, Aug. 8, 1945, 59 Stat. 1544. The ICC Statute at Article 33 provides that superior orders may constitute a full defense where the defendant was under a legal obligation to obey orders, the person did not know that the order was unlawful, and the order was not manifestly unlawful.

Article 7(3) [superior responsibility] of the [ICTY] Statute. Where both [forms of] responsibility are alleged under the same count, and where the legal requirements pertaining to both of these heads of responsibility are met, a Trial Chamber should enter a conviction on the basis of Article 7(1) only, and consider the accused's superior position as an aggravating factor in sentencing.[16]

Because of the difficulty of proving effective control and the knowledge element of the doctrine of superior responsibility, prosecutors before the international criminal tribunals are increasingly utilizing the theory of the joint criminal enterprise to address crimes committed by multiple individuals, even individuals within a formal chain of command where the doctrine of superior responsibility would also apply. Rather than holding superiors liable for failing to control their subordinates in a vertical fashion, the theory of the joint criminal enterprise allows — under certain circumstances — for the lateral imposition of liability on all members of a group acting with a common purpose when any member commits a criminal act.

COMPLICITY AND JOINT CRIMINAL ENTERPRISE

Most international crimes are committed as part of an armed conflict or large-scale atrocities involving many people, both perpetrators and victims. Such crimes are often the result of concerted action by groups of individuals. Sometimes these groups are formally organized (within a state bureaucracy or military organization); other times they are less formal or more spontaneous. How should the law ascribe individual criminal

---

This provision will be applicable mainly in the war crimes context, as the Article notes that orders to commit genocide or crimes against humanity are manifestly unlawful as a matter of law.

responsibility when various members of a group have contributed to the commission of international crimes in differing degrees? Which members of such organizations should be held criminally liable when other members are involved in international crimes? When should members of a group be liable for acts that were not part of the goal of the group, but were nonetheless committed in the context of concerted action toward that goal? In addition, how wide should the net be cast? We have so far mentioned the principal actor (i.e., the person who pulls the proverbial trigger) and that person's military or civilian superior. What about colleagues? Support staff? The architect of the concentration camp? The driver who transports civilians to be executed? The person who provides financing to the organization?

Complicity

The Allied Powers at the end of World War II were confronted directly with the challenge of applying individual accountability for atrocities made possible by organized and cooperating individuals. To respond to this phenomenon, the U.S. negotiators in particular argued for the inclusion of complicity and conspiracy as applicable forms of responsibility.* The reference to complicity liability in the Nuremberg charter

---

*The United States also argued for the recognition of the concept of criminal organizations. According to this theory, the Prosecution would seek a declaration from the Nuremberg Tribunal on the illegality of indicted organizations — such as the *Schutzstaffel* (SS), an elite paramilitary unit, and the Gestapo, the secret police. Each member of those organizations would be subject to arrest and prosecution before national courts based solely on his or her membership in a convicted organization. The Tribunal's declaratory judgment would be *res judicata* in individual proceedings against organization members. The burden would then shift to the individual defendants to prove either that membership in the organization was involuntary or that they did not know the organization's criminal object and purpose. This doctrine of collective responsibility was adopted, but underutilized in the post–World War II period and has not been revived with the rest of the Nuremberg legacy.

was, like most of its provisions, general: that "[l]eaders, orga-nizers, instigators and accomplices participating in the formu-lation or execution of a common plan or conspiracy to commit any of the foregoing crimes [crimes against the peace, war crimes, and crimes against humanity] are responsible for all acts performed by any persons in execution of such plan." The Nuremberg and Tokyo tribunals also recognized a substantive crime of conspiracy to prepare, initiate, and wage aggressive war, although this charge remained controversial.

The World War II-related judgments adopted a liberal view of the *actus reas* of complicity liability, an approach that has been generally followed by the present-day ad hoc tribunals. For example, moral support provided by the mere presence of an individual during the commission of a crime, without any other specific act, may be sufficient to trigger liability if the presence of the accused provides encouragement to those directly involved in the criminal act.[17] This was the position taken by the ICTR Trial Chamber in *Akayesu,* which found that the presence and verbal encouragement of Akayesu dur-ing the rape and mistreatment of civilians were sufficient to impose accessory liability on him for those crimes.[18] The standard adopted by today's tribunals is that an individual who provides knowing assistance that has "a substantial effect" on the commission of the crime may be found liable for aiding and abetting the underlying criminal act. There is general agreement on this formulation of the test for complicity liabil-ity; the challenge faced by the tribunals is determining what actions have a "substantial" effect on the outcome of the crime.

The *mens rea* required to hold an accessory liable is also controversial and has attracted considerable academic debate. The issue is whether the accomplice must have the same *mens rea* as the principal. This question is particularly acute in the case of genocide. In other words, must the prosecution dem-onstrate that an accessory to genocide had the specific intent to destroy, in whole or in part, a protected group of people?

The jurisprudence is now clear that an accomplice does not need such specific intent to be convicted of complicity in genocide. Some prominent commentators, however, argue that only those accomplices who have genocidal intent should be held liable for genocide.[19] The argument for not requiring specific intent is threefold. First, it is argued that broadening the scope of liability for genocide beyond those with genocidal intent creates greater deterrence and appropriately punishes individuals who knowingly contribute to international crimes. Second, this approach captures the complexity of international crimes by recognizing that they are more difficult to commit without the assistance of many. Third, it creates an additional incentive for potential accomplices to ascertain the nature of the activity they are assisting or supporting on the ground that they may still be prosecuted for genocide even if they themselves do not possess genocidal intent. The other side to this argument asserts that broadening the scope of liability runs the risk of diluting the special stigma associated with genocide; narrowing the scope of liability by requiring genocidal intent for accomplices as well as direct perpetrators preserves the special nature of genocide and is consistent with the distinction ICL makes between crimes against humanity and genocide.

Joint Criminal Enterprise

The concept of joint criminal enterprise (often abbreviated JCE and in some jurisdictions referred to as the common purpose doctrine) has been present since the dawn of modern ICL at Nuremberg and Tokyo, but is still the subject of controversy and doctrinal uncertainty. The modern articulation of JCE is found in an ICTY appeals chamber decision.* The

---

*The common purpose doctrine is also found in several of the modern terrorism treaties. For example, a person commits an offense under the Terrorist Bombing Convention when he or she "in any other way contribute[s] to the commission of any offenses by a group of persons acting with a common purpose."

appeals chamber identified three categories of JCE liability: The first category is sometimes referred to as basic JCE liability, the second category is systematic JCE liability, and the third category is an extended form of JCE liability.[20] The first category describes an enterprise in which all participants share the same *mens rea* with respect to the criminal activity. A recent decision of the ICTY described the *mens rea* of the first category of JCE as follows: "the accused must both intend the commission of the crime and intend to participate in a common plan aimed at its commission."[21] Thus, an individual who drives soldiers to a village knowing and intending that the civilian villagers will be killed can be found liable under this first category. The second category is illustrated with the prosecution of those involved in the Nazi concentration camps. The *mens rea* for the second category of JCE is intentional and knowing participation in an organized system or institution undertaking some criminal purpose. Courts have been particularly quick to imply the intent to further the criminal enterprise in cases involving individuals with authority in the organization.

The third category is the most controversial, and has been the subject of differing, and confusing, doctrinal pronouncements by contemporary ICL tribunals. This extended form of liability attributes to members of an organization responsibility for an act of another member of that organization that was not part of the original common plan, but that was a "natural and foreseeable" consequence of implementing the common plan. The ICTY Appeals Chamber gave the following example of the third category of JCE liability:

> An example of [category three liability] would be a common, shared intention on the part of a group to forcibly remove

---

Article 2(3), International Convention for the Suppression of Terrorist Bombings, Jan. 12, 1998, G.A. Res. 52/164, U.N. Doc. A/RES/52/, reprinted at 37 I.L.M. 249 (1998). This common purpose liability exists where the person either has the intent to further the general criminal activity or purpose of the group or plays some role with the knowledge of the intention of the group to commit the offense.

members of one ethnicity from their town, village or region (to effect "ethnic cleansing") with the consequence that, in the course of doing so, one or more of the victims is shot and killed. While murder may not have been explicitly acknowledged to be part of the common design, it was nevertheless foreseeable that the forcible removal of civilians at gunpoint might well result in the deaths of one or more of those civilians. Criminal responsibility may be imputed to all participants within the common enterprise where the risk of death occurring was both a predictable consequence of the execution of the common design and the accused was either reckless or indifferent to that risk.[22]

Does the requirement of foreseeability have any limiting power? Or, in a situation of mass violence or armed conflict, are all international crimes foreseeable? Consider the example just presented. What other international crimes are the natural and foreseeable result of a campaign of ethnic cleansing? Is the commission of rape, torture, or genocide natural and foreseeable under these circumstances?

The Appeals Chamber more recently clarified the *mens rea* required for the third category of JCE:

[T]he accused can only be held responsible for a crime outside the common purpose if, under the circumstances of the case: (i) it was *foreseeable* that such a crime might be perpetrated by one or other members of the group and (ii) the accused *willingly took that risk (dolus eventualis)*. The crime must be shown to have been foreseeable to the accused in particular.[23]

The ICTY has suggested that in the case of the third category of JCE, the prosecutor does not need to prove that there was a specific agreement to further the common purpose between the accused and the person who committed the foreseeable act. In other words, the link between the accused and the person who committed the underlying act may be quite tenuous.

JCE and the common purpose doctrine are designed in part to capture the organizational reality of mass atrocities. Although the first two categories of JCE liability will raise difficult issues concerning the type of assistance that triggers liability, it is the third category that has led some ICL experts and human rights advocates to argue for a narrowing of the doctrine to better reflect principles of personal fault. As you read through JCE decisions, ask yourself whether the doctrine has become too expansive by holding individuals responsible not only for acts they did not commit, but for acts committed outside of the common plan by individuals they might not even know. In the alternative, is such expansive liability appropriate when addressing mass atrocities, particularly if it may increase the reluctance of individuals to join such enterprises?

~ 11 ~

International Criminal Law and Its Alternatives: Truth, Justice, Reconciliation, and Memory

The fundamental purpose of any system of law is to further desirable social policy outcomes. Most texts in the field of international criminal law (ICL) assume the worthiness of the project to expand individual criminal responsibility for acts that violate international law, regardless of whether the offenders are state agents or private actors. That said, it is worth reflecting for a moment on the articulated justifications for a regime of ICL.[1] The goals of ICL—as advanced over time by its practitioners and supporters—are as varied as they are ambitious: to deter future offenses, mete out just punishment, promote accountability, incapacitate offenders, rehabilitate victims and perpetrators, provide a substitute for vigilante justice, reconcile divided communities, individualize guilt to avoid collective recriminations, reinforce the rule of law, and heal shattered societies. In this way, ICL embodies some of the goals traditionally associated with domestic criminal law (retribution, deterrence, and rehabilitation). At the same time, it embodies others that transcend those more localized concerns and reflect expanded interests of the international community.[2] The system of ICL is thus more than the extension of the domestic criminal law model onto the international plane.

This chapter reviews some of the articulated purposes of ICL, and weighs them against alternative models of justice and accountability, both legal and nonlegal. The goal is to better contextualize ICL vis-à-vis these alternative responses to situations of armed conflict, mass violence, and repression. As you consider the various situations in which states, acting individually or collectively, have resorted to international criminal justice, consider to what extent the criminal justice model employed in response to "ordinary" crimes on the domestic level is effective on the international level in response to the "extraordinary" crimes of genocide, war crimes, and crimes against humanity. In addition, consider what other options were available to these actors and whether these other responses might have achieved more desirable outcomes. Finally, consider these issues from the perspective of victims and the local affected communities: Which responses do you think best reflect their interests and priorities? To what extent should the international community seek to incorporate victims' rights and perspectives into the design and implementation of transitional justice mechanisms?

THE OBJECTIVES OF INTERNATIONAL CRIMINAL LAW

Although more ambitious justifications have been associated with the project of international criminal justice, the two main justifications for ICL, as articulated by the international community today, are retribution and deterrence. Rehabilitation remains a goal of international human rights law and many domestic systems; however, it is less salient in ICL, at least at the moment. The original ad hoc tribunals envisioned contributing to the reconciliation of warring communities. Over time, the tribunals' ability to accomplish this has been questioned in light of modern research.

Retribution

Theories of retribution are premised on the idea that individuals who disturb the public order must be punished for their actions. This, it is surmised, helps to return society to a prior state of equilibrium. For retributivists, a regime of international criminal justice is justified by the need to avenge acts that disturb international public order. Punishment also serves the purposes of signaling the global society's condemnation of the disruptive conduct. As an alterative to execution or exile, criminal justice creates heightened stigma by ensuring that responsible individuals are publicly condemned as war criminals. Indeed, accountability and anti-impunity are frequent refrains of proponents of international criminal justice.

Punishment can also provide a sense of satisfaction to victims when they see their tormentor reprimanded. The imperative of providing criminal justice is often justified as a way to avoid cycles of recrimination and other forms of vigilante self-help that may occur when malefactors enjoy impunity. The law thus acts as a channel for personal and collective vengeance to prevent the cycle of violence that plagues societies without rigorous systems of criminal justice.

Retributive impulses and efforts are inherently retrospective — they are focused on meting out just punishment for prior bad acts. The punishment is calibrated to the offender's moral culpability and the harm caused to the body politic. In the context of mass crimes, however, this calculation remains a challenge. Of Hermann Göring, Hitler's designated successor and the highest ranking defendant at Nuremberg, political theorist Hannah Arendt once wrote: "It may well be essential to hang Göring, but it is totally inadequate. That is, this guilt, in contrast to all criminal guilt, oversteps and shatters any and all legal systems."[3] Similarly, how can those responsible for the deaths of more than 800,000 people in Rwanda be adequately punished? The international criminal tribunals are often criticized for sentencing individuals accused of heinous crimes too leniently. Dražen Erdemović, for example, was convicted for his involvement in a firing squad that massacred hundreds of Muslim men. Mathematically, he alone was probably responsible for at least 70 of those deaths, yet the International Criminal Tribunal for the Former Yugoslavia (ICTY) sentenced him to five years' imprisonment. The tribunals appear to reserve their harshest sentences (life imprisonment) to the intellectual authors or leaders who order or facilitate international crimes, rather than those who implement such criminal plans. How does one compare the punishment of a person who killed 70 people with that of the leaders who created the conditions that led to those killings?

Deterrence

As compared with the retributivist approach to criminal justice, theories of deterrence are forward looking in their perspective. Deterrent approaches focus on the prevention of future crimes rather than the punishment of crimes that have already been committed. Deterrence is premised on the interplay between the moral philosophies of utilitarianism (the theory that conduct should be directed toward achieving the greatest happiness for the greatest number of people) and consequentialism (the theory that decisions should be made on the basis of the expected outcomes or consequences of the action). By this account, the criminal prosecution and punishment of responsible individuals prevents future crimes by triggering two types of deterrence: specific and general. Specific deterrence operates against individuals who have already engaged in undesirable conduct and works through the dual forces of rehabilitation and incapacitation. The goal of specific deterrence is to ensure that the perpetrator not engage in additional wrongful acts. By contrast, general deterrence is directed at society at large. The social condemnation of bad acts coupled with the visible punishment of the convicted individual are thought to prevent others from engaging in comparable conduct.

Both theories of deterrence assume a rational actor who will refrain from committing criminal acts after weighing the fear of negative consequences associated with the action (prosecution and punishment) against the gains to be had by engaging in criminal behavior. More idealistically, deterrence assumes that social norms will eventually be internalized and good conduct habitualized, so that individuals will no longer consider the possibility of engaging in breaches. By this account, a vigorous regime of criminal justice contributes to greater social utility overall. This assumes, of course, that the source of the social norms and any prosecutorial power will be perceived as legitimate and morally credible. Genuine internalization of norms will be resisted where the norms are deemed illegitimate or exogenously imposed and where they are contrary to entrenched attitudes backed by community support.

For utilitarians, a regime of international criminal justice is thus justified as an effort to prevent future violations. Yet testing this hypothesis continues to vex criminologists, as it is virtually impossible to construct a rigorous empirical study to quantify the deterrent effect of prosecutions. Even in the more established domestic context, we are left to theorize how deterrence works with few firm data on which to draw.

What we do know is that effective deterrence requires first and foremost a credible threat of punishment. Indeed, most studies show that ensuring the perception of the *predictability* of punishment (rather than its severity) is the most efficacious means of promoting deterrence. If this is true, ICL has a long way to go. Even now, at the height of the ICL renaissance, the existing tribunals are considering only a tiny fraction of the world's international crimes. Although they are high profile, ICL prosecutions may be too episodic, selective, and unsystematic to exert any general deterrent effect. Often, the indicted individuals seem randomly chosen — ill-fated losers in an accountability lottery.

Even assuming the most robust enforcement, these cases involve extreme conduct that is perhaps less susceptible to processes of deterrence. Until legal censure is more certain, the narratives that explain why seemingly ordinary people do evil things in the context of war or state-sponsored repression — because they are beset by prejudices, intoxicated by power, manipulated by elites, terrified into submission by superior orders or threats of retaliation for their inaction, or caught up in a maelstrom of violence — likely still overwhelm any cost-benefit analysis in which individual perpetrators may engage. As a result, the deterrent effect of ICL prosecutions remains speculative.

Where deterrence might be at its most effective is at the level of regime elites — those who may deliberately choose to sponsor international crimes to consolidate their power. As international tribunals increasingly focus on prosecuting leaders, rather than low-level followers, political and military elites may face a more daunting cost-benefit analysis that weighs in favor of desistence. As such prosecutions become an expected and anticipated part of international affairs, the possibility of deterrence becomes more credible.[4]

Rehabilitation

For many years, the rehabilitation of offenders was an express goal of many domestic penal systems. Over time, however, rehabilitation fell out of vogue in many systems (the United States most prominently), and its demise seems to be premised on the conclusion that it is unworkable, unattainable, and unrealistic. Nonetheless, human rights groups continue to urge states to give priority to rehabilitation in designing and implementing their criminal justice systems. So, for example, Article 10(3) of the International Covenant of Civil and Political Rights urges states to ensure that "[t]he penitentiary system comprise[s] treatment of prisoners the essential aim of which shall be their reformation and rehabilitation." From the perspective of penalties under ICL, the Statute of the International Criminal Court (ICC) at Article 77 does seem to contemplate the possibility of rehabilitation. According to that provision, which mirrors domestic legislation in many continental systems, the default maximum sentence is 30 years, although life imprisonment is contemplated where warranted by the extreme gravity of the crime and the individual circumstances of the convicted person.

For the moment, it is too early to evaluate fully the ability of the international criminal justice regime to prevent recidivism and enable convicted defendants to rejoin society. Defendants convicted by the ICTY are only just now beginning to complete their sentences. (For example, Erdemović — one of the first defendants to be sentenced after pleading guilty to the charges against him — has been released. He provided valuable testimony for the prosecution.) Many individuals will undoubtedly serve their sentences in national systems that still have faith in the promise of rehabilitation. Most important perhaps, many individuals will be released after the circumstances that led to the violence in which they participated — a brutal war or repressive government — have ended. Where minimum order and a functioning domestic legal system have been restored, and where the moral order is re-established, criminal behavior that had become "normalized" may once again be considered deviant, and ICL defendants may return to their prior, law-abiding lives with little difficulty. Others, of course, will remain unrepentant. They, and their supporters, may forever consider their prosecution and incarceration to be a profound injustice.

Peace and Reconciliation

Although many developed legal systems are increasingly turning to mechanisms of "alternative dispute resolution" (conciliation, mediation, and arbitration) in the noncriminal context, social reconciliation is not an express objective of many developed criminal justice systems. By contrast, some domestic systems in the developing world do rely on processes and traditions that focus more on the restoration of community balance and less on the punishment of the guilty to enforce societal rules and norms. Where crimes occur within communities that must continue to live together, as compared with anonymous criminal acts between strangers who will never likely interact with each other again, reconciliation becomes a relevant penological goal.

Since World War II, many of the world's incidents of mass violence have occurred within the borders of a single state, albeit with dramatic spillover effects at times. This violence has often pitted different groups within society—defined by ethnicity, race, religion, political persuasion, language, class or socioeconomic status, and tradition—against each other and resulted in the destruction of much of the societal infrastructure. When violence turns inward, entire communities that once intermarried and lived peacefully together can be torn asunder. Under these circumstances, proponents of international criminal justice posit that criminal trials can help societies achieve peace and reconciliation in the wake of mass violence. The UN Security Council resolution establishing the ICTY therefore predicted that the tribunal would "contribute to the restoration and maintenance of peace."[5] Likewise, the

Statute for the International Criminal Tribunal for Rwanda (ICTR) promised that the tribunal would "contribute to the process of national reconciliation."[6] The fact that the Security Council can trigger the ICC's jurisdiction by activating Chapter VII of the UN Charter in response to threats to the peace reflects this faith in the power of justice to bring about peace.

The presumed connection between justice and reconciliation is that the assignment of individual criminal responsibility will effectively individuate guilt and short-circuit attitudes of collective responsibility. As a result, it is assumed that Bosnian Muslims will recognize that it was Dusko Tadić who was responsible for a particular act of violence against members of their community and not all Bosnian Serbs. Although proponents of international criminal justice have touted reconciliation as a key goal of the system, many remain skeptical that international criminal justice can bring about social repair and reconciliation. Indeed, at least one empirical study in Bosnia suggests that the ICTY has contributed little toward the reconciliation of that country's various ethnic groups.[7] In addition, the outcomes of certain cases remain contentious. The acquittal of high-level members of the Kosovo Liberation Army by the ICTY came as a stunning blow to many Serbian court watchers. It has been opined that the judgment increased bitterness between the Kosovar and Serbian populations of the region and reignited radical Serbian groups.[8]

THE CRITIQUES OF INTERNATIONAL CRIMINAL JUSTICE

While proponents of international criminal justice have advanced these goals and expectations, opponents and skeptics have questioned whether the international community should rely on criminal trials in the face of mass violence at the expense of other preventative and reactive options. These naysayers raise a number of critiques of international criminal justice that go to the very heart of the ICL project. This section sets out a few of the arguments that have been made against contemporary efforts to further international criminal justice.

Victor's Justice

An early critique of international criminal justice was the observation that only the vanquished are punished. Hermann Göring once charged that "The victor will always be the judge, and the vanquished the accused." His words ring true with respect to the Nuremberg and Tokyo proceedings. The establishment of those tribunals was possible only because Germany and Tokyo had been completely defeated in World War II. As a result, those tribunals considered only crimes committed by German and Japanese defendants.

This led to some uncomfortable hypocrisies, as none of the Allies came to the work of the tribunals with entirely clean hands. Most notably, it seemed incongruous to allow a Soviet prosecutor and a Soviet judge to participate in the prosecution of German crimes against civilians and prisoners of war in light of the Katyn Forest Massacre, which Soviet troops secretly committed against thousands of Polish citizens. In a stunning move, the Soviets actually attempted to pin this atrocity on the Germans. The United Kingdom could have been asked to answer for, among other things, the 1945 firebombing of the city of Dresden, an arguably indiscriminate attack that resulted in the deaths of tens of thousands of civilians and the total destruction of the city's baroque center — all for little military gain. With respect to the United States, the Nuremberg Tribunal awarded German defendant Karl Dönitz, commander of the German Navy, a relatively light sentence in part because the United States had engaged in the same unrestricted submarine warfare with which Dönitz had been charged. (Indeed, U.S. Admiral Chester Nimitz submitted an affidavit in Dönitz's case to this effect.) Debate continues, moreover, as to whether the bombing of Hiroshima and, *a fortiori* Nagasaki, constituted war crimes.

One response to this critique of the World War II proceedings is that although the Nuremberg and Tokyo Tribunals meted out victors' justice, it was good justice. These were not sham trials with predetermined outcomes pursued only for their propaganda value. Defendants were generally given due process guarantees, such as the right to counsel and to cross-examine witnesses and evidence, and the tribunals demonstrated the true possibility of acquittal. It seems clear that had the Germans and Japanese won the war, no such process would have been provided had tribunals even been convened for Allied personnel.

The greater involvement of the international community in the establishment of today's tribunals and the existence of a permanent international criminal court help to dispel this concern with respect to the ICL renaissance. As a result, the critique has shifted to decry the selective prosecution of perpetrators from weaker states and the relative impunity of perpetrators from powerful states. That so far only Africans have been indicted by the ICC fuels this argument.

Prevention in Lieu of Justice

Deterrence through criminal prosecutions is not, of course, the only way to prevent crime. Many would prefer to see the international community invest in more robust prophylactic measures and strategies *ex ante* to obviate prosecutorial responses *ex post*. A genuine commitment to prevention requires the provision of international aid and development in times of peace, the creation of structural measures to avert the escalation of violence, and the support of programs to establish the rule of law around the world.

Where these more inchoate measures fail, a prevention mandate also forces a consideration of the historic and contested doctrine of humanitarian intervention. Humanitarian intervention involves the armed intervention into a state by another state or a collective of states, with or without authorization from the UN Security Council, for the promotion or protection of basic human rights where the territorial state is perpetuating abuses or is unable or unwilling to provide the necessary protection to its inhabitants. In a major new initiative, the UN recognized:

> The emerging norm that there is a collective international responsibility to protect, exercisable by the Security Council authorizing military intervention as a last resort, in the event of genocide and other large-scale killing, ethnic cleansing or serious violations of international humanitarian law which sovereign Governments have proved themselves powerless or unwilling to prevent.[9]

The Responsibility to Protect (R2P) recognizes that although it is preferable to prevent and deter violations of human rights by nonforceful means, such as mediation and sanctions, the use of proportional force in accordance with international norms and in defense of individuals in jeopardy may be necessary as a last resort.

The ICTY — established in the midst of the ongoing conflict in the former Yugoslavia — was roundly criticized by many as a feeble substitute for a more robust military response to atrocities. Likewise, the ICTR — established after the international community stood by while genocide engulfed Rwanda — was criticized as too little, too late. Proponents of prevention often argue that today's ad hoc criminal tribunals were established primarily to atone for the guilt of not intervening in yesterday's bloodshed. Under these circumstances, justice emerges as a consolation prize for communities wracked by violence.

Justice and Diplomacy

A tension exists between efforts to seek justice and efforts to achieve peace. In particular, where tribunals are in existence while abuses are ongoing, they may complicate efforts to negotiate with potential, or even indicted, war criminals. Indeed, a strong argument posits that the international community should not support any measures that delay peace and thereby increase the number of victims. According to one commentator, who wrote anonymously about the implications of simultaneously pursuing peace and justice in the former Yugoslavia:

> Targeting violators of human rights and bringing them to justice is essential. Accusation, however, comes more easily than making peace. The quest for justice for yesterday's victims of atrocities should not be pursued in such a manner that it makes today's living the dead of tomorrow. That, for the human rights community, is one of the lessons from the former Yugoslavia. Thousands of people are dead who should have been alive — because moralists were in quest of the perfect peace. Unfortunately, a perfect peace can rarely be attained in the aftermath of a bloody conflict.[10]

While the Dayton Peace Accords were being negotiated, two men who had the real capability of improving conditions on the ground — Radovan Karadžić (the self-proclaimed president of the Serb enclave in Bosnia) and Ratko Mladić (chief of staff of the Bosnian Serb Army) — had both been indicted by the ICTY. (Slobodan Milošević had not yet been formally indicted, although he was under investigation.) They were excluded from the peace negotiations and were presumably less inclined to go along with the results because they risked prosecution once peace was achieved.

The potential for legal accountability to be subordinated to efforts to achieve peace on the ground gave rise to the adage "no peace without justice." This became a rallying cry of human rights activists. As a response to the charge that the quest for justice prolonged the war, human rights activists point the finger at the international community for lacking the resolve to follow through on their threats to intervene and thus emboldening war criminals to keep fighting. They also charge that any peace without justice is not a viable or durable peace, because the presence of war criminals enjoying impunity prevents the peaceable stabilization of societies.

With the establishment of the ICTY, the Security Council seemed to prioritize justice over an immediate peace. The ICC, however, suggests a more nuanced relationship between these two ideals. Article 16 of the ICC Statute allows the UN Security Council, acting within its Chapter VII mandate to respond to threats to and breaches of the peace, to defer an ICC investigation or prosecution for a renewable period of 12 months.

ALTERNATIVES TO INTERNATIONAL CRIMINAL JUSTICE

In situations in which ICL is applicable — during or following armed conflict, repression, or mass violence — there are a multitude of other ways a state or the international community can respond. These choices mark the field of transitional justice. A full discussion of transitional justice is beyond the scope of this text; however, it may be useful at this point to consider what other alternatives to criminal prosecutions are available to address the commission of international crimes. As you review these various options, consider what commends them and what problems they may present.

Do Nothing

One option is, of course, to do nothing. Where the past is controversial and painful, societies may prefer to draw a thick line and essentially start over rather than grapple with what happened and who was responsible. This is essentially what happened in fascist Spain after World War II. Francisco Franco, *el generalissimo,* remained in power until his death in 1975. He rose to power in 1936, in the midst of the Spanish Civil War. During World War II, he was supportive of the Axis side, but managed to largely stay out of the war; he declared total neutrality by 1943 when the tide was turning against Germany. His focus was more internal, overseeing a repressive apparatus that some historians say was responsible for up to 80,000 executions. Because he was not involved in acts of international aggression, the Allies largely left him alone after World War II, although Spain was for a time quite marginalized in Europe. Only recently has Spain begun to reckon with its past, passing legislation that calls for the exhumation of mass graves to determine the fate of the disappeared and the removal of what monuments to Franco remain. In 2007, the most senior bishop of the Catholic Church formally apologized for the Church's support of Franco.

Amnesty

As discussed further in Chapter 9, national governments often resort to amnesty laws in the face of prior abuses by government officials. Such laws prevent the investigation and punishment of individuals who committed abuses. An amnesty law may provide a useful incentive to encourage members of a repressive regime to relinquish power by eliminating the possibility of prosecutions. Early amnesty laws passed in Latin America and elsewhere were generally blanket self-amnesties that prevented any form of reckoning with prior crimes. Such blanket amnesties may frustrate victims, who are denied any form of civil or criminal redress. More recently, South Africa utilized a conditional, or individualized, amnesty in connection with opportunities for victims and perpetrators to give testimony about what they experienced under apartheid. The amnesty law administrated by that country's Truth and Reconciliation Commission (TRC) protected individuals from prosecution and civil liability in exchange for their cooperation in establishing the full truth about the past.

Human rights organizations generally oppose the use of amnesties in any circumstances, arguing that they further impunity and undercut domestic and international efforts to deter future gross violations of human rights. Most domestic courts that have reviewed their own amnesties have upheld their legality, although some states in Latin America have begun to deviate from this norm by reversing amnesties that were passed in the 1970s and 1980s. By contrast, all international tribunals that have evaluated the legality of amnesties have found them to violate fundamental principles of justice, including the right of victims to have their rights adjudicated by a court of law. For example, the Inter-American Court of Human Rights has ruled that the Pinochet "self-amnesty" is incompatible with the American Convention on Human Rights. It is generally agreed that blanket self-amnesties, such as that adopted by Pinochet, are probably illegal under international law. Conditional amnesties, like that adopted in South Africa, raise the question of whether a quasi-legal process that results in legal protection, rather than punishment, provides a minimum level of justice that satisfies international law. No international tribunal has evaluated the legality of such an amnesty, although the ICC has been faced with the question with respect to an amnesty in Uganda that is a weaker form of conditional amnesty than that adopted in South Africa.

Truth and Investigatory Commissions

The phenomenon of the truth commission emerged initially as a response to mass violence in countries (mostly in Latin America) where prosecutions were precluded by the operation of an amnesty law, the lack of political will, a still-entrenched military, or other obstacles. Thus, truth commissions have often represented a compromise between "former abusers and their victims, who settle for the limited satisfaction of truth, rather than receive actual redress through punishment."[11] Commissions are often presided over by respected public figures rather than trained lawyers or judges. They take the testimony of victims and experts and draft a final report of their findings. Truth commissions provide an alternative form of justice by establishing a historical record of abuses, providing a forum for victims (and at times perpetrators) to bear witness, investigating the fate of the disappeared, creating an environment more ripe for reconciliation and forgiveness than an adversarial trial, issuing or recommending reparations, and proposing institutional reforms to prevent a repeat of past violence. By generating a "definitive" history of abuses, truth commissions can undercut revisionist accounts that might develop about a country's past history of violence. As Michael Ignatieff famously observed, truth commissions reduce the number of lies that may legitimately circulate as part of the public discourse.[12]

Some truth commissions, such as the commission established in El Salvador, identify individual perpetrators; others are content to present causes, patterns, and consequences of violence. In South Africa, the TRC granted amnesty so long as the perpetrator revealed the full truth of his or her crimes and such crimes were politically motivated. Although the conditional amnesty of the South African TRC was one of the most innovative developments in the field, few countries have followed its lead.

Truth commissions have the advantage over criminal trials of focusing on the victims and their experiences rather than on the defendants. Where they "name names," truth commissions can also achieve some measure of stigma and accountability, although the *ex parte* designation of individuals as responsible for human rights violations with limited opportunities to be heard raises due process concerns. Truth commissions can also award compensation to victims, assuming there is a fund from which to draw. Finally, where truth commissions invite the participation of both victims and perpetrators, they can encourage acts of contrition and forgiveness that may lay the groundwork for a more community-wide reconciliation.[13]

Lustration

Those complicit in past oppression can also be barred from political office or other positions of influence. The term *lustration* derives from the Latin word for "purification." Following World War II, the Allies launched a de-Nazification program in Germany and its former spheres of influence. After the fall of communism, similar efforts were launched in Eastern Europe to address the systemic bureaucratic repression that characterized life within the former Soviet client states. There, thousands of individuals were disqualified from public life and even from some private enterprises and industries. Most recently, in May 2003, the Coalition Provisional Authority in Iraq began lustrating members of the Ba'ath Party—a party considered to be synonymous with the Saddam Hussein regime. Under this policy, all senior members of the party were banned from public life (including employment as doctors at hospitals, as university professors, and other ostensibly nonpolitical posts); some more junior people could appeal their exclusion. As we can now see in Iraq, lustration can contribute to destabilization by leaving important posts empty or filled by untrained or inexpert individuals.

Civil Trials

Criminal trials are pursued by the state (or the international community) on behalf of the polity whose peace has been breached by criminal behavior. In the process of vindicating social norms, the victims of crime appear as mere witnesses for the prosecution. By contrast, victims are front and center in civil (tort) actions against responsible individuals. As an alternative to initiating criminal suits, states have the option of enabling victims of international crimes to obtain civil redress. Tort liability often exists alongside penal liability. Indeed, tort liability may be broader than penal liability where a state has not codified international crimes in its penal code, but recognizes private rights of action over violations of international law.

Individual civil (tort) liability for violations of ICL is most developed in the United States, although victims of international crimes are increasingly seeking civil reparations in the context of criminal prosecutions in civil law jurisdictions that allow this. In the United States, the ancient Alien Tort Statute (ATS), 28 U.S.C. § 1350, and its more youthful sibling, the Torture Victim Protection Act (TVPA), 28 U.S.C. § 1350 note, allow U.S. federal courts to assert jurisdiction over certain international torts. In the modern era, the ATS was first successfully invoked in the human rights context in *Filártiga v. Peña-Irala,*[14] in which a federal court found a Paraguayan national liable for acts of torture and summary execution committed in Paraguay against another Paraguayan national, whose sister had serendipitously discovered the defendant living in the United States.

Since that pioneering case, dozens of cases have been brought against natural and legal persons (including major multinational corporations) involving allegations of various forms of involvement in ICL violations committed abroad. In 1991, the U.S. Congress passed the TVPA in connection with its ratification of the Convention Against Torture and Other Cruel, Inhuman or Degrading Treatment or Punishment, which obligates state parties to adopt measures to ensure that torturers are held legally accountable for their acts. The TVPA corrected an anomaly of the ATS; the latter was only available to non-U.S. citizens as plaintiffs, resulting in a situation in which U.S. victims were denied an opportunity to vindicate international human rights that was available to foreign victims. The Anti-Terrorism Act (ATA), 18 U.S.C. § 2333, allows for similar civil suits involving acts of "international terrorism" as defined by the statute.

To be sure, when serious international crimes are at issue, a monetary judgment will never be commensurate to the harm suffered. Indeed, such judgments perpetuate the fiction that money is equivalent to healing and that for every pain suffered, there will be an amount that will compensate. The enforcement of damage awards against human rights abusers has been a challenge in many civil human rights suits in the United States, as defendants rarely have adequate and attachable assets within the forum. Nonetheless, a damage award — even where unenforced — marks a symbolic victory over an oppressor, recognizes concrete damage to individuals, and is symbolic of a plaintiff's loss. Where an award can be enforced, awarded money damages provide economic support to enable rehabilitation and reintegration into society and confer a measure of social standing on plaintiffs.

State Responsibility

In addition to civil suits against individuals, money damages are available in limited circumstances against states deemed responsible for international crimes. The International Court of Justice (ICJ), the judicial branch of the United Nations, can hear claims between states that have accepted its jurisdiction. It has jurisdiction primarily over states (not individuals) and can thus exercise jurisdiction over states accused of being responsible for the commission of international crimes. For example, Article IX of the Genocide Convention provides that disputes "between the Contracting Parties relating to the interpretation, application or fulfillment of the present Convention, including those relating to the responsibility of a State for genocide or any of the other acts enumerated in Article III [conspiracy, incitement, attempt, complicity], shall be submitted to the International Court of Justice."

Pursuant to Article IX, Bosnia-Herzegovina sued the Federal Republic of Yugoslavia (Serbia and Montenegro) for committing genocide during the breakup of the former Yugoslavia. The Court, largely mimicking the ICTY's genocide jurisprudence, determined that Serbia was liable for failing to *prevent* genocide at Srebrenica, where Bosnian Serb troops massacred more than 7,000 Bosnian Muslim boys and men in July 1995, but that Serbia itself was not liable for the *commission* of genocide.[15] Another notable example is the case of *Nicaragua v. United States*. There, Nicaragua attempted to hold the United States responsible for violations of the laws of war committed by the *Contra* rebel forces, who were receiving considerable U.S. assistance. When the Court ruled in preliminary proceedings that it had jurisdiction over the parties and the dispute, the United States defaulted and withdrew its acceptance of ICJ jurisdiction. Nonetheless, the ICJ proceeded against the United States and determined that, although the United States was liable for financing and otherwise supporting the *Contras,* violations committed directly by the *Contras* were not attributable to the United States.[16] In these suits where state responsibility for international crimes is at issue, the petitioner state must often meet close to a "beyond a reasonable doubt" standard of proof. In the Bosnia case, the ICJ indicated that:

> 209. The Court has long recognized that claims against a State involving charges of exceptional gravity must be proved by evidence that is fully conclusive. The Court requires that it be fully convinced that allegations made in the proceedings, that the crime of genocide or the other acts enumerated in Article III have been committed, have been clearly established. The same standard applies to the proof of attribution for such acts.[17]

The ICJ has jurisdiction only over suits between states. Individuals have no standing to advance claims against responsible states (although the nationality state may espouse claims of their citizens). Various human rights institutions, created either by treaty or as part of the UN edifice, can receive complaints against states by individuals under certain circumstances. These human rights bodies have varying powers of enforcement and thus effectiveness.

Europe, the Americas, and Africa boast regional human rights commissions or courts that can accept jurisdiction over individual petitions brought by victims of human rights violations alleging violations of the institutions' constitutive treaties. In Europe, the European Court of Human Rights (ECHR), based in Strasbourg, France, exercises jurisdiction over states that are party to the European Convention for the Protection of Human Rights and Fundamental Freedoms and its Protocols. The Inter-American system has a Commission based in Washington, DC, and Court based in San José, Costa Rica (IACHR) that exercise this function with respect to the American Declaration on the Rights and Duties of Man and the American Convention on Human Rights. Africa long had a Commission with jurisdiction over the African Charter on Human and People's Rights. A corresponding court — the African Court of Human and People's Rights (ACHPR) — was recently established and will be housed in Arusha, Tanzania. There is no regional human rights system in Asia or the Middle East, although there are promising developments toward this end in Southeast Asia.

In addition, particular human rights treaties have created a web of enforcement bodies with varying adjudicative powers. The Human Rights Committee (HRC), for example, is a creature of the International Covenant on Civil and Political Rights (ICCPR). It has the power to entertain communications from individuals claiming to be victims of violations of any of the rights set forth in the ICCPR committed by states that have ratified the Covenant's First Optional Protocol. The Committee then forwards its "views" to the state concerned to promote compliance. Similar quasi-adjudicative bodies hear petitions from victims claiming violations of other multilateral human rights conventions.

These institutions assess states' compliance with human rights obligations — those basic rights and freedoms that all states owe individuals within their territories or under their jurisdictions. Many of the human rights norms adjudicated by these bodies, especially those civil rights dealing with the right to life and physical integrity, have analogs in ICL. So, for example, the IACHR found the state of Honduras liable for a practice and policy of disappearances in the seminal case of *Velasquez Rodriguez v. Honduras.*[18]

Domestic tribunals exercise only limited jurisdiction over states for breaches of international law. Historically, states were absolutely immune from suit before the courts of sister sovereigns. By the middle of the twentieth century, however, this immunity began to weaken as the role of the state in international relations diversified and the principle of sovereignty eroded. A new norm of restrictive, or qualified, immunity gradually emerged, which accords immunity for public acts (*acta jure imperii*), but not for acts in which a state is acting in a private or commercial capacity (*acta jure gestionis*). Although some international law instruments address this defense, foreign sovereign immunity is now largely governed by national law. For example, the U.S. Congress enacted the Foreign Sovereign Immunities Act (FSIA), 28 U.S.C. § 1330 *et seq.,* in 1976 to "depoliticize" determinations of sovereign immunity and provide courts with concrete standards with which to make immunity determinations. The FSIA was recently amended at § 1605A to withhold sovereign immunity from, and provide a cause of action against, designated "state sponsors of terrorism" for acts of torture, extrajudicial killing, aircraft sabotage, or hostage taking committed outside the United States where the victim or the claimant is a U.S. national. This amendment has repoliticized the doctrine of sovereign immunity, as claims can only be brought against a state that the U.S. government has designated as a "state sponsor of terrorism." A number of suits have been brought against such "state sponsors of terrorism" (mainly Cuba and Iran) in U.S. federal courts.

JURISDICTIONAL CONCURRENCE

The various judicial and quasi-judicial mechanisms discussed earlier coexist. The result is a high degree of jurisdictional concurrence between international and domestic institutions and criminal and civil processes. If we were to take a snapshot of the system of ICL today, here is what we would see. The international community has promulgated a web of human rights and ICL treaties that condemn various forms of violence toward people, toward property, in war, and in peace. Examples include the international "bill of rights" (comprising the Universal Declaration of Human Rights, the ICCPR, and the International Covenant on Economic, Social, and Cultural Rights), the four Geneva Conventions, and their progeny. At the same time, academics, advocates, and jurists continue to refer to a wide-ranging body of customary norms that supplement and, in some cases, exceed codified norms. The international community has created a variety of enforcement mechanisms for these norms, some more robust and judicial than others. These include bodies with jurisdiction over individual states — such as the HRC, which supervises compliance with the ICCPR — and over individuals, such as the various international criminal courts.

These various options for the enforcement of ICL norms can be graphically portrayed in the matrix shown in Table 11.1 using U.S. statutory law as exemplary.

Table 11.1
Options for the Enforcement of ICL Norms

Tort Liability			Criminal Liability		
Respondent/ Defendant	Int'l Forum	Domestic Forum	Int'l Forum	Hybrid Forum	Domestic Forum
Individual	Ø	Suits under the ATS/ TVPA/ ATA	Prosecutions before the ICTY, ICTR, ICC	Prosecutions before the Special Court for Sierra Leone	Prosecutions for international crimes codified in Title 18
State	Suits and proceedings before the ICJ, ECHR, IACHR, ACHPR, HRC	Suits under the FSIA	Ø	Ø	Ø

As Table 11.1 reveals, no international body has automatic tort jurisdiction over individuals. Individuals may by contract consent to have disputes resolved before international arbitration bodies, although this is rare and more often done by corporations engaged in international business transactions. States may also espouse the claims of their nationals before the ICJ. Individuals may receive money damages within the context of criminal prosecutions. Drawing from a feature of many civil law jurisdictions, the ICC Statute is the first international tribunal to allow victims to have partial party standing and to seek reparations in the context of criminal proceedings before the ICC.

State criminal liability does not currently exist under international law. Commentators have decried this accountability gap. In particular, they note the seemingly unjust asymmetry arising from the fact that petitioners must meet a higher standard of proof when they assert claims based on ICL against a state without having the potential to generate aggravated penalties. The International Law Commission (ILC)—a body of experts created by the General Assembly to engage in the codification and progressive development of international law—considered the question of state criminal responsibility in connection with its Draft Articles on State Responsibility.[19] Draft Article 19, later eliminated on the grounds that a sovereign state could not be criminally punished, had recognized a distinction between state responsibility for international delicts (the Roman and Germanic law analogue of torts) and international crimes. The most compelling argument for state criminality is the need to condemn a state whose highest echelons of power have devised and implemented a policy to commit international crimes and obstruct justice. To be sure, it is difficult to conceptualize a state's *mens rea,* although notions of corporate criminality exist under domestic law that may provide useful analogs. Moreover, punitive penalties (such as exemplary damages) are not traditionally awarded in proceedings against states, even for willful behavior. Nonetheless, recognizing state criminality might generate heightened stigma and perhaps amplified deterrence.

This typology of culpability with its two axes—individual versus state responsibility and tort versus criminal liability—illustrates that liability may exist concurrently at the state and individual level and before domestic and international tribunals. So far, the enforcement of ICL has been so scattered and exceptional that there has been little overlap. The cases against Serbian defendants before the ICTY and against Serbia and Montenegro in the ICJ present a notable recent exception. Nonetheless, given this level of jurisdictional concurrence, a high potential exists for divergent outcomes that could lead to significant uncertainty about, and distrust of, the international justice system.

CONCLUSION

This chapter has explored the question of what a regime of international criminal justice can reasonably be expected to accomplish. Where judicial mechanisms fall short, societies and the international community must consider other available mechanisms to address the misdeeds of the past. Indeed, many of the measures discussed here can be adopted alongside criminal prosecutions before domestic or international tribunals as part of a comprehensive response to situations of societal breakdown, ethnic conflict, and massive violence. For example, in Sierra Leone, the Special Court operated simultaneously with a Truth and Reconciliation Commission as an element of the Lomé Peace Accord "to address impunity, break the cycle of violence, provide a forum for both the victims and the perpetrators of human rights violations to tell their story, [and] get a clear picture of the past in order to facilitate genuine healing and reconciliation." Depending on the circumstances, these various mechanisms may complement or complicate each other. Although conflicts developed between the two Sierra Leonean institutions, there is a growing consensus that pursuing such a two-track process may more adequately address the demands of victims, international justice, peace, and reconciliation than any one approach on its own. Modern research in this area confirms that there is no one-size-fits-all model. Efforts at transitional justice must be holistic, reflecting the priorities and constraints of different segments of societies and responding to different goals and objectives.

Endnotes

CHAPTER 1

1. *See* Meir Dan-Cohn, *Decision Rules and Conduct Rules: On Acoustic Separation in Criminal Law*, 97 Harv. L. Rev. 625 (1984).

2. 2 St. Thomas Aquinas, *Question 40 of War*, *in* Summa Theologica 1359-1360 (Fathers of the English Dominican Province trans., Benzinger Brothers, Inc. 1947).

3. Convention on the High Seas, Apr. 29, 1958, 13 U.S.T. 2312, 450 U.N.T.S. 82.

4. United Nations Convention on the Law of the Sea, Dec. 10, 1982, 1833 U.N.T.S. 3, *reprinted in* 21 I.L.M. 1261 (entered into force Nov. 16, 1994).

5. Convention Respecting the Laws and Customs of War on Land, Oct. 18, 1907, 36 Stat. 2277, 205 Consol. T.S. 2.

6. *See* John H. E. Fried, *War Crimes.* Grolier Online, http://www.grolier.com/wwii/wwii_warcrimes.html.

7. *See* The Law of Armed Conflicts 21 (Dietrich Schindler & Jiri Toman eds., 2004).

8. Letter from Capt. Hy Wirz to Maj. Gen. J. H. Wilson (May 7, 1865). This letter, the indictment, and judgment against Wirz are *reprinted in* http://cdl.library.cornell.edu/cgi-bin/moa/sgml/moa-idx?notisid=ANU4519-0121.

9. Commission on the Responsibility of the Authors of the War and on Enforcement of Penalties, *reprinted in* 14 Am. J. Int'l L. 118 (1920).

10. *Id.* at 120.

11. Treaty of Versailles, June 28, 1919, reprinted in 13 Am. J. Int'l L. 151 (Supp. 1920).

12. Allison Marston Danner, *When Courts Make Law: How the International Criminal Tribunals Recast the Laws of War*, 59 Vand. L. Rev. 1, 2 (2006).

13. General Treaty for the Renunciation of War as an Instrument of National Policy, Aug. 27, 1928, 46 Stat. 2343, 94 L.N.T.S. 57.

14. Declaration of the Four Nations on General Security ("Moscow Declaration"), signed at Moscow, October 30, 1943, 9 U.S. Dep't of State Bulletin 308

(1943) (entered into force 30 October 1943). The Moscow Conference, October 19-30, 1943 (Declaration of German Atrocities), 1 November 1943, 1943 For. Rel. (I) 749 at 768, *reprinted in* 38 Am. J. Int'l L. 3, 7 (1944) (Supp).

15. The full IMT judgment is *reprinted in: Judicial Decisions Involving Questions of International Law — International Military Tribunal (Nuremburg), Judgment and Sentences,* 41 Am. J. Int'l L. 172 (1947) [hereinafter Judgment].

16. United States v. Araki, 101 The Tokyo Major War Crimes Trial (R. John Pritchard, ed. 1998).

17. Judgment, 41 Am. J. Int'l L. at 221.

18. *Id.*

19. *Id.*

20. Convention on the Prevention and Punishment of the Crime of Genocide, Dec. 9, 1948, 78 U.N.T.S. 277 (entered into force Jan. 12, 1951).

21. The Geneva Conventions and their drafting history are available on the Web site of the International Committee of the Red Cross at http://www.icrc.com.

22. International Convention for the Protection of All Persons From Enforced Disappearance, E/CN.4/2005/WG.22/WP.1/REV.4 (Sept. 23, 2005).

23. International Covenant on Civil and Political Rights, Dec. 16, 1966, 999 U.N.T.S. 171.

24. International Covenant on Economic, Social and Cultural Rights, Dec. 16, 1966, 993 U.N.T.S. 3.

25. Attorney General of Israel v. Eichmann, *reprinted in* 36 I.L.R. 5 (Jm. 1961), *aff'd*, 36 I.L.R. 277 (S. Ct. 1962).

26. *Federation Nationale des Deportes et Internes Resistants et Patriotes v. Barbie, reprinted in* 78 I.L.R. 125 (Court of Cassation 1985), *aff'd* 100 I.L.R. 331 (Court of Cassation 1988).

CHAPTER 2

1. *See* Prosecutor v. Ahmad Muhammad Harun ("Ahmad Harrun") *and* Ali Muhammad Ali Abd — Al-Rahman ("Ali Kushaya"), Case No. ICC-02/05-01/07, Decision on the Prosecution Application under Article 58(7) of the Statute, ¶¶ 19-25 (Apr. 27, 2007).

2. Prosecutor v. Kallon, Case No. SCSL-2004-15-AR72(E), Decision on Challenge to Jurisdiction: Lomé Accord Amnesty (Mar. 13, 2004).

3. Prosecutor v. Kallon, Case No. SCSL-2004-15-AR72(E), Decision on Constitutionality and Lack of Jurisdiction (Mar. 13, 2004).

4. Prosecutor v. Taylor, Case No. SCSL-2003-1-I, Decision on Immunity from Jurisdiction (May 31, 2004).

5. *See* Prosecutor v. Tadić, Case No. IT-94-1-A, Judgment (July 15, 1999).

6. *See* Democratic Republic of the Congo v. Belgium, 2002 I.C.J. Rep. 3 (Feb. 14) (Joint Sep. Op. Higgins, Kooijmans, & Buergenthal) (Arrest Warrant of 11 April 2000); *Princeton Principles on Universal Jurisdiction, Princeton Project on Universal Jurisdiction* (Princeton University Press, 2001).

7. Antonio Cassese, *Is the Bell Tolling for Universality? A Plea for a Sensible Notion of Universal Jurisdiction,* 1 J. of Int'l Crim. J. 589 (2003).

8. *See, e.g.*, *Ex Parte* Quirin, 317 U.S. 1 (1942); *In Re* Yamashita, 327 U.S. 1 (1946); *and* Johnson v. Eisentrager, 339 U.S. 763 (1950).

9. Hamdan v. Rumsfeld, 548 U.S. 557 (2006).

10. Boumediene v. Bush, 553 U.S. ___ (2008).

11. Pub. L. No. 104-106, 1342, 110 Stat. 486 (1996).

12. *See* Agreement on Surrender of Persons Responsible for Serious Violations of International Humanitarian Law in the Territory of the Former Yugoslavia, http://www.un.org/icty/legaldoc-e/index.htm.

13. See Jorge A. F. Godinho, *The Surrender Agreements Between the U.S. and the ICTY and ICTR: A Critical View*, 1 J. Int'l Crim. J. 502 (2003) for a discussion.

14. United States v. Alvarez-Machain, 504 U.S. 655, 670 (1992).

15. Sosa v. Alvarez-Machain, 542 U.S. 692 (2004).

16. *See* Prosecutor v. Dragon Nikolić, Case No. IT-94-2-Pt, (Oct. 9, 2002). (Decision on Defense Motion Challenging the Exercise of Jurisdiction by the Tribunal).

17. *Id*. at ¶ 114.

18. Committee Against Torture, Consideration of Reports Submitted by States Parties Under Article 19 of the Convention, Conclusions and Recommendations of the Committee Against Torture (United States), U.N. Doc. No. CAT/C/USA/CO/2, 36th Sess. (July 25, 2006), *available at* http://www.ohchr.org/; For more on rendition, *see* Joan Fitzpatrick, *Rendition and Transfer in the War Against Terrorism: Guantánamo and Beyond*, 25 Loy. L.A. Int'l & Comp. L. Rev. 457 (2003).

19. *See* Case of Lilian Celiberti de Casariego, UN GAOR, 36th Sess., Supp. No. 40, UN Doc. A/36/40 (1981), at 185; Case of Sergio Ruben Lopez Burgos, UN GAOR, 36th Sess., Supp. No. 40, UN Doc. A/36/40 (1981), at 76; Case of Almeida de Quinteros, Comm. No. 107 (1981), July 21, 1983 and Garcia v. Ecuador, Comm. No. 319/1988, UN Doc. A/47/40 (1994), at 290; *See also* Manfred Nowak, *U.N. Covenant on Civil and Political Rights: CCPR Commentary* 31 (1993) ("Also considered manifestly arbitrary are kidnappings by secret service agents abroad . . . insofar as these can be attributed to the State") and Rosemary Rayfuse, *International Abduction and the United States Supreme Court: The Law of the Jungle Reigns*, 42 Int'l & Comp. L. Q. 8827 (1993).

CHAPTER 3

1. Alain Pellet, *"Applicable Law," in* The Rome Statute of the International Criminal Court: A Commentary, 1058-1059 (Cassese, Gaeta, and Jones eds.) (2002).

2. 1969 Vienna Convention on the Law of Treaties ("Vienna Convention"), May 23, 1969, 1155 U.N.T.S. 331 (entered into force Jan. 27, 1980).

3. Reservations to the Convention on the Prevention and Punishment of the Crime of Genocide, 1951 I.C.J. 15 (May 28).

4. Human Rights Committee, *General Comment No. 24 (Issues Relating to Reservations Made Upon Ratification or Accession to the Covenant or the Optional Protocols Thereto, or in Relation to Declarations under Article 41 of the Covenant)*. U.N. Doc. CCPR/C/21/Rev.1/Add.6 (Nov. 4, 1994).

5. *See, e.g.*, Cassese, Gaeta, and Jones (eds.), The Rome Statute of the International Criminal Court (2002); Commentary on the Rome Statute of the International Criminal Court (Otto Triffterer ed., 1999).

6. Fourth Geneva Convention, Art. 4 (emphasis added).

7. Prosecutor v. Delalić, Mucić, Delić & Landžo, Case No. IT-96-21-A, Judgment (Feb. 20, 2001).

8. Prosecutor v. Delalić, Mucić, Delić & Landžo, Case No. IT-96-21-T, Judgment, ¶¶ 503, 515 (Nov. 16, 1998).

9. Prosecutor v. Tadić, Case No. IT-94-1-A, Judgment, ¶ 287 (July 15, 1999) ("[I]n case of doubt and whenever the contrary is not apparent from the text of a statutory or treaty provision, such a provision must be interpreted in light of, and in conformity with, customary international law").

10. The Charming Betsy, 6 U.S. 64 (1804).

11. Prosecutor v. Tadić, Case No. IT-94-1-AR92, Decision on the Defense Motion for Interlocutory Appeal on Jurisdiction, ¶ 134 (Oct. 2, 1995).

12. Prosecutor v. Norman, Case No. SCSL-2004-14-AR72(E), Decision on Preliminary Motion Based on Lack of Jurisdiction (May 31, 2004).

13. *Id. at* ¶ 12 (Sep. Op. Robertson J.).

14. Prosecutor v. Erdemović, Case No. IT-96-22-A, Joint Separate Opinion of Judge McDonald and Judge Vohrah (Oct. 7, 1997), ¶ 61.

15. International Military Tribunal at Nuremberg, *in The Trial of German Major War Criminals, Proceedings of the International Military Tribunal Sitting at Nuremberg, Germany*, Part 4, p. 34.

16. Prosecutor v. Furundžija, Case No. IT-95-17/1-T, ¶¶ 182-183 (Dec. 10, 1998).

17. Prosecutor v. Kupreškić, Case No, IT-95-16-T, Judgment, ¶ 717 (Jan. 14, 2000).

18. *See, e.g.*, Prosecutor v. Kupreškić, Case No. IT-95-16-T, Judgment (Jan. 14, 2000) ("generally speaking, and subject to the binding force of decisions of the Tribunal's Appeals Chamber upon the Trial Chambers, the International Tribunal cannot uphold the doctrine of binding precedent (*stare decisis*) adhered to in common law countries.").

19. Sosa v. Alvarez-Machain, 542 U.S. 692 (2004).

20. United States v. Altstötter, 3 Trials of War Criminals Before the Nuremberg Military Tribunals Under Control Council Law No. 10 at 3, 983 (1951).

CHAPTER 4

1. Prosecutor v. Tadić, Case No. IT-94-1-T, Opinion and Judgment, ¶¶ 650-652 (May 7, 1997) (hereinafter Tadić Judgment).

2. Prosecutor v. Tadić, Case No. IT-94-1-A, Judgment, ¶¶ 273-305 (July 15, 1999) (hereinafter Tadić Appeals Judgment).

3. Article 4, Geneva Convention Relative to the Protection of Civilian Persons in Time of War, Aug. 12, 1949, 6 U.S.T. 3516, 75 U.N.T.S. 287.

4. Tadić Appeals Judgment at ¶ 166 ("While previously wars were primarily between well-established States, in modern inter-ethnic armed conflicts such as that in the former Yugoslavia, new States are often created during the conflict and

ethnicity rather than nationality may become the grounds for allegiance. Or, put another way, ethnicity may become determinative of national allegiance. Under these conditions, the requirement of nationality is even less adequate to define protected persons. In such conflicts, not only the text and the drafting history of the Convention but also, and more importantly, the Convention's object and purpose suggest that allegiance to a Party to the conflict and, correspondingly, control by this Party over persons in a given territory, may be regarded as the crucial test").

5. Tadić Judgment, ¶ 573(May 7, 1997).

6. Prosecutor v. Delalić et al., Case No. IT-96-21-T, Judgment, ¶ 193 (Nov. 16, 1998).

7. United Nations War Crimes Commission, *History of the United Nations War Crimes Commission and the Development of the Laws of War* 179 (1948).

8. Larry May, *Crimes Against Humanity: A Normative Account* 110 (2004).

9. Rome Statute of the International Criminal Court, Jan. 16, 2002, UN Doc. A/CONF. 183/9, 37 ILM 1002 (1998), 2187 U.N.T.S. 90.

CHAPTER 5

1. Antonio Cassese, International Criminal Law 72 (2003).

2. Prosecutor v. Delalić, Case No. IT-96-21-T, Judgment, ¶ 403 (Nov. 16, 1998).

3. Cassese, *supra*, at 72.

4. Judgment, 22 Trial of the Major War Criminals Before the International Military Tribunal, Nuremberg 14 November 1945-1 October 1946 at 462 (1948) [hereinafter Nuremberg Judgment].

5. Delalić, *supra*, at ¶ 313.

6. Prosecutor v. Norman, Case No. SCSL-2004-14-AR72(E), Decision on Preliminary Motion Based on Lack of Jurisdiction (May 31, 2004) (Sep. Op. Robertson J).

7. Nuremberg Judgment, *supra*, at 463.

8. *Id.* at 462.

9. Prosecutor v. Tadić, Case No. IT-94-1-AR92, Decision on the Defence Motion for Interlocutory Appeal on Jurisdiction, ¶ 94 (Oct. 2, 1995).

10. Caso Scilingo, Sentencia Audiencia Nacional, No. 16/2005 (Apr. 19, 2005) (Sp.) [hereinafter Scilingo Judgment]; *See generally* Christian Tomuschat, *Issues of Universal Jurisdiction in the* Scilingo *Case*, 3 J. Int'l Crim. J. 3 (2005); Alicia Gil Gil, *The Flaws of the* Scilingo *Judgment*, 3 J. Int'l Crim. J. 1082 (2005); Giulia Pinzauti, *An Instance of Reasonable Universality: The* Scilingo *Case*, 3 J. Int'l Crim. J. 1092 (2005).

11. Case Scilingo, STS No. 789/2007 (Nov. 8, 2007) (Sp.).

12. Bundesverfassungsgericht [BVerfG] [Federal Constitutional Court] Dec. 12, 2000, 2 BvR 1290/99, NJW 2001, S. 1848 [1849], (F.RG.), English translation *available at* http://www.bverfg.de/entscheidungen/rk20001212_2bvr 129099en.html [hereinafter Jorgić].

13. *Id.* at ¶ 7.

14. *Id.* at ¶ 10.

15. Prosecutor v. Krstić, Case No. IT-98-33-T, Judgment, ¶¶ 576-580 (Aug. 2, 2001) (rejecting notion of cultural genocide).

16. See Jorgić v. Germany, Application no. 74613/01, Judgment (July 12, 2007), *available at* http://www.echr.coe.int/eng.

17. The Attitude of States Toward the Development of Humanitarian Law, in The New Humanitarian Law of Armed Conflict: Proceedings of the 1976 and 1977 Conferences 221, 257 (Antonio Cassese ed., 1980) (emphasis omitted).

18. Prosecutor v. Hadžihasanović, Case No. IT-01-47-PT, Decision on Joint Challenge to Jurisdiction, ¶ 62 (Nov. 12, 2002).

19. *Id.* at ¶ 64; *See also* Prosecutor v. Aleksovski, Case No. IT-95-14/1-A, Judgment, ¶ 146 (Mar. 24, 2000) (noting that the object and purpose of the Fourth Geneva Convention is to ensure the "protection of civilians to the maximum extent possible").

CHAPTER 6

1. Charter of the International Military Tribunal Art. 6(a), Aug. 8, 1945, 59 Stat. 1546, 82 U.N.T.S. 279.

2. Judgment, 1 *Trial of the Major War Criminals Before the International Military Tribunal, Nuremberg 14 November 1945-1 October 1946* at 186 (1947), *reprinted in* 41 Am. J. Int'l L. 172 (1947) [hereinafter Nuremberg Judgment].

3. The Security Council has branded only a handful of situations as "acts of aggression" or "aggression," including acts committed by South Africa and Southern Rhodesia against its neighbors, by Israel against Tunisia, and by Iraq against Kuwait. *See* Niels Blokker, *The Crime of Aggression and the United Nations Security Council*, 20 Leiden J. Int'l L. 867, 880 (2007).

4. *See* Int'l Comm. on Intervention & St. Sovereignty, *The Responsibility to Protect* (Dec. 2001), *available at* http://www.iciss.ca/pdf/Commission-Report. pdf.

5. Carl von Clausewitz, I *On War* 101 (1968).

6. *See* 1985 Yearbook of the International Law Commission (Vol. II), at 8 (reproducing the 1954 Draft Code).

7. G.A. Res. 3314(XXIX), U.N. GAOR, 29th Sess., U.N. Doc. A/RES/3314 (1974).

8. Article 3(g) was declared customary international law by the ICJ in the Nicaragua case. *See Military and Paramilitary Activities in and Against Nicaragua* (Nicar. v. U.S.), Merits, 1986 I.C.J. 14, 103 (June 27, 1986).

9. For a discussion of the handful of domestic proceedings involving crimes of terrorism, *see* Antonio Cassese, *On Some Problematical Aspects of the Crime of Aggression*, 20 Leiden J. Int'l L. 841, 842-843 (2007). In particular, *see* R. v. Jones et al., (2006) UKHL 16 (Mar. 29, 2006) (U.K.) (finding that aggression was criminalized under customary international law, but not U.K. law).

10. Coalition for the International Criminal Court, *Crime of Aggression Background*, *available at* http://iccnow.org/?mod=aggressionbackground.

11. Drafters are working from a consolidated Discussion Paper. *See* Discussion Paper Proposed by the Chairman, International Criminal Court (ICC), Official Records of the Assembly of State Parties, Resumed Fifth Session, U.N. Doc. No. ICC-ASP/5/SWGCA/2 (2007) [Hereinafter "Discussion Paper"].

12. *See* Discussion Paper, Annex, ¶ 1 (Articles 8*bis* (a)).

13. Nicar. v. U.S., *supra* (finding that the United States had used unlawful force in violation of customary law by mining Nicaraguan ports, undertaking naval attacks, and arming and training the *Contras*); Oil Platforms Case (Iran v. U.S.), 2003 I.C.J. 161 (Nov. 6, 2003) (finding that the United States was not entitled to use armed force in self-defense pursuant to Article 51 of the Charter); Case Concerning Armed Activities on the Territory of the Congo (Dem. Rep. of Congo v. Uganda), Merits, 2005 I.C.J. 165 (Dec. 19, 2005) (finding Uganda guilty of an act of aggression within the meaning of Resolution 3314).

14. Benjamin Ferencz, *Address to the Diplomatic Conference of Plenipotentiaries on the Establishment of an International Criminal Court*, 11 Pace Int'l L. Rev. 341, 342 (1999).

15. Prosecutor v. Tadić, Case No. IT-94-1, Decision on the Defence Motion for Interlocutory Appeal on Jurisdiction, ¶ 70 (Oct. 2, 1995) [hereinafter Tadić Decision on Jurisdiction].

16. *See, e.g.*, Prosecutor v. Tihomir Blaškić, Case No. IT-95-14-T, Judgment (Mar. 3, 2000) (finding Republic of Croatia exercised overall control over Bosnian Croats embattled in Bosnia-Herzegovina).

17. Tadić Decision on Jurisdiction, *supra*, at ¶ 83.

18. *Id.* at ¶ 97 ("Why protect civilians from belligerent violence, or ban rape, torture or the wanton destruction of hospitals . . . when two sovereign States are engaged in war, and yet refrain from the same bans or providing the same protection when armed violence has erupted 'only' within the territory of a sovereign State?").

19. Hamdan v. United States, 548 U.S. 557 (2006).

20. Prosecutor v. Delalić, Case No. IT-96-21-T, Judgment, ¶ 193 (Nov. 16, 1998).

21. Prosecutor v. Tadić, Case No. IT-94-1-T, Opinion and Judgment, ¶ 573 (May 7, 1997).

22. Prosecutor v. Akayesu, Case No. ICTR-96-4-T, Judgment, ¶ 643 (Sept. 2, 1998).

23. Prosecutor v. Kayishema, Case No. ICTR-95-1-T, Judgment, ¶ 603 (May 21, 1999).

24. *Id.* at ¶ 616.

25. Prosecutor v. Kunarac, Case No. IT-96-23-A & IT-96-23/1-A, Judgment, ¶ 58 (June 12, 2002).

26. *Id.* at ¶ 58.

27. For more on the question of combatant classification, see Derek Jinks, *The Declining Significance of POW Status*, 45 Harv. Int'l L. J. 367 (2004).

28. Prosecutor v. Delalić, Case No. IT-96-21-A, Judgment, ¶ 166 (Feb. 20, 2001).

CHAPTER 7

1. G.A. Res. 46/51, U.N. Doc. A/RES/46/51 (Jan. 27, 1992).

2. Convention for the Prevention and Punishment of Terrorism, League of Nations Doc. C.94.M.47.1938.V (1937).

3. International Convention for the Suppression of Terrorist Bombings. Jan. 9, 1998, S. Treaty Doc. No. 106-6, 37 I.L.M. 251 ("a place of public use, a State or government facility, a public transportation system or an infrastructure facility with the intent to cause death or serious bodily injury or with the intent to cause extensive destruction of such a place, facility or system, where such destruction results in or is likely to result in major economic loss").

4. International Convention for the Suppression of the Financing of Terrorism, G.A. Res. 109, U.N. GAOR 6th Comm., 54 Sess., 76th mtg., Agenda Item 160, U.N. Doc. A/54/109 (1999).

5. U.N. SCOR Res. 1373, U.N. Doc. S/RES/1373 (Sept. 28, 2001).

6. U.N. SCOR Res. 1624, U.N. Doc. S/RES/1624 (Sept. 14, 2005).

7. *See* http://www.un.org/apps/news/infocus/lebanon/tribunal/.

8. U.N. SCOR Res. 1757, U.N. Doc. S/RES/1757 (2007).

9. *See* Nidal Nabil Jurdi, *The Subject-Matter Jurisdiction of the Special Tribunal for Lebanon*, 5 J. Int'l Crim. J. 1125 (2007).

10. Christian Munch, *The International Criminal Court (ICC) and Terrorism as an International Crime*, 14 Mich. St. J. Int'l L. 121, 133 (2006).

11. Mahnoush H. Arsanjani, *The Rome Statute of the International Criminal Court*, 93 Am. J. Int'l L. 22, 29 (1999).

12. *See* Art. 147, Convention (IV) Relative to the Protection of Civilian Persons in Time of War (Aug. 12, 1949).

13. Prosecutor v. Tadić, Case No. IT-94-1, Decision on the Defence Motion for Interlocutory Appeal on Jurisdiction, ¶ 70 (Oct. 2, 1995).

14. *Id.*

15. Prosecutor v. Galić, Case No. IT-98-29-T, Judgment (Dec. 5, 2003). *See also* Prosecutor v. Fofana and Kondewa, Case No. SCSL-04-14-T, Judgment, ¶ 170 (Aug. 2, 2007).

CHAPTER 8

1. David Luban, *A Theory of Crimes Against Humanity*, 29 Yale J. Int'l L. 85, 86 (2004).

2. The Appeals Chamber of the ICTY has taken this position. As noted later in this chapter, the Tribunal concluded that Goran Jelisić was on "a one-man genocide mission, intent upon personally wiping out the protected group;" *See also* Prosecutor v. Jelisić, Case No. IT-95-10-T, Judgment ¶ 108 (Dec. 14, 1999).

3. Declaration of France, Great Britain and Russia, May 24, 1915, *quoted in* Egon Schwelb, *Crimes Against Humanity*, 23 Brit. Y.B. Int'l L. 178, 181 (1946).

4. Commission on the Responsibility of the Authors of the War and on Enforcement of Penalties, *Report Presented to the Preliminary Peace Conference* (Mar. 29, 1919), *reprinted in* 14 Am. J. Int'l L. 95, 177 (1920).

5. 1919 Versailles Treaty of Peace Between the Allied and Associated Powers and Germany, June 28, 1919, 225 Consol. T.S. 188.

6. Hannah Arendt, Eichmann in Jerusalem: A Report on the Banality of Evil 268 (1965).

7. *See* Revised and updated report on the question of the prevention and punishment of the crime of genocide prepared by Mr. Whitaker, Commission on

Human Rights, Sub-Commission on Prevention of Discrimination and Protection of Minorities, 38th Sess. U.N.Doc. E/CN.4/Sub.2/1985/6 (July 2, 1985) at 20 ("'[G]enocide' in popular modern usage covers many more cases of mass killings than those covered in the Convention.").

8. *Id.* at 10 ("It could seem pedantic to argue that some terrible mass-killings are legalistically not genocide, but on the other hand it could be counterproductive to devalue genocide through over-diluting its definition.").

9. France *et al. v.* Göring, 1 Trial of the Major War Criminals Before the International Military Tribunal 27, 43-44 (1946).

10. *See* GA Res. 96(I).

11. In the Rome Statute, for example, these elements are found in the first paragraph under Article 6 for genocide, and Articles 7(1) and 7(2)(a) for crimes against humanity.

12. Prosecutor v. Kambanda, Case No. ICTR-97-23-S, Judgment, ¶ 16 (Sept. 4, 1998).

13. Art. 7, *Report of the Preparatory Commission for the International Criminal Court; Addendum: Finalized Draft Text of the Elements of Crimes*, U.N. Doc. PCNICC/2000/INF/3/Add.2 (July 6, 2000).

14. *See* Prosecutor v. Kayishema & Ruzindana, Case No. ICTR-95-1-T, Judgment, ¶ 134 (May 21, 1999).

15. Prosecutor v. Akayesu, Case No. ICTR-96-4-T, Judgment, ¶ 477 (Sept. 2, 1998) [hereinafter Akayesu Trial Judgement].

16. Prosecutor v. Karadžić & Mladić, Case Nos. IT-95-5-R61, IT-955-R61, Review of the Indictments Pursuant to Rule 61 of the Rules of Procedure and Evidence, ¶ 94 (July 11, 1996).

17. Prosecutor v. Krstić, Case No. IT-98-33-T, Judgment, ¶ 80 (Aug. 2, 2001).

18. *See* Prosecutor v. Jelisić, Case No. IT-95-10-T, Judgment (Dec. 14, 1999) [hereinafter Jelisić Trial Judgment].

19. *Id.* at ¶ 108.

20. Prosecutor v. Jelisić, Case No. IT-95-10-A, Judgment ¶ 66 (July 5, 2001).

21. *See* Prosecutor v. Blagojević & Jokić, Case No. IT-02-60-A, Judgment (May 9, 2007); Prosecutor v. Krstić, Case No. IT-98-33-A, Judgment, (April 19, 2004).

22. Prosecutor v. Kunarac, Case No. IT-96-231, Judgment, ¶ 90 (June 12, 2002).

23. Prosecutor v. Kordić & Čerkez, Case No. IT-95-14/2, Judgment, ¶ 180 (Feb. 26, 2001).

24. Prosecutor v. Kupreškić et al., Case No. IT-95-16, Judgment, ¶ 549 (Jan. 14, 2000); *see also* The Barbie Case, French Court of Cassation (Criminal Chamber), Dec. 20 1985, 78 ILR 125.

25. Prosecutor v. Blaškić, Case No. IT-95-14, Judgment, ¶ 214 (Mar. 3, 2000).

26. William J. Fenrick, *Should Crimes Against Humanity Replace War Crimes?*, 37 Colum. J. Transnat'l L. 767, 780 (1999).

27. Kayishema & Ruzindana, *supra*, at ¶ 98.

28. *See* Prosecutor v. Nikolić, Case No. IT-94-2-R61, Review of Indictment Pursuant to Rule 61 of the Rules of Procedure and Evidence, ¶ 27 (Oct. 20, 1995).

29. Jelisić Trial Judgment, *supra*, at ¶ 70.

30. Prosecutor v. Musema, Case No. ICTR 96-13, Judgment, ¶ 162 (Jan. 27, 2000).

31. See Akayesu Trial Judgment, *supra*, at ¶ 39.

32. *Id*. at ¶ 30 n.56; *see also Id*. at ¶ 113 (defining all enumerated groups).

33. *Id*.

34. *Id*. at ¶ 39.

35. *Id*.

36. *Id*. at ¶ 40.

37. Karl D. Jackson, *The Khmer Rouge in Context*, in Cambodia, *1975-1978*: Rendezvous with Death 3, 3 (Karl D. Jackson ed., 1989).

38. Prosecution v. Tadić, Case No. IT-94-I-T, Decision on the Defence Motion, ¶ 32 (Aug. 10, 1995).

39. Prosecutor v. Tadić, Case No. IT-94-1, Judgment, ¶ 251 (July 15, 1999) (emphasis in original) [hereinafter Tadić Judgment].

40. Kunarac, *supra*, at ¶ 98.

41. Blaškić, *supra*, at ¶ 257.

42. Tadić Judgment, *supra*, at ¶ 272.

43. Prosecutor v. Mrkšić, Case No. IT-95-13-R61, Judgment, ¶ 30 (Apr. 3, 1996).

44. Doe v. Alvaro Rafael Saravia, 348 F. Supp. 2d 1112, 1156 (E.D. Cal. 2004).

45. *See* Kayishema & Ruzindana, *supra*, at ¶ 95 (noting that the genocide prohibition covers acts falling short of death).

46. *See, e.g.*, Prosecutor v. Rutaganda, Case No. ICTR 96-3 Judgment and Sentence, ¶ 51 (Dec. 6, 1999).

47. Musema, *supra*, at ¶ 157.

48. Prosecutor v. Kvočka, Case No. IT-98-30/1, Judgment, ¶ 208 (Nov. 2, 2001).

49. The Prosecutor v. Kupreškić *et al.*, Case No. IT-95-16, Judgment, ¶ 818 (Oct. 23, 2001).

50. *Id*. at ¶ 566.

51. The Prosecutor v. Kupreškić *et al.*, Case No. IT-95-16, Judgment, ¶ 393 (Mar. 7, 2003).

52. Prosecutor v. Naletilić & Martinović, Case No. IT-98-34-T, Judgment, ¶ 636 (Mar. 31, 2003).

53. Prosecutor v. Kvočka, Case No. IT-98-30/1-T, Judgment, ¶ 195 (Nov. 2, 2001).

54. Prosecutor v. Krnojelac, Case No. IT-97-25-T, Judgment, ¶ 434 (Mar. 15, 2002).

55. Prosecutor v. Stakić, Case No. IT-97-24-T, Judgment, ¶ 306 (July 31, 2003).

56. Krstić, *supra*, at ¶ 685. By contrast, cumulative convictions were entered for genocide and persecution.

57. *Id*. at ¶ 497 (noting requirement of mass destruction).

58. *Id*. at ¶ 229.

CHAPTER 9

1. R v. Bow Street Metropolitan Stipendiary Magistrate and others ex parte Pinochet Ugarte [1999], 2 All ER 97, 114 (House of Lords). It should be noted, however, that only one of the Lords, Lord Millet, held that immunity is always overridden by ICL; the others who found no immunity based their decision on the provisions of the Convention Against Torture and thus only narrowly found that official immunity would be inapplicable to charges of torture.

2. Dapo Akande, *International Law Immunities and the International Criminal Court*, 98 Am. J. Int'l L. 407, 411 (2004).

3. *See generally* U.S. v. Noriega, 746 F. Supp. 1506 (1990).

4. *See* ICTY Statute, Art. 7(2); ICTR Statute, Art. 6(2); SCSL Statute, Art. 6(2); and the Nuremberg Charter, Art. 7. The Tokyo Charter had a similar provision (Art. 6), but it noticeably and deliberately does not refer to heads of state, presumably reflecting the earlier decision not to prosecute the Emperor of Japan. The ICC provision on immunities, Article 27, has two provisions that track the distinction between functional and personal immunity. The functional immunity subsection (Art. 27(1)) replicates that found in the earlier treaties; the personal immunity subsection (Art. 27(2)) is unique to the ICC Statute, leading some commentators to suggest that the earlier immunity provisions may only cover functional, and not personal, immunity. *See* James Miglin, *From Immunity to Impunity: Charles Taylor and the Special Court for Sierra Leone*, 16 Dal. J. Leg. Stud. 21, 37-38 (2007).

5. Geneva Convention Relative to the Treatment of Prisoners of War, Aug. 12, 1949, 6 U.S.T. 3316, 75 U.N.T.S. 135, Art. 4(2).

6. *Id.* at Art. 5.

7. Rasul v. Bush, 542 U.S. 466 (2004).

8. *See* Dapo Akande, *The Application of International Law Immunities in Prosecutions for International Crimes, in* Bringing Power to Justice?: The Prospects of the International Criminal Court 62-68 (J. Harrington, M. Milde, and R. Vernon eds., 2006) (setting out different interpretations of Article 98 and referring to the domestic implementing legislation of Canada, the United Kingdom, Malta, Ireland, New Zealand, South Africa, and Switzerland).

9. Case Concerning the Arrest Warrant of 11 April 2000 (Democratic Republic of the Congo v. Belgium) (2002) ICJ Report 3, ¶¶ 58-61; For a critique of the *Arrest Warrant* decision that argues that the Court did not adequately or clearly address the question of immunities (by not, for example, making a clear distinction between functional and personal immunities, and by confusing the basis for lifting functional immunity for acts that constitute international crimes), *see* Miglin, *supra* at 32-34.

10. In fact Milošević himself did not raise the issue; it was raised on his behalf by *amici* who were effectively acting as his counsel. *See* Prosecutor v. Milošević, Case No. IT-02-54, Decision on Preliminary Motions (Nov. 8, 2001).

11. The ICTR had previously indicted, tried, and convicted (via a guilty plea) the Rwandan Prime Minister Jean Kambanda, although the indictment was issued after Kambanda was no longer in office. *See* Prosecutor v. Kambanda, Case No. ICTR-97-23-S, Judgment and Sentence (Sept. 4, 1998).

12. Prosecutor v. Taylor, Case No. SCSL-2003-01-I, Decision on Immunity from Jurisdiction (May 31, 2004).

13. *See, e.g.*, Azapo v. President of South Africa, CCT 17/96, 1996 (4) SALR 671 (CC). The recent exceptions concern amnesties passed in Argentina and Chile, which have been overturned within their respective countries and are not recognized by other states in the context of transnational criminal prosecutions.

14. *See* Prosecutor v. Kallon & Kamara, Case Nos. SCSL 2004-15-AR72(E) & SCSL 2004-16-AR72(E), Decision on Challenge to Jurisdiction: Lomé Accord Amnesty (Mar. 13, 2004).

15. Prosecutor v. Gbao, Case No. SCSL 2004-15-AR72(E), Decision on preliminary motion on the invalidity of the agreement between the United Nations and the Government of Sierra Leone on the establishment of the Special Court (2004), ¶ 9 (emphasis added).

16. *Id.* at ¶ 10.

17. Robert Cryer, *Commentary, in* Annotated Leading Cases of International Criminal Tribunals: The Special Court for Sierra Leone *2003-2004* 60 (André Klip and Göran Sluiter eds., 2006).

18. *See* Office of the Prosecutor, *Policy Paper on the Interests of Justice* 1-4 (Sept. 2007) (noting the difference between the interests of justice and peace, and that any efforts to secure peace must be undertaken consistent with the legal requirements of the Rome Treaty to hold accountable those most responsible for violations of international criminal law).

19. *Id.* at 8.

20. Human Rights Watch, The Meaning of "The Interests of Justice" in Article 53 of the Rome Statute (June 2005).

21. Carsten Stahn, *Complementarity, Amnesties and Alternative Forms of Justice: Some Interpretative Guidelines for the International Criminal Court,* 3 J. Int'l Crim. J. 695, 717-718 (2005).

22. *Id.* at 709.

23. *Judgment Concerning the Legality of the General Security Service's Interrogation Methods,* 38 I.L.M 1471 (1999).

24. *Id.* at ¶ 36.

25. Miriam Gur-Arye, *Can the War Against Terror Justify the Use of Force in Interrogation? Reflections in Light of the Israeli Experience, in* Torture: A Collection 191 (Sanford Levinson ed., 2004).

CHAPTER 10

1. *See Report Presented to the Preliminary Peace Conference, in* 1 The Law of War: A Documentary History 842, 853-54 (Leon Friedman ed., 1972).

2. *In Re* Yamashita, 327 U.S. 1, 16 (1946).

3. *Id.* at 27-28 (Murphy, J., dissenting).

4. *See* Jenny S. Martinez, *Understanding* Mens Rea *in Command Responsibility: From* Yamashita *to* Blaškić *and Beyond,* 5(3) J. Int'l Crim. Justice 638 (2007).

5. The High Command Case, 11 Trials of War Criminals Before the Nuremberg Military Tribunals Under Control Council Law No. *10* 543-544 (1951).

6. The Hostage Case, 11 Trials of War Criminals Before the Nuremberg Military Tribunals Under Control Council Law No. *10, 757,* 1260 (1950).

7. Protocol Additional to the Geneva Conventions of 12 August 1949, and Relating to the Protection of Victims of International Armed Conflicts (Protocol I), June 8, 1977, 1125 U.N.T.S. 3.

8. *See* Prosecutor v. Hadžihasanović, Case No. IT-01-47-AR72, Decision on Interlocutory Appeal Challenging Jurisdiction in Relation to Command Responsibility, ¶ 18 (July 16, 2003).

9. Prosecutor v. Delalić, Case No. IT-96-21-T, Judgment, ¶ 354 (Nov. 16, 1998).

10. *Id.* at ¶ 378.

11. *Id.* at ¶ 377.

12. *Id.* at ¶ 610.

13. *See, e.g.*, Prosecutor v. Blaškić, Case No. IT-95-14-T, Judgment, ¶ 302 (Mar. 3, 2000).

14. *See* Prosecutor v. Akayesu, Case No. ICTR-96-4, Judgment, ¶ 691 (Sept. 2, 1998) (acquitting defendant mayor on superior responsibility counts for lack of evidence that he controlled *interahamwe* death squads operative in his commune).

15. Prosecutor v. Halilović, Case No. IT-01-48-T, Judgment, § 54 (Nov. 16, 2005).

16. Prosecutor v. Blaškić, Case No. IT-95-14, Judgment, ¶ 91 (July 29, 2004).

17. *See* discussion of related cases during the World War II era involving mere presence *in* Prosecutor v. Furundžija, Case No. IT-95-17/1-T, Judgment, ¶¶ 205-209 (Dec. 10, 1998) (citing to the Synagogue and Pig-cart Parade cases).

18. Akayesu, *supra*, at ¶ 693.

19. William Schabas argues that genocidal intent should be required to hold someone liable as an accessory to genocide. *See* William A. Schabas, *Genocide in International Law* 259 (2000).

20. Prosecutor v. Tadić, Case No. IT-94-1-A, Judgment (July 15, 1999).

21. Prosecutor v. Brdjanin, Case No. IT-99-36-A, Judgment, ¶ 365 (April 3, 2007).

22. Prosecutor v. Tadić, *supra*, at ¶ 204.

23. Brdjanin, *supra*, at ¶ 365 (emphasis in original).

CHAPTER 11

1. Good discussions of this topic may be found here: Immi Tallgren, *The Sensibility and Sense of International Criminal Law*, 13 Europ. J. Int'l L. 561 (2002); Robert D. Sloane, *The Expressive Capacity of International Punishment: The Limits of the National Law Analogy and the Potential of International Criminal Law*, 43 Stanford J. Int'l L. 39 (2007); and Mark A. Drumbl, *Atrocity, Punishment, and International Law* (2007).

2. For a discussion of the traditional justifications of the criminal law, see Miriam J. Aukerman, *Extraordinary Evil, Ordinary Crime: A Framework for Understanding Transitional Justice*, 15 Harv. Hum. Rts. J. 39 (2002).

3. Hannah Arendt and Karl Jaspers, Correspondence 1928-1968 54 (1992).

4. For more on deterrence, *compare* David Wippman, *Atrocities, Deterrence, and the Limits of International Justice*, 23 Fordham Int'l L.J. 473, 476, 483 (1999) ("Even if we assume that those committing atrocities engage in rational cost-benefit calculations (weighing the risk of prosecution against the personal and political gain of continued participation in ethnic cleansing and similar acts), most probably view the risk of prosecution as slight. . . . Even if successful, the contribution of such mass prosecutions to deterrence is uncertain at best."), *with* Payam Akhavan, *Beyond Impunity: Can International Criminal Justice Prevent Future Atrocities?*, 95 Am. J. Int'l L. 7, 12 (2001) ("Where leaders engage in some form of rational cost-benefit calculation, the threat of punishment can increase the costs of a policy that is criminal under international law."). *See also* Julian Ku and Jide Nzelibe, *Do International Criminal Tribunals Deter or Exacerbate Humanitarian Atrocities?*, 84 Wash. U. L. Rev. 777 (2006).

5. U.N. SCOR Res. 808, pmbl., U.N. Doc. S/RES/808 (Feb. 22, 1993).

6. U.N. SCOR Res. 955, pmbl., U.N. Doc. S/RES/955 (Nov. 8, 1994).

7. For more on reconciliation, *see* Laurel E. Fletcher and Harvey M. Weinstein, *Violence and Social Repair: Rethinking the Contribution of Justice to Reconciliation*, 24 Hum. Rts. Q. 573, 606-617 (2002).

8. Prosecutor v. Haradinaj, Case No. IT-04-84-T, Judgment (Apr. 3, 2008).

9. Intl. Comm. on Intervention & State Sovereignty, The Responsibility to Protect (Dec. 2001), *available at* http://www.iciss.ca/report-en.asp.

10. Anonymous, *Human Rights in Peace Negotiations*, 18 Hum. Rts. Q. 249 (1996). (It has been speculated that this article was written by Bertrand Ramcharan, former acting High Commissioner for Human Rights and once an assistant to Thorvald Stoltenberg, Special Representative of the UN Secretary-General for the former Yugoslavia.) For a response, *see* Felice D. Gaer, *U.N.-Anonymous: Reflections on* Human Rights in Peace Negotiations, 19 Hum. Rts. Q. 1 (1997).

11. Ivan Simonovic, *Attitudes and Types of Reaction Toward Past War Crimes and Human Rights Abuses*, 29 Yale J. Int'l L. 343, 346 (2004).

12. Michael Ignatieff, *Articles of Faith*, Index on Censorship, Issue 5 (1996).

13. For more on truth commissions, *see* Charles Villa-Vicencio and Wilhelm Verwoerd, *Looking Back Reaching Forward: Reflections on the Truth and Reconciliation Commission of South Africa* (2000); Priscilla B. Hayner, *Unspeakable Truths: Facing the Challenge of Truth Commissions* (2001); Peter A. Schey, Dinah L. Shelton, and Naomi Roht-Arriaza, *Addressing Human Rights Abuses: Truth Commissions and the Value of Amnesty*, 19 Whittier L. Rev. 325 (1997).

14. Filártiga v. Peña-Irala, 630 F.2d 876 (2d Cir. 1980),

15. Application of the Convention on the Prevention and Punishment of the Crime of Genocide (Bosn. & Herz. v. Serb. & Monten.).

16. Military and Paramilitary Activities in and against Nicaragua (Nicaragua v. United States of America) Merits, Judgment, I.C.J. Reports 1986.

17. Bos. & Herz. v. Serb. & Mont., *supra*.

18. Velasquez Rodriguez Case, Judgment of July 29, 1988, Inter-Am.Ct.H.R. (Ser. C) No. 4 (1988).

19. *See* International Law Commission, http://www.un.org/law/ilc/.

Glossary

Acta jure gestionis. Activities of a commercial nature that are carried out by a state or one of its subdivisions or agencies, but that also could be carried out by a private person. Such acts are not immune from the jurisdiction and process of foreign courts under the modern doctrine of restrictive foreign sovereign immunity.

Acta jure imperii. Acts in which a state is acting in its governmental, and not private or commercial, capacity. Activities of a state that only a sovereign is capable of conducting.

Actus reus. "Guilty act." The physical act (which can also be an omission) that, in combination with the necessary mental state (*mens rea*), constitutes a crime.

Ad hoc tribunal. A criminal tribunal formed to prosecute those responsible for atrocities committed during a particular war or episode of repression. Usually has limited temporal, subject matter, or personal jurisdiction.

Aggression. The threat of force or use of force against a state that violates international law. In international criminal law, modern parlance for the crimes against peace prosecuted after World War II at Nuremberg and Tokyo. The crime of aggression is within the jurisdiction of the International Criminal Court, but has yet to be defined.

Amnesty. Prospective protection from criminal or civil liability for an already completed wrongful act. Often contrasted with pardons, which come after a finding of liability or guilt.

Assassination. Usually refers to the targeted killing of a specific person, such as a leader, for political purposes.

Aut dedere aut judicare. "Extradite or adjudicate." A provision found in many international criminal law treaties, such as the Convention Against Torture, that requires state parties to either extradite or prosecute someone within their territory suspected of committing the international crime in question.

Combatants. Members of an armed force that enjoy the privilege of engaging in military activities and the protections of international humanitarian law. They include persons authorized by a sovereign to participate in an armed conflict, as well as members of a military force not authorized by a sovereign but who otherwise meet the specific requirements for combatant status found in the 1949 Geneva Conventions and their 1977 Protocols.

Comity. The principle that one nation state will extend goodwill, respect, and courtesies to other nations (or other jurisdictions within the same nation), particularly by recognizing the validity and effect of executive, legislative, and judicial acts. The term refers to the idea that courts should not act in a way that demeans the jurisdiction, laws, or judicial decisions of another jurisdiction. Part of the presumption of comity is that other jurisdictions will reciprocate the courtesy shown to them.

Common Article 3. Article 3, the text of which is repeated in all four of the 1949 Geneva Conventions, is the sole treaty provision that applies expressly to noninternational armed conflicts. Called a "treaty in miniature," common Article 3 sets forth the minimum protections and standards of conduct to which the state and its armed opponents must adhere.

Common law crimes. Crimes created through the common law as opposed to by statute. Although still present in the United Kingdom, common law crimes have mostly been abolished in the United States.

Complementarity. The foundational principle setting forth the relationship between the International Criminal Court (ICC) and national jurisdictions, as contained in Articles 17 through 19 of the ICC Statute. Under the principle of complementarity, the ICC may only assert jurisdiction if national jurisdictions are unwilling or unable to do so. This includes situations in which a national jurisdiction purports to assert jurisdiction, but is in reality unwilling to investigate or prosecute thoroughly.

Convention. A binding agreement or treaty, often multilateral, concluded among states.

Courts martial. Military courts governed by military law. In the United States, courts martial are governed by the Uniform Code of Military Justice.

Crime against the peace. The term set forth in the Nuremberg and Tokyo Charters after World War II to refer to the commission of an illegal or aggressive war; that is, violations of the *jus ad bellum*. Referred to as the crime of aggression in the ICC Statute.

Crimes against humanity. A constellation of acts made criminal under international law when they are committed within the context of a widespread or systematic attack against a civilian population. Unlike most other international crimes, crimes against humanity are not the subject of a dedicated convention. As a result, the definition of the crime varies among international statutes and domestic penal codes.

Cultural genocide. The deliberate destruction of the cultural heritage of a protected group with the intent to destroy that group. Cultural genocide is not recognized as a separate crime under international law, although acts that are referred to as cultural genocide may also qualify as war crimes or crimes against humanity and may provide evidence of genocidal intent.

Cultural property. Works of art or monuments, buildings dedicated to education or culture, and property of historical significance. Entitled to special protection in armed conflict.

Customary international law. Consists of two elements: (1) collective state practice (2) undertaken out of a sense of legal obligation. This formula thus comprises an objective element (state practice) and a subjective element (*opinio juris*). A body of widely accepted yet uncodified law that has binding force and effect.

Declaration of war. A formal statement indicating the intention of a state to commence hostilities. Declarations of war are rarely used in international relations today and are not necessary to trigger the application of humanitarian law.

Diplomat. A class of persons including ministers and ambassadors who are sent by their government to a foreign state to represent the sending state in its international relations.

Diplomatic immunity. The customary protection accorded by the host country to diplomats on an official mission of the sending state.

Disappearances. The practice by which individuals, often real or perceived enemies of the state, are kidnapped, detained, mistreated, and then killed without any acknowledgment to the family or friends of the victim.

Distinction. A principle of humanitarian law that states that military attacks should distinguish between legitimate military targets on the one hand and noncombatants, those *hors de combat*, and civilian objectives on the other hand.

Dolus specialis. Specific intent. An intent to produce a particular prohibited consequence by committing a criminal act.

Double criminality rule. A principle of extradition law adopted by states that allows for the extradition of individuals only where the crimes charged exist in the penal codes of both the requesting state and the requested state.

Economic, social, and cultural rights. Rights protecting individuals in their economic, social, and cultural activities. The most authoritative source of such rights is found in the Covenant on Economic, Social and Cultural Rights, which includes the right to work in just and favorable conditions, the right to education, the right to health care, and the right to self-determination.

Ejusdem generis. "Of the same kind." A principle of legal interpretation that governs where a list of specific items is followed by a more general or open-ended reference; the latter is to be interpreted so as to apply to the same types of things already listed.

Entry into force. The point at which a treaty becomes binding on those states that have ratified it. Multilateral treaties usually require the ratification of a specific number of states to enter into force.

Erga omnes. "In relation to everyone." The phrase was used by the International Court of Justice in the *Barcelona Traction* case to refer to certain rules of international law, such as the prohibition against genocide, the violation of which by any state is of concern to all states.

Ethnic cleansing. The phrase used to describe the forced displacement, deportation, and commission of related violence against an ethnic group to obtain the territory occupied by that group or achieve ethnic homogeneity. The term was used to describe much of the violence that occurred in the former Yugoslavia in the 1990s.

Extradition. The formal process by which an accused (or convicted defendant) is transferred from one state (the requested state) to another state (the requesting state). The process of extradition is frequently governed by bilateral extradition treaties, although Europe does have a multilateral extradition treaty.

Extraordinary Chambers in the Courts of Cambodia. Sometimes referred to as the Khmer Rouge Tribunal, the special chambers created within the Cambodian legal system by agreement between the Cambodian government and the United Nations to prosecute those responsible for the most serious crimes committed during the Khmer Rouge era (1975–1979).

Extraordinary rendition. A term employed to refer to the secret rendition (the transfer of an individual without the use of an extradition agreement or other formal legal process) of an individual between states. Extraordinary rendition is often undertaken for the purpose of having the individual interrogated by means that would be illegal if conducted by the original custodial state (including through the use of torture).

Extraterritorial jurisdiction. The application of a state's laws to, or the exercise of authority over, activity conducted outside of its own territory.

Francs-tireurs. A term used to refer to guerrilla forces. First coined during the Franco-Prussian War (1870–1871) to describe irregular military forces that took up arms against the Germans.

General Assembly. One of the principal organs of the United Nations consisting of representatives of all UN member states. Capable of issuing resolutions and declarations that may contribute to the creation of international law or provide evidence of the existence of a rule of customary international law.

General principles of law. Principles common to the major legal systems of the world; constitutes a source of international law.

Geneva Law. Shorthand reference to the rules of international humanitarian law found in the four 1949 Geneva Conventions and their two 1977 Protocols. Geneva Law protects particularly vulnerable groups, such as civilians and prisoners of war.

Genocide. A set of prohibited acts committed with the intent to destroy, in whole or in part, a national, ethnic, racial, or religious group. Most definitions of genocide track that which is found in the 1951 Convention on the Prevention and Punishment of Genocide, although some states (e.g., Spain) altered the definition in important ways (by, for example, expanding the list of protected groups).

Grave breaches. Violations of the 1949 Geneva Conventions that give rise to individual criminal responsibility and are subject to universal jurisdiction.

Hague Law. Shorthand reference to the rules of international humanitarian law primarily codified in a series of treaties created in The Hague in the late nineteenth and early twentieth centuries, most notably in 1899 and 1907. Hague Law generally contains rules governing the means and methods of warfare.

Hors de combat. In international humanitarian law, individuals who do not participate directly in hostilities, including combatants who no longer present a military threat because they are wounded, have laid down their weapons, or have surrendered. Individuals who are *hors de combat* are not a legitimate military target and must be treated humanely.

Hostis humani generis. "Enemy of all humankind." Most famously used to describe pirates and to justify the use of universal jurisdiction to prosecute acts of piracy. Today, applied to torturers, war criminals, *génocidaires*, and those who commit crimes against humanity.

Humanitarian intervention. Efforts by states, acting unilaterally or collectively, to halt abuses committed in another state against that state's own citizens.

Hybrid tribunal. Tribunals that have a mix of national and international elements. Hybrid tribunals are generally situated within the host state as opposed to being established abroad and are staffed by international and domestic personnel (judges, prosecutors, investigators, defense counsel, and support staff) working in tandem. These tribunals apply a mixture of international and domestic law, including local criminal law.

Immunity *rationae materiae*. Used to refer to functional immunity of a government official under international law, which protects a government official from prosecution for his or her official actions taken while in office.

Immunity *rationae personae*. Used to refer to personal immunity of a government official under international law. Provides immunity to the person for any act so long as he or she is holding a government position. Personal immunity ceases once the individual leaves office.

Incitement. An attempt to persuade another person to commit a criminal offense.

Indiscriminate attack. Bombardments that are not directed against any military objective.

International Committee of the Red Cross (ICRC). A private Geneva-based body that generates and monitors compliance with international humanitarian law.

International Court of Justice (ICJ). The principal judicial organ of the United Nations. The Court's role is to settle, in accordance with international law, legal disputes submitted to it by states and to give advisory opinions on legal questions referred to it by states, authorized UN organs, and specialized agencies. The Court is composed of 15 judges, who are elected for nine-year terms by the UN General Assembly and the Security Council.

International Criminal Court (ICC). The first permanent international criminal court, created by the Rome Treaty of 1998, which came into force on July 1, 2002. The ICC is located in The Hague.

International Criminal Tribunal for Rwanda (ICTR). The ad hoc tribunal created by UN Security Council Resolution 955 to prosecute persons responsible for genocide and other serious violations of international humanitarian law committed in the territory of Rwanda between January 1, 1994 and December 31, 1994. Its Chambers are located in Arusha, Tanzania, although there is a prosecutorial office in Kigali, Rwanda. The ICTR shares an Appeals Chamber in The Hague with the International Criminal Tribunal for the Former Yugoslavia.

International Criminal Tribunal for the Former Yugoslavia (ICTY). The first ad hoc tribunal since World War II. The UN Security Council created the ICTY through Resolution 827 to prosecute serious violations of international criminal law and humanitarian law committed in the territory of the former Yugoslavia since 1991. The tribunal is located in The Hague.

International humanitarian law (IHL). The law regulating armed conflict, sometimes also referred to as "the law of armed conflict" or "the law of war." International humanitarian law is a set of rules that seeks, for humanitarian reasons, to limit the effects of armed conflict. IHL protects persons who are not or who are no longer participating in hostilities (Geneva Law) and restricts the means and methods of warfare (Hague Law).

International Law Commission. A body of experts established by the UN General Assembly to promote the progressive development of international law.

International Military Tribunal for the Far East (IMTFE). Also known as the Tokyo Tribunal, the ad hoc tribunal formed to prosecute Japanese defendants for international crimes committed during World War II. U.S. General Douglas MacArthur, the Supreme Allied Commander of the Far East, created the IMTFE by a special proclamation with the acquiescence of the other Allied Powers.

International Military Tribunal for the Trial of German Major War Criminals (IMT). Best known as the Nuremberg Tribunal, the ad hoc tribunal established by the London Agreement of August 8, 1945 among the four victorious powers of World War II to prosecute German defendants for international crimes committed during the war.

Invasion. The movement of a hostile force across a boundary for the purpose of attacking or occupying a foreign state's territory.

Juge d'instruction. In France, a magistrate responsible for conducting the investigative hearing that precedes a criminal trial. In this hearing, the major evidence is presented, witnesses are heard, and depositions are taken. If at the end of the hearing the magistrate is not convinced that the evidence of guilt is sufficient, no trial occurs. This process is comparable to the grand jury hearing in the Anglo-American system.

Jus ad bellum. The set of rules regulating the decision to use military force in international relations. The *jus ad bellum* addresses the legality of going to war and historically took the form of theological and secular "just war" theories.

Jus cogens. "Cogent law." Peremptory norms of international law, from which no state is allowed to deviate.

Jus in bello. The set of rules regulating the means and methods of armed conflict and the protection of war victims. The *jus in bello* aims to limit the destructiveness of war, forbids the use of certain weapons, prohibits the attack of certain targets, protects civilians, and limits the area and range of fighting. The *jus in bello* is encompassed in both Hague Law and Geneva Law. The rules regulating the conduct of the armed conflict (*jus in bello*) are independent of the legality of the decision to engage in an armed conflict (*jus ad bellum*).

Law of armed conflict. *See* International humanitarian law (IHL).

League of Nations. The international organization established by the peace treaties that ended World War I. Like its successor, the United Nations, its purpose was the promotion of international peace and security. It disbanded in 1946 when its functions were transferred to the UN.

Lex specialis derogat legi generali. A choice of law rule that states that a law governing a specific subject matter (*lex specialis*) trumps an otherwise applicable law that governs only general matters (*lex generalis*).

Male captus, bene detentus. The doctrine that an improper or illegal capture of an individual does not invalidate that individual's detention or subsequent trial.

Malum in se. "Wrong or evil in itself."

Martens Clause. A clause in the preamble to the 1899 Hague Convention (II) governing the laws and customs of war on land that refers to the idea that there are general principles of conduct that apply to all armed conflicts absent any specific codification. The clause was based on a declaration read by Professor von Martens, the Russian delegate at the Hague Peace Conference of 1899.

Mens rea. "Guilty mind." The mental state required to hold an individual criminally liable for an act, the latter referred to as the *actus reus*.

Mercenary. A hired foreign soldier who participates in armed conflict primarily out of financial motivation.

Military commission. Courts established under military law and used to prosecute enemy combatants during an armed conflict where civilian courts or courts martial are not available.

Military necessity. A humanitarian law principle stating that the only legitimate object of war is to weaken the enemy's military forces and capacity.

Nationality principle. Assertion of extraterritorial jurisdiction by a state over the actions of its own nationals outside its territory.

Ne bis in idem. "Not twice for the same." Analogous to double jeopardy, the principle under international criminal law that prohibits an individual from being tried twice for the same crime. Codified at Article 20 of the ICC Statute.

Necessity. A criminal law defense permitting an otherwise illegal act in the face of exigent circumstances not attributable to the defendant.

Non liquet. "It is not clear." In international law, refers to the situation in which there is no clear rule of international law that applies.

Nulla poena sine lege. "No punishment without law." A variation of *nullum crimen sine lege* states that for every act made criminal there should be a preexisting penalty.

***Nullum crimen sine lege* (NCSL).** "No crime without law." A fundamental principle of justice that applies to all criminal law systems and requires that penal law be prospective and not retroactive, and that it also be specific and easily ascertained, thus providing adequate notice to individuals that certain conduct may result in criminal sanction.

Occupation. The holding of foreign territory, either as an incident of an armed conflict or with the consent of the occupied state. Humanitarian law imposes duties on occupying states that exist after the cessation of active hostilities.

Opinio juris. A belief that there is a legal obligation to act in a certain way; an element of customary international law.

Pardon. An executive act that sets aside a criminal conviction.

Passive nationality principle. Also referred to as the passive personality principle. The principle by which a state may assert jurisdiction over a crime committed against one of its own nationals, regardless of where the crime was committed or the nationality of the offender. Many national terrorism statutes are based on this principle.

Perfidy. A deliberate breach of faith; a calculated violation of trust; treachery. Perfidy is prohibited by international humanitarian law.

Permanent Court of International Justice (PCIJ). The judicial arm of the League of Nations and the precursor to the International Court of Justice.

Persecution. Colloquially, identity-based mistreatment or discrimination. Also an enumerated crime against humanity that encompasses the intentional and severe deprivation of a fundamental right.

Pillage. The unlawful or unauthorized appropriation of property in a time of war.

Piracy. An act of depredation committed on a ship or aircraft, usually for private ends on the high seas or outside the jurisdiction of any state.

Political offense exception. A provision found in extradition treaties indicating that crimes of a political nature (e.g., acts of revolution or insurrection) are not subject to extradition.

Propio motu. "On his or her own motion." One of three trigger mechanisms before the ICC. The prosecutor of the ICC has the power to bring an indictment *proprio motu*, subject to approval by the ICC's Pre-Trial Chamber.

Protocol. An international agreement that may be independent, but is more often supplemental to an extant treaty drawn up by the same negotiators to explain, interpret, or expand on the provision of the original treaty.

Quarter. Not killing an enemy when he or she has surrendered, been captured, or is otherwise *hors de combat*. The order to give no quarter violates humanitarian law.

Ratification. The process by which a state becomes a full party to a treaty.

Reparations. The payment by a state party to another state for damages sustained by the latter because of an international law violation of the former. Also refers to compensation provided to a victim or group of victims who have suffered a violation of international criminal law. Monetary damages or restitution of previously seized property is a common form of this second type of reparation, but such reparations may also include community service or a public memorial. The ICC is the first international criminal tribunal to formally provide a mechanism for the provision of reparations to victims.

Reprisal. A form of self-help in ancient humanitarian law. Reprisals involve the commission of breaches of international law by a state that has been the victim of similar breaches undertaken to compel compliance by the first offender.

Reservations, declarations, and understandings (RUDs). Statements attached to a treaty by a party when ratifying the treaty. A reservation is a statement that alters the legal effect of a treaty provision with respect to that state. Understandings clarify, but do not alter, the legal meaning or effect of a provision. A statement labeled an understanding that in fact alters the legal effect of a treaty provision is a reservation. Declarations can indicate a state's agreement to an optional part of a treaty, such as subjecting itself to a formal complaints mechanism. As with understandings, a statement labeled a declaration that in fact clarifies or alters the legal effect of a treaty provision is either an understanding or reservation, respectively.

Rome Treaty. The treaty completed in Rome on July 17, 1998, that created the International Criminal Court. As of June 2008, 106 states are party to the treaty. Also called the ICC Statute.

Security Council. The principal executive body of the United Nations. Consists of five permanent members (China, France, Russia, the United Kingdom, and the United States) and ten nonpermanent members who are chosen by the General Assembly for two-year terms. The Security Council is charged with maintaining peace and security in the international system, and is the only UN body that may issue resolutions that are binding on all states.

Self-defense. A customary right of states to utilize force in response to acts of aggression committed against them. Also, a criminal law defense enabling individuals to utilize force to repel an imminent attack or to protect themselves from harm by another.

Special Court for Sierra Leone (SCSL). The hybrid tribunal established by an agreement between the Government of Sierra Leone and the United Nations to prosecute those who bear the greatest responsibility for serious violations of international humanitarian law and Sierra Leonean law committed in the territory of Sierra Leone since November 30, 1996.

Special Panels in East Timor. The hybrid tribunal created by the United Nations and the Government of East Timor to prosecute crimes committed in 1999 related to a referendum in which the citizens of East Timor voted overwhelmingly for independence from Indonesia.

Special Tribunal for Lebanon (STL). An ad hoc tribunal created by the United Nations Security Council to prosecute those responsible for the assassination of the former Lebanese prime minister, Rafik Hariri, and other related political assassinations.

State immunity. The immunity afforded to states and their instrumentalities under either international or domestic law. Also called foreign sovereign immunity. Many states have statutes defining the scope of foreign sovereign immunity and setting forth exceptions.

Status of forces agreement. A treaty that controls the consensual placement of foreign troops by one state in the territory of another state.

Statute of limitation. Also called prescription in international law. The lifetime of criminal liability for a particular offense. Many international crimes have no statute of limitation.

Superior responsibility. The doctrine by which military and civilian superiors may be held liable for the acts of their subordinates.

Territorial principle. The principle that a state may assert jurisdiction over activities that occur within its own territory. This is the most widely accepted basis for a state's assertion of jurisdiction. Territorial jurisdiction is sometimes broken into two types: the objective territorial principle, which refers to acts committed on the territory of the state, and the subjective territorial principle, which justifies a state's assertion of jurisdiction over acts that are initiated outside of its territory but have an effect within its territory.

Transitional justice. The process by which states and societies address prior periods of war, repression, or mass violence to prevent a return to violence.

Transnational crimes. Crimes that are primarily defined by domestic law and prosecuted domestically, but take place in or affect more than one state. Examples include drug trafficking, money laundering, and many acts of terrorism.

Travaux préparatoires. The drafting history of a treaty. The *travaux* may be consulted to clarify the meaning of a treaty provision as an interpretive aid.

Tu quoque. "You also." At one time, a defense under international humanitarian law whereby a state could be exonerated for a violation of a rule by showing that the accusatory state had violated the same rule.

Uniform Code of Military Justice. The code of military law in the United States found in Title 10, Chapter 47, of the U.S. Code.

Universal jurisdiction. The jurisdictional principle that allows a state to assert jurisdiction over a crime regardless of the location of the criminal act, the nationality of the alleged perpetrator, or the nationality of the victim. Universal jurisdiction applies only to the most serious international crimes, such as genocide, crimes against humanity, and certain war crimes. International criminal law treaties may also enable the exercise of universal jurisdiction.

Victor's justice. Justice accorded by a victorious state against agents of a vanquished state, rather than pursuant to a neutral rule of law.

World Court. *See* International Court of Justice (ICJ).

Index